מסורה

ArtScroll® Series

Rabbi Nosson Scherman / Rabbi Gedaliah Zlotowitz

General Editors

Rabbi Meir Zlotowitz ז״ל, *Founder*

THE Weekly

SEFER BEREISHIS • ספר בראשית

Rabbi Nachman Zakon

Illustrated by Tova Katz

Published by

ARTSCROLL®

Mesorah Publications, ltd

The Jaffa Family Edition

Parashah

An illustrated retelling of the Chumash with Midrash

We express special appreciation to
Jacob Schottenstein
for suggesting the concept of this book.
Mature beyond his years, he is already well on the way to embracing his family legacy.

ARTSCROLL® SERIES

"THE WEEKLY PARAHAH — SEFER BEREISHIS"

First edition – First impression: September 2019

Published by **MESORAH PUBLICATIONS, LTD.**
4401 Second Avenue / Brooklyn, N.Y 11232 / (718) 921-9000 / Fax: (718) 680-1875
www.artscroll.com

Distributed in Israel by **SIFRIATI / A. GITLER**
POB 2351 / Bnei Brak 5112, Israel

Distributed in Europe by **LEHMANNS**
Unit E, Viking Business Park, Rolling Mill Road / Jarrow, Tyne and Wear / England NE32 3DP

Distributed in Australia and New Zealand by **GOLDS WORLD OF JUDAICA**
3-13 William Street / Balaclava, Melbourne 3183, Victoria, Australia

Distributed in South Africa by **KOLLEL BOOKSHOP**
Northfield Centre / 17 Northfield Avenue / Glenhazel 2192 / Johannesburg, South Africa

Printed in Canada
Custom bound by Sefercraft, Inc. / 4401 Second Avenue / Brooklyn N.Y. 11232

ISBN-10: 1-4226-2367-X
ISBN-13: 978-1-4226-2367-1

It is a privilege to dedicate this volume
to our unforgettable friend and mentor

Rabbi Meir Zlotowitz ז״ל
הרב מאיר יעקב בן הגאון הרב אהרן ז״ל

He changed the world and spread Torah study to an unprecedented degree. It is fitting that this *Sefer Bereishis* is dedicated to him, because his multivolume commentary of *Bereishis* has been an unparalleled classic for forty years.

He made the study of *Bereishis* accessible to everyone — scholar, layman, student, *everyone*! — and this new work will do the same in a unique and joyous way.

ArtScroll/Mesorah was his vision and he made it his reality. Under the leadership of our beloved friend, Rav Gedaliah, it carries on Rav Meir's dream. With Hashem's help, may he and the rest of the ArtScroll family — *Rav Meir's family* — continue to bring Torah, *yiras Shamayim*, and inspiration to multitudes and generations of our people,

The Jaffa Family

Acknowledgments

My fondest memories of my father are of him telling us the stories of the weekly parashah, with Midrashim. My fascination with the stories of the Torah was born in the glow of the Shabbos candles, lit by my mother. I am gratefully dedicating this book to my parents, Aharon Yosef ben Yochanan HaKohen and Breindel Reizel bas Nachman *a"h*.

As an adult, my appreciation for Chumash and Midrash grew by leaps and bounds through the inspirational *shiurim* of my rebbi, Rav Nachman Bulman *zt"l*.

My writing career has been due to my life's partner, Miriam, who has been an indispensable fountain of help, guidance, and encouragement. This *sefer* is another product of our partnership.

I must thank my *chavrusa*, Dr. Pinchas Ackerman, for his unlimited patience throughout the writing of this *sefer*.

Teaching Torah requires accuracy to ensure that it properly reflects our *mesorah*, the traditions handed down from generation to generation. Rabbi Pinchas Waldman *shlita*, my rebbi and mentor, checked the accuracy of this *sefer* and verified the sources, ensuring the quality and authenticity of the text. I am grateful for all that he has done for our family.

The text went through the expert editorial hands of Rabbi Nosson Scherman and Shmuel Blitz, whose suggestions and edits fine-tuned the original manuscript, putting a polish on it so it sparkles.

Thanks to the other members of ArtScroll's professional and caring staff: Rabbi Gedaliah Zlotowitz, for giving me this wonderful opportunity; Mrs. Faygie Weinbaum and Mrs. Esther Feierstein, for their meticulous proofreading; Mrs. Chana Sternglantz, for providing expert technical assistance; Rabbi Avrohom Biderman, for his input on the illustrations; Mendy Herzberg, for shepherding the many files so efficiently; Rabbi Dovid Morgenstern, for reviewing the work and making important suggestions.

Tova Katz's illustrations have enhanced this work immeasurably, and she was a pleasure to work with. Yonina Hartstein of Divine Design did a beautiful job designing and laying out the book, and creating the extraordinary cover.

After years of telling over the parashah to my young *talmidim* in a way that would excite and fascinate them, I thank the Almighty that He has given me this opportunity to reach so many more *talmidim* than I could ever have in the classroom.

Rabbi Nachman Zakon

Welcome!

We love our Torah so much.

On Simchas Torah in shul, we dance with it. We hug it. And when someone carries it near us, we kiss it.

Who else in the world kisses their books and dances with them?

We love the Torah, because it is not just a book. The Torah is Hashem's words to us. It's the way He speaks to us.

As we read about the Torah, we'll be taking a journey that will tell us how the Jewish people came to be. We will discover what our mission is and what our mitzvos are. We will learn what Hashem wants from us. Along the way there will be fascinating facts, amazing questions, and exciting stories.

Every parashah will come alive as we read what Hashem is telling us.

So let's get started. It's going to be a great trip!

Table of Contents

Parashas Bereishis / פָּרָשַׁת בְּרֵאשִׁית	1
Parashas Noach / פָּרָשַׁת נֹחַ	23
Parashas Lech Lecha / פָּרָשַׁת לֶךְ לְךָ	43
Parashas Vayeira / פָּרָשַׁת וַיֵּרָא	67
Parashas Chayei Sara / פָּרָשַׁת חַיֵּי שָׂרָה	95
Parashas Toldos / פָּרָשַׁת תּוֹלְדוֹת	113
Parashas Vayeitzei / פָּרָשַׁת וַיֵּצֵא	137
Parashas Vayishlach / פָּרָשַׁת וַיִּשְׁלַח	159
Parashas Vayeishev / פָּרָשַׁת וַיֵּשֶׁב	181
Parashas Mikeitz / פָּרָשַׁת מִקֵּץ	197
Parashas Vayigash / פָּרָשַׁת וַיִּגַּשׁ	219
Parashas Vayechi / פָּרָשַׁת וַיְחִי	235
Glossary	259
Sources	260

פָּרָשַׁת בְּרֵאשִׁית

Parashas Bereishis

Bereishis • בְּרֵאשִׁית

Parashah Pointers

- Hashem creates the world in six days.
- He rests on the seventh day: Shabbos.
- Hashem creates Adam and Chavah, the first man and woman, on Erev Shabbos. They live in Gan Eden, the Garden of Eden. It's a perfect place!
- Hashem tells Adam that he and his family can eat whatever grows in Gan Eden. There is only one tree they may not eat from: the Eitz Hada'as, the Tree of Knowledge of Good and Bad.
- The snake fools Chavah and gets her to eat from the Eitz Hada'as. She gives it to Adam, and he eats it too. This is the very first sin.
- Hashem punishes Adam and Chavah for eating from the tree.
- After Shabbos, Hashem sends Adam and Chavah out of Gan Eden. They are not allowed to live there any longer.
- They have two children, Kayin and Hevel.
- Kayin kills his brother Hevel!
- One hundred and thirty years after Kayin and Hevel were born, Adam and Chavah have another child. They name him Sheis. Many more generations are born.
- Noach is born. He has three sons: Shem, Cham, and Yefes.
- The world becomes evil. Hashem decides that if people don't behave better, He will bring a Mabul (Flood) that will destroy all life on earth!

Bereishis — In the Beginning

In the beginning, there was no earth, planets, moon, sun, stars, or galaxies. There was no universe and no life. Nothing! There was only Hashem, and His Torah.

When the time came to create the world, Hashem looked into His Torah. Using its letters, He created the world.

The First Day

At first, there was nothing. Not even air!

Then Hashem said, "Bereishis — In the beginning" — and everything in the entire universe came into existence. Out of nothing! There was heaven and earth and darkness. But there was no order. Everything in creation was mixed up with everything else.

Hashem then made light and separated it from the darkness. He called the light "day," and the darkness He called "night." That was the first day of Creation.

Why Beis?

Why does Torah and Creation start with the letter "beis" of Bereishis? Shouldn't it have started with the letter "aleph," the first letter of the Jewish alphabet?

"Beis" is the first letter in the word "berachah," the Hebrew word for "blessing." This is telling us that Hashem started the world with a blessing.

Another reason is because the number value of "beis" is two. This reminds us that there are two worlds: this world that we live in, which we can see and touch, and the other world, Olam Haba, where souls go when they leave this world. That is the world where Hashem will reward us for the mitzvos we do.

The Light Was Good

Hashem saw that the light was good. The light of Creation was so good that a person could see from one end of the world to the other.

But Hashem knew that wicked people didn't deserve such an awesome light. He decided to hide it away until Mashiach comes. Then this special light will once again light up the world for the benefit of holy tzaddikim and good people.

QUESTIONS, ANYONE?

In the verses that tell us what happened on the first day of Creation, the word "ohr" (light) is repeated five times. Why?

Those words stand for the Five Books of the Torah that light up our world. Without the Torah, the world would indeed be a sad and dark place.

TORAH IN OUR LIVES

Unlike non-Jews, who start their holidays in the morning (such as July Fourth or Presidents' Day), our holidays and Shabbos start at night. Why is that?

Because the Torah says, at the end of the first day of Creation, "It was evening and then morning, one day." Evening comes first, and it starts the day.

The Second Day

On the second day, Hashem divided the world's waters in half. He put the sky in place to separate between the water on earth and in the sky. He called the sky Shamayim — heaven.

The angels were also created on this day. Gehinnom, the place where evil souls go to be punished after they leave this world, was also created.

Because the waters of the world were divided on the second day of Creation, it is the only day of Creation that Hashem doesn't say that it was "good." What's not good about dividing something? When people get along with each other, that is very good. But sometimes, they argue and get "divided" into groups that don't get along and hate each other. That is very bad. So when Hashem "divided" the waters, He didn't want to call it "good."

The Third Day

Hashem commanded that the world's oceans, seas, rivers, and lakes should appear. Then there was dry land on the earth's surface. Hashem called the dry part of the world "eretz," which means land.

Then Hashem told the earth to produce fruit trees and everything else that grows from the ground, like flowers, grass, and vegetables.

The Fourth Day

Hashem put the sun and moon in the sky.

In the beginning the sun and moon were the same size, with the same amount of light. But the moon was not happy that they were both ruling together, one by day and one by night. It wanted to be the only light. The moon complained to Hashem, "I am like a king, ruling over the world, and the sun is like a king, ruling over the world. How can there be two kings over the same place?"

"You're right," Hashem said. And then He made the moon smaller!

But so the moon shouldn't feel too bad that it was made smaller, Hashem gave the stars to the moon, to help light up the night sky.

Questions, Anyone?

Is there water in the sky?

That water is something so holy that we can't know what it is until our souls go to Olam Haba.

Why did Hashem call the sky Shamayim?

Hashem made the Shamayim with fire and water. He mixed them together and the Shamayim appeared.

The word shamayim is a combination of the two Hebrew words "eish" (fire) and "mayim" (water).

Fascinating Facts

When Hashem created the seas He made them promise to split in the future, when it was time for the Jews to escape from Pharaoh and his army.

TORAH IN OUR LIVES

What happens when the sun hits the exact place in the sky that it was when it first started shining? We go outside, look at it, and make a berachah, thanking Hashem for Creation. This is called Bircas HaChamah, Blessing the Sun.

It doesn't happen often, only once every twenty-eight years! The last time the berachah was made was in 2009. The next time will be in 2037. How old will you be then?

FASCINATING FACTS

Hashem created humanity to rule over all life on earth. The world — its trees, plants, animals, fish, and birds — are there to serve people. But only if the people are worthy. When people don't behave properly the world can turn against them. There can be exploding volcanoes, harmful earthquakes and hurricanes, and other natural disasters.

The Fifth Day

The sky became filled with birds of all types, while the seas swarmed with fish, and all sorts of sea creatures, large and small.

Hashem created a pair of colossal fish, a male and a female. They are called the Levyasan. These were bigger than a whale. Much bigger!

Hashem realized that if these sea giants would have children, pretty soon the whole world would be full of them and the world wouldn't last. So He killed the female and preserved it in salt. It will be eaten by the tzaddikim when Mashiach comes.

The Sixth Day

All the world's animals — cows, tigers, elephants, sheep, and many, many more — rose out from the earth. Bugs, reptiles, spiders, and worms did, too.

We don't build a house because we want a nice place to put furniture or because we need walls to hang pictures. We build a house for people who will live there. But people move in only after the house is finished.

Hashem built the world the same way. The first man and woman were the most important. But first Hashem made sure they would have a beautiful home. It would be a world full of color, nice smells, and many different kinds of animals, birds, and fish. A universe of sun, moon, stars, and space.

Now it was time for Hashem to create Adam, the first man.

Adam Is Created

Everything in Creation came into being by the word of Hashem. But to create the first human being, Hashem did it Himself. Creating the first people would be more like an artist carving a shape.

Have you ever seen your mom make challah? She takes flour and water and mixes it together. She then kneads it into dough and shapes it into a challah. Hashem did something like that to make Adam.

Hashem took earth from the place in Yerushalayim where the Mizbei'ach (Altar) of the Beis HaMikdash would stand many years in the future. Then, He mixed it together with bits of earth from all over the world, north, south, east, and west. He took water from all over, and mixed it with the earth. Then, Hashem kneaded the earth and water into the form of a human being. He created a head, hands, internal organs, feet — everything. This was a lump of earth in the shape of a person. It looked human, but there was no life in it.

Then, finally, Hashem blew a soul (neshamah) into Adam's nose — and the first person, Adam, came to life. This soul gave Adam the power to speak and think.

In His Image

Hashem had made Adam in His image. Of course we don't look like Hashem. What that means is that we have choices — we can choose to obey Hashem or not. Hashem's other creations, like the sun and moon, don't have that choice. They orbit the earth, as Hashem commanded them, day after day. They can't tell Hashem, "Enough! I won't do this anymore."

Also, humans can think. We don't do things by instinct like the animal kingdom. If a lion sees a lamb, he eats it without thinking. If a boy with strong muscles sees a little kid eating an ice cream, he can choose to grab it away (bad choice!) or choose to be nice to him (good choice!).

Meet Adam

When Adam came to life he knew that Hashem had made him. Even when he was only a few minutes old, he looked like he was twenty. He understood everything about the world around him and spoke in Lashon Hakodesh. He was on such a high level that Hashem spoke to him.

Busy Day

Friday, the sixth day of Creation, was a very busy day. Not only were Adam and the animals created that day, but a lot of other things happened as well. Good things like the creation of Chavah, the first woman. Terrible events like the first sin, and much more.

FASCINATING FACTS

The world was created in six days. But it would become permanent only if, in the future, on the sixth day of Sivan, the Jews would accept the Torah. If they didn't accept the Torah, the world would disappear.

Fortunately we did accept the Torah … and the world is still here!

There is a hint to this in the Torah itself. When it discusses the sixth day of Creation, instead of writing, "there was evening, there was morning, a sixth day" (yom shishi), the Torah added the Hebrew letter "hei" to the word "shishi." The "hei" changes the meaning of the words from "**a** sixth day" to "**the** sixth day." This means that there is **a very special sixth day**.

What day is that? The sixth day, when the Torah was given. The sixth day of Sivan.

Created Last

Right before the seventh day began, Hashem created items that would be used for miracles.

Moshe's stick: The stick Moshe used to bring the ten Makkos (plagues) on Egypt.

Miriam's well: A stone that gushed with water for the Jews in the desert.

Bilaam's donkey: When the time came, it had the power to speak to Bilaam.

Mahn: The food that fell from heaven, which the Jews ate in the desert.

Luchos: Two square blocks of stone on which Hashem would write the Aseres HaDibros (Ten Commandments).

The Seventh Day — Shabbos

At the end of Friday, exactly when the seventh day began, Hashem stopped creating the universe. Everything that needed to be created had already been created.

And now it was time for Shabbos!

Shabbos is like the world's battery pack. It is the day that the ``batteries" of the world are recharged, so the whole world can continue to exist. On Sunday, the world turns on again, because of Shabbos.

This happens every single week. Six days pass. Shabbos comes, and the world rests.

In other words, Shabbos is the world's soul. Our souls give us life. Shabbos gives the world life.

Blessed and Holy

Hashem blessed the Shabbos and made it holy. One way He made it holy was by not allowing the mahn to fall in the desert on Shabbos. He blessed it by having twice as much mahn fall on Friday, enough for Friday and Shabbos.

What this means is that Hashem made the Shabbos a day of no work. It would be used only for holiness. No collecting mahn on Shabbos. No going to work.

Isn't Shabbos food the best? Ever try to eat cholent or kugel during the week? It doesn't taste nearly as good as it tastes on Shabbos! Because Hashem blessed the Shabbos, food tastes better when it is eaten on Shabbos.

We prepare more food for Shabbos than for any other day of the week. How can we afford to spend so much money preparing for Shabbos?

That is because of another blessing that Hashem gave Shabbos. Just like on Friday twice as much mahn fell as during the rest of the week, Hashem helps us earn more during the week so we can afford to shop for Shabbos!

Rain!

Let's go back and see what else happened on the sixth day of Creation, after Hashem made Adam.

When Adam looked around after he came to life there were no trees or bushes, nothing was growing out of the ground anywhere.

What happened to the trees, grass, and bushes that He created on the third day? They were all there, but they were underground, waiting to burst forth over the earth.

FASCINATING FACTS

Every day of the week has a "partner." Sunday has Monday, Tuesday has Wednesday, and Thursday has Friday.

The seventh day — Shabbos — said to Hashem, "All the days have a partner except for me."

Hashem answered, "The Jewish people are your partner."

The Jewish people are the ones who observe Shabbos. We and Shabbos are partners!

Hashem knew that in the future the nations of the world would tell the Jews, "Eretz Yisrael is not yours! Who says you can live there? You stole the land from others!"

So instead of starting the Torah with the first mitzvah, Hashem began the Torah with the story of Creation. This way, when the nations of the world complain, we can open the Torah to the very beginning and say to them, "Look. It says right here that Hashem created the whole world. It belongs to Him, so He can give any part of it to whomever He wants. He gave Eretz Yisrael to us, the Jewish people, FOREVER!"

What was missing to get them to come out? Prayer!

Adam knew if he wanted food on earth he would have to pray for it. He started to pray and the very first rainfall came pouring out of the sky.

Suddenly, all over the world, trees rose out of the earth. They grew taller and taller, reaching for the sky. They were full of fruit. A sweet smell filled the air as flowers broke through the earth. Vegetables grew. Adam's prayers had brought the earth to life!

In Paradise

Imagine living in a hotel for free. All meals are served and you don't have to clean up afterward. Mom and Dad don't have to go to work because there are no bills to pay. Everything is free! A place of no worry. Paradise, right?

Well, that was the kind of place Hashem invited Adam to live in. It was a special place created just for him, a garden on the eastern side of a place called Eden. The garden was called Gan Eden.

The garden had many different trees full of mouthwatering fruit. When Adam wanted a snack, all he had to do was to pick fruits and eat. Delicious fresh rolls also grew on the trees. If he wanted something more, angels would roast meat for him that dropped from heaven. They also served him wine.

There was no illness, no death. The garden was a place where Adam would have no worries. He could spend all his time serving Hashem.

Adam didn't even need to water the garden. It got its water from a river that flowed through Gan Eden.

Name It!

When they were created, the animals and birds didn't have any names. They weren't called lions, tigers, or parrots. Then Hashem brought the animals and birds to Adam and told him to give each one its name.

After Adam had named the animals, Hashem said to Adam, "What's your name?"

"My name should be Adam, because I was made from adamah, earth."

Chavah, the First Woman

Now that the animals had names, Hashem sent each animal and its partner to parade past Adam. When Adam saw that each animal was created with a male and female, he asked Hashem to give him a partner as well, a wife.

Why didn't Hashem put the trees and plants on the earth before Adam prayed?

To teach us the power and importance of prayer. To show us how much Hashem wants to hear us ask for what we need to live in His world.

What holiday do we celebrate on the day that Adam came to life?

Rosh Hashanah, which comes out on the first day of the Hebrew month of Tishrei. That was the sixth day of Creation.

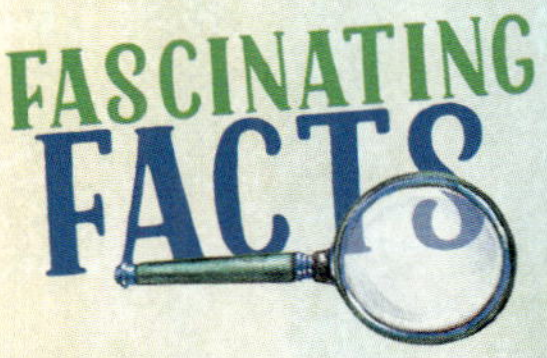

When the river in Gan Eden left the garden it split into four rivers: Pishon, Gichon, Chidekel, and Euphrates.

In Hebrew, Adam is spelled aleph, dalet, mem. These letters stand for:
א Aleph: Adam
ד Dalet: [King] David
מ Mem: Mashiach

Hashem put Adam into a deep sleep. Hashem took a rib out of Adam's side and used it to create the very first woman on earth. When Adam woke up he found the wife Hashem had created just for him. She was very beautiful.

Adam's wife needed a name. He chose to name her Chavah because his wife would be the mother of all of us. Chavah means "life giver," from the Hebrew word for life, "chayah."

The Wedding

When Adam and Chavah got married they were the only people on earth. So it wasn't a large wedding with many guests.

But it was the first wedding ever, and it was magnificent!

In preparation for her wedding Hashem braided Chavah's hair. He gave her 24 different pieces of sparkling jewelry.

When she was ready, Hashem Himself brought Chavah to her chupah. Her chassan, Adam, was waiting for her. He was standing under ten chupahs, one above the other! Each chupah was dazzling. The chupahs were made of expensive jewels, precious stones, and gold.

The powerful and famous angels Gavriel and Micha'el stood next to Adam. Instead of a band, angels sang and danced for them.

Hashem gave Adam and Chavah a blessing, and commanded them to have many children and descendants.

Mazel Tov! Mazel Tov! Mazel Tov!

About an hour after they were married, Adam and Chavah became parents. If there had been people in the world then, they would have given the new parents not just one mazel tov, but many. Chavah had twins and then triplets! Five children! She had a boy who was born with a twin sister, and triplets, a boy and two girls.

Imagine taking care of five babies all at once! What a challenge! But Chavah didn't have that challenge. In Gan Eden there was no need to raise children. They were born adults. There was also no need to wait nine months for a baby to be born. The children were all born the same day.

The oldest son was named Kayin and the younger son was named Hevel. We don't know the names of Adam and Chavah's daughters.

Eat!

In the center of the Garden was a tree called Eitz Hada'as — the Tree of Knowledge of Good and Bad. Next to it was a huge tree called the Eitz HaChaim, the Tree of Life.

Hashem commanded Adam, "Eat from any tree in the Garden, except

FASCINATING FACTS

Some say that when Hashem created Adam, one side of him was a man, and the other side was a woman. The two sides were connected back to back. Later, Hashem separated them.

QUESTIONS, ANYONE?

What is the very first of the Torah's six hundred and thirteen mitzvos?

To have children. It was Adam and Chavah's first mitzvah.

FASCINATING FACTS

The population of the entire world on the sixth day of Creation was seven! Compare that to today: The world's population today is way over seven billion!

For 1,656 years, from Adam until the Mabul (you'll read about that soon), humans were allowed to eat only what grew from the ground: fruits, vegetables, and grains. They were not allowed to kill any living creature for food.

for the Eitz Hada'as! Because on the day you eat from the Eitz Hada'as, you will die."

Besides the command not to eat from the Eitz Hada'as, Hashem gave Adam six other commandments. All non-Jews have to keep these mitzvos.

The Six Commandments

- Don't worship idols or bow down to them.
- Don't curse Hashem.
- Appoint judges and courts of law.
- Don't murder.
- Be moral.
- Don't steal.

QUESTIONS, ANYONE?

What kind of fruit tree was the Eitz Hada'as?

No one really knows for sure. There are many opinions. It was one of the following: esrog, wheat, figs, or grapes. (Many people think it was an apple, but that is a mistake.)

Chavah Meets the Snake

A snake lived in Gan Eden. But it didn't look like today's snakes. It had feet. It didn't crawl or slither, it walked erect like you and me. It was the cleverest of all the animals, the king of beasts. And it was evil.

The snake wanted to make Chavah sin.

The snake started a conversation with Chavah. (I told you it wasn't like today's snakes!) "Did Hashem tell you not to eat from any of the trees in the garden?" he asked.

"No, just not from the Eitz Hada'as. If we touch it, we will die."

"No you won't," said the snake. "Hashem doesn't want you to eat from it because He is afraid that if you do, you will be like Him and be able to create worlds."

Disaster!

The snake's words were all lies and lashon hara against Hashem! Still, the snake was able to convince Chavah, who believed his lies. He gave her a little push and she touched the Eitz Hada'as.

Chavah reached out to the tree, picked the forbidden fruit from the Eitz Hada'as, and ate it.

As soon as she ate it she discovered that everything the snake had told her was a lie! She couldn't create worlds! For what she had done, she would have to die.

Chavah then gave the forbidden fruit to Adam and to the animals to eat!

What a disaster! On the sixth day of Creation, with only three hours left to the start of the world's first Shabbos, Adam and Chavah had disobeyed Hashem.

It didn't take Adam and Chavah too much time before they disobeyed Hashem. From the time Hashem commanded them not to eat from the Eitz Hada'as, until they ate from it, was only about an hour!

They had eaten from the *only* tree that Hashem had told them not to eat from. It was the first sin and it brought tragedy and death to the world. If Adam and Chavah had not eaten from the tree, we would never get sick and everyone would live forever.

FASCINATING FACTS

Did Hashem say no one should touch the tree? No, He just said not to eat from it. Chavah got in trouble because she said something that was not true.

"You see?" said the snake. "You touched the tree and you didn't die! You can eat from it, too!"

Where Are You?

Are animals embarrassed that they don't wear clothes? Before the sin, Adam and Chavah weren't embarrassed, even though they were not wearing clothes. Once they had sinned they became embarrassed. So they made themselves clothing from fig leaves and covered themselves with them.

Then they heard the angels saying that Hashem is coming to the garden to punish them.

What do small children who have just done something really bad do when they hear their father coming? They run and hide! They are ashamed of what they did and are afraid of what's going to happen.

When Adam and Chavah heard their Father in Heaven coming, they ran and hid, afraid and ashamed of what they had done.

"Where are you?" Hashem called out to Adam.

"I was afraid so I hid."

"Did you eat from the tree?"

Testing, Testing

Now of course Hashem knows all and sees all. He knew what had happened and where Adam was. But it was a test. Would Adam admit that he had sinned and done wrong? If he admitted doing the sin, he would get a light punishment.

What did Adam do when Hashem asked if he had sinned?

Adam answered, "The woman You gave me — she gave it to me and I ate it."

In other words, Adam was telling Hashem: "It's not my fault. It's Your fault for giving me Chavah. And it's Chavah's fault for giving it to me."

Adam didn't pass his test. Instead of admitting his sin, he played the "blame game." He was saying: "I didn't sin, it's someone else's fault." That was not what Hashem wanted to hear.

Chavah's Defense

Hashem said to Chavah, "What have you done?"

Instead of admitting that she had done wrong, she told Hashem, "The snake tricked me and I ate."

Cursed

The entire story of the first sin started with the evil snake.

Hashem said to the snake, "Because of what you did, you are more cursed than all the animals. From now on you will crawl on your belly and eat dust from the ground. You and mankind will be eternal enemies."

Pain and Sweat

Now Hashem gave Chavah her punishment. He told her that having children won't be as easy as it was. Now it would be painful. And the children will have to be raised and taken care of until they grow up.

Adam was told that since he ate from the tree, the earth will be cursed because of him. Thorns and weeds will grow on their own. He and

Questions, Anyone?

All the animals, male and female, were created at the same time. Not Adam and Chavah. Adam was created first, and then Hashem created Chavah. Why?

Hashem wanted Adam to ask Hashem to give him a wife. When Adam sinned and said that it's Hashem's fault for giving him a wife who fed him the forbidden fruit, Hashem would answer: "But you asked for her."

Torah in Our Lives

When we do something wrong, it's so easy to blame someone else. But the first step in doing teshuvah (repenting) is to be strong and admit our mistake. Not taking the blame just makes things worse.

So when Shira and Rivky are caught doing something wrong, Shira shouldn't say, "Rivky made me do it."

When Shlomie throws the ball and breaks a window, he should admit it.

Is it embarrassing? It sure is! Will they get in trouble? No doubt. But is it the right thing to do? Absolutely. Doing what our Creator wants us to do is always best!

his descendants will have to work long and hard to grow wheat and other foods.

Death

Hashem told Adam, "From the earth you came and to the earth you will return." That was Hashem's way of saying that people will now die and be buried in the ground.

Though they were punished, Hashem was actually merciful to them. Adam and Chavah had been told that if they ate from the tree they would die. And that was true — because of their sin they would die. But not right away. Hashem in His mercy let them live a long, long time after they sinned before they died.

The leaves that Adam and Chavah used to make clothes for themselves wouldn't last. So Hashem made them clothes. Adam's clothing had the power to attract animals and birds.

Shabbos

Finally, the sixth day was over and the seventh day, Shabbos, started. Even though they had sinned, Hashem allowed Adam and his family to stay in Gan Eden over Shabbos. That first Shabbos, even at night, was as bright as day.

As soon as Shabbos ended, the world got dark, pitch black. Adam was terrified. He had never seen the world go black before. He was created in the daytime and all Shabbos there was light.

Hashem put an idea into Adam's head. He knocked two rocks together and made fire, which lit up the night. Adam was so excited and relieved that he made a berachah over the fire. That is the same berachah we make over the Havdalah candle after Shabbos.

Hashem said, "If I leave Adam in Gan Eden he may eat from the Tree of Life and live forever." So when Shabbos was over, Hashem sent Adam and his family out of Gan Eden. He sent two angels with swords to the entrance of Gan Eden. Their job was to prevent Adam or anyone else from entering the Garden.

Where did Adam and his family go after they left Gan Eden? To the mountain on which the future Beis HaMikdash would be built in Yerushalayim. He would live and work the land in the place where he was created.

The First Murder

How did the first murder in the world happen? This is a sad story.

Kayin was a farmer. His younger brother, Hevel, was a shepherd.

FASCINATING FACTS

Hashem was going to run the world He created with strict judgment. That meant that the minute someone sinned, he or she would be punished as they deserved. He realized, though, that the world could not last that way. Instead, Hashem decided to judge the world with mercy as well. So when a person sins, Hashem doesn't punish him right away. He allows a person time to change bad behavior, do teshuvah, and be forgiven.

QUESTIONS, ANYONE?

How old was Adam when he died?

Nine hundred and thirty years old. He was supposed to live 1,000 years, but he saw that in the future, King David was destined to die at birth. So Adam gave King David seventy years of his own life!

FASCINATING FACTS

The reason we make a berachah over the fire of the Havdalah candle after Shabbos is because that is when fire was created.

Kayin decided to bring a korban (offering) to Hashem to thank Him for the food he grew. That was a good idea. But instead of bringing his best fruits as a korban, he chose the poorest-quality ones. That was bad.

Imagine a family gets a box of mishloach manos on Purim. They take out all the fancy chocolates and yummy candies to keep for themselves. What's left in the box? Some dried-up raisins, black jelly beans, and packages of stale popcorn that no one wanted. Then they go and send these leftovers as mishloach manos to their best friends. That is not nice!

That is a lot like what Kayin did. That is what he gave to Hashem.

The Best

Hevel also brought a korban. He looked at his flocks and chose the best sheep of all of them, as a korban to Hashem.

When Hevel put it on the Mizbei'ach a miracle happened.

A ball of fire suddenly came shooting down from heaven. It landed on the Mizbei'ach and burnt the korban. This was a sign that Hashem was very happy with what Hevel had done and accepted his service to Him.

Jealousy

Kayin saw the miracle Hashem had done for his brother's korban. Hashem had not performed a miracle for his korban, and Kayin got very jealous of his brother. He was also angry that Hashem had not treated him the same as He treated his brother.

Instead of blaming himself for giving Hashem the bad fruits, Kayin blamed Hashem and his brother!

Suddenly Kayin heard Hashem speak to him.

"Why are you angry? Do good and you will be forgiven."

Fight!

Kayin and Hevel had the entire world to themselves. But Kayin wanted it all. He didn't want to share it with his brother. He wanted to get rid of Hevel. Kayin looked for an excuse to argue with his brother so he could kill him.

"Let us divide the world between us," Kayin said to Hevel. "I'll take the land and what grows on it and you take everything else." Hevel agreed.

Then Kayin started shouting at him, "Get off the land. It's mine!"

So Hevel went to graze his sheep in the mountains. Kayin ran after him, telling him to get off his land. They argued and the argument turned into a fight!

Kayin and Hevel were fighting until finally Hevel won. Kayin was on the floor, and Hevel was holding him down.

FASCINATING FACTS

Kayin had killed one-seventh of the world's population when he murdered his brother!

QUESTIONS, ANYONE?

The Torah actually writes "your brother's bloods are crying out" using the plural bloods, instead of writing your "brother's blood." Why?

Kayin had killed Hevel, whose blood was crying out for justice. But in a way Kayin killed more people: all of the children, grandchildren, and descendants of Hevel, who would not be born because Kayin had killed him.

Their blood was also crying for justice. So the Torah uses the word bloods in the plural. It's a hint to teach us that a murderer doesn't just kill one person, but all the future generations as well.

FASCINATING FACTS

Some opinions say Hashem gave Kayin a dog to protect him.

Murder!

Kayin asked for mercy. He begged Hevel to let him get up. Hevel felt bad and let Kayin get up. That's when Kayin grabbed a stone, hit Hevel with it, and killed him!

Kayin heard Hashem speak. "Where is Hevel, your brother?" Hashem asked him.

Of course, Hashem knew exactly what happened. He knows everything that happens. Once again, He wanted to give Kayin a chance to admit he sinned. Hashem wanted Kayin to say he was sorry and do teshuvah.

Kayin thought that he could fool Hashem. If Hashem was asking where Hevel was, maybe He didn't know what had happened.

Kayin lied. "I don't know where he is. Am I my brother's keeper?"

Hashem spoke again. "What have you done?! Your brother's blood is crying out to Me from the ground!"

Kayin's Judgment

Hashem passed judgment on Kayin.

"You are cursed to work the earth very, very hard before it will grow food. You will become a wanderer and an exile on earth."

Kayin would never be able to live in one place. He would always be on the move, going from place to place.

Surrounded

After hearing how he would be punished, Kayin finally regretted committing murder. He admitted he had done wrong.

He was surrounded by growling animals who wanted to kill him because of what he did. Kayin turned to Hashem and begged for mercy.

Hashem announced that whoever kills Kayin will die. Kayin himself will live for seven generations. Then the animals surrounding him left.

Hashem put a letter of His Name on Kayin's forehead to protect him from being killed.

Hevel Is Buried

Adam and Chavah discovered their son's body lying on the ground. But since no one had ever died before, they didn't know what to do with the body!

Then they saw a bird burying a dead bird. Adam and Chavah realized this was a message from Hashem. Now they knew what to do with the body. They buried Hevel.

Adam and Chavah's Grave

Adam died at the age of 930. He is buried in the city of Chevron, in the Me'aras HaMachpeilah. That is the very famous cave where Avraham and Sarah, Yitzchak and Rivkah, and Yaakov and Leah, our Fathers and Mothers, are buried. It is visited by many thousands every year. Chavah was buried there as well.

Adam lived a long time, and saw many things happen during his life. Below are some of the events that happened while he was alive.

QUESTIONS, ANYONE?

How old was Hevel when he died?

Only forty days old!

Talented and Creative

Lemech was Kayin's sixth-generation descendant. His children were very talented and creative. He had three sons: Yovol, Yuval, and Tuval-Kayin, and one daughter, Naamah.

Yovol came up with the idea of raising animals while wandering in the desert and living in tents.

Yuval invented musical instruments: harps and flutes.

Tuval-Kayin sharpened and polished copper and iron weapons for warriors.

Naamah was a good woman who married Noach. She, her husband Noach, and their children were the only ones to survive the Mabul that wiped out all life on earth. (You'll read about it in the next parashah.) Every human being alive today is a descendant of Naamah.

Lemech killed Kayin by accident. He shot an arrow at what he thought was an animal and it hit Kayin.

After Kayin died, Adam and Chavah became parents again. Their son Sheis was born. Chavah called him Sheis because, "Hashem has given me another son to take the place of Hevel." The Hebrew word for "given" is "shos."

Sheis's son was Enosh.

FASCINATING FACTS

The name Naamah means pleasant.

Yovol and Yuval worshiped idols. Some write that Yovol built temples for them and his brother played music for them.

The Big Mistake

Enosh and the people living in his time made a big mistake. They decided that since the sun and moon are Hashem's creations, people should bow down to them and pray to them as a way to show respect to Hashem. This was a mistake, because it led people to forget Hashem.

It wasn't long before some people began to say that the sun had spoken to them. They said that the sun wanted them to build temples with sun images in them. Others said that animals had told them that those who worship the image of this or that animal will have good luck. They were all liars, of course. But they wanted to be famous.

People believed what these liars said. They started bowing down and asking statues of wood and stone to help them. The world forgot that Hashem existed!

It happened so fast. The world wasn't even three hundred years old!

Mabul!

Hashem wanted to help them to remember Him. He raised the water level of the oceans. The waves flooded and destroyed one-third of the world!

You would think that after such a terrible tragedy people would ask themselves what they were doing wrong, and return to Hashem. It didn't happen. They just continued their bad ways.

QUESTIONS, ANYONE?

How were Chanoch and Noach related?

Chanoch was Noach's great-grandfather.

What happened to the clothes that Hashem made for Adam?

He gave them to his son Sheis, who gave them to Mesushelach, who gave them to Noach. Noach took them with him into the Teivah.

Special People

The Torah lists ten generations between Adam and Noach. On the list are some very special people who were not like the rest of the world. They believed in Hashem and were tzaddikim. Here they are:

- Chanoch — He was such a holy man that Hashem turned him into an angel! When the time came for Chanoch to die, Hashem took him straight up to Heaven, alive. There He turned him into Matatron, one of the strongest and most powerful angels in heaven.

  Adam died 57 years before Chanoch was taken to Heaven. Chanoch was chosen to bury Adam in the Me'aras HaMachpeilah.

- Mesushelach — He was Noach's grandfather, a tzaddik who lived longer than any human on earth. He died at the age of 969! That's even longer than Adam lived! Mesushelach served Hashem so well that as long as he was alive, Hashem did not send the great Mabul. His good deeds protected the world from being destroyed.

  The Mabul started seven days after he died. In his honor Hashem waited for the end of the seven days of mourning before bringing the Mabul.

FASCINATING FACTS

Chanoch, the man who became an angel, worked as a shoemaker, making shoes for other people.

Noach Is Born

Mesushelach's son Lemech had a son called Noach. Once Noach was born, the ground wasn't as cursed as it had been before. It made it easier to be a farmer. Because of that, the people had more time to rest. So Lemech called his son Noach, from the Hebrew word to rest, "nach."

Noach himself invented tools to plow the ground. That made being a farmer even easier.

Noach got married and didn't have children for many years. Finally, when he was five hundred years old, he had his first son, Yefes, followed by two more, Shem and Cham.

What Took So Long?

Why didn't Noach have children right away? He had to wait hundreds of years! That's a long time!

Imagine if Noach had children when he was young. By the time the Mabul came they would have families of their own.

It was hard enough to build one Teivah. Can you imagine if Noach would have had to build three more? Having children later made his job easier. He had to build only one Teivah.

And if his children would grow up to be wicked, they would have died in the Mabul. That would cause Noach great pain. Because his children were born later, they were too young to be punished with death and were saved under their father Noach's protection.

Evil

The world had become evil. Hashem decided that if people didn't improve the way they behaved, He would bring a Mabul that would destroy all life on earth!

Even though things had gotten so bad that the world had to be destroyed, Hashem was merciful. He gave them 120 years to improve. That's a long time!

All Is Not Lost

If the Mabul came, all life that started with Bereishis would be lost! Fortunately, there was one person who found favor in Hashem's eyes: Noach.

He and his family would be rescued and survive the Mabul. All would not be lost and life would start over again.

The fascinating and exciting story of Noach's rescue and a world reborn is what the next parashah is about.

TORAH IN OUR LIVES

Sometimes we hear about good people who are going through really tough times. We wonder, why should these terrible things be happening to them? We can find the answer in the story of Noach.

He suffered hundreds of years, waiting for children. His friends were grandparents before he even had one child. Noach was a tzaddik! Why did he have to suffer?

When the Mabul came Noach understood that Hashem had done him a favor. His sons didn't die in the Mabul, and he had to build only one Teivah.

Have faith and trust in Hashem. He loves us, and He has a good reason for sometimes doing things to good people that seem to be bad for them.

He always knows what's best for us. Always!!!

פָּרָשַׁת נֹחַ

Parashas Noach

Noach • נֹחַ

Parashah Pointers

- Noach is a tzaddik living at a time when almost everyone is very evil.
- Hashem tells Noach that because people are evil, He will destroy the world in a Mabul, a huge Flood.
- Hashem commands him to build a "Teivah," a large ship.
- Noach and his family go into the Teivah. One male and one female of all non-kosher animals also go in, as well as seven males and seven females of all kosher animals and birds.
- The Mabul comes. For forty days and nights the rain comes pouring down and floods the earth. Even the mountaintops are covered! All the people and animals drown. Only the people and animals in the Teivah are saved. Also, the fish did not die.
- The rain stops but it takes a long time for the earth to dry. Noach sends a raven and then a dove to check if the land is dry enough for everyone to leave the Teivah.
- Finally, a year after the Mabul began, Hashem tells Noach to leave the Teivah, together with his family and all the animals.
- Hashem promises Noach not to destroy the world again. He puts a rainbow in the sky as a sign of this promise.
- Noach plants a vineyard. He drinks too much, gets drunk, and lies down. Canaan, Cham's son and Noach's grandson, sees his grandfather and tells his father.
- Cham comes into his father's tent and sees his father lying there. He goes out to his brothers and makes fun of their father.
- Shem and Yefes, Noach's two other sons, go in and treat their father with respect. They cover him.
- Noach knew what had happened. He blesses Shem and Yefes for their good deed. He curses Canaan, that he will be a slave to Shem and Yefes.
- Many people are born and they build a city. Once again the world becomes evil and the people decide to build a tower to the sky. They think they can climb up to the sky and fight with Hashem.
- Until this time, everyone in the world spoke Hebrew. But to punish the people for their building the tower, Hashem brings 70 languages to the world, and spreads the people all over.
- Avram is born. Sarai is born. They get married.

An Evil World

The whole world was evil. No one believed in Hashem. People were stealing from each other and murdering each other. But not Noach. He was different. He was a tzaddik. He and his family believed in Hashem, and they didn't do bad things or steal. He had three sons: Shem, Cham, and Yefes.

Hashem created the world for people to be good to each other. But the people had become so bad and selfish that Hashem decided He must destroy the earth and start all over again! Noach and his family would survive the world's destruction and rebuild it.

One More Chance

Before destroying the world, Hashem, Who loves people, decided to give the world one more chance to save itself. He would send a warning to the world to stop being evil or their world would come to an end. If they would hear the message and change their ways, He wouldn't have to destroy them.

Hashem chose Noach to send the warning.

A Worldwide Mabul

Hashem spoke to Noach and said, "The end of all life is coming because the world is filled with robbery, and I am going to destroy it. I will flood the world with water, a Mabul, to destroy all life on earth.

"Make a Teivah." The ship that Noach was commanded to build is called a "Teivah." In English, "Teivah" is usually translated as an "Ark," which means a container used to protect something valuable. "You, your family, and a male and female of every animal, bird, and whatever crawls on earth will survive in the Teivah."

Hashem told Noach exactly how large to build the Teivah. It was enormous! It was the size of a large palace. It would take Noach 120 years to build it.

Everyone Is Talking About It

Hashem wanted to give the people a chance to do teshuvah. So how did He get His message out to the world? Simple — word of mouth! One person tells another, who tells another. Pretty soon everyone is talking about it. This is how it worked for Noach.

Noach started to build the Teivah. All day long he was banging away, building his Teivah, using wood beams. When they heard the noise, people came out to find out what was going on.

Questions, Anyone?

Who was the greatest of Noach's sons?

Shem. That is why even though he was Noach's third child, he is listed first. Yefes was the oldest, and Cham was the second.

Why does the Torah say Noach was a tzaddik "in his generation"?

Some say it's to tell us that if Noach became a tzaddik even though he lived among such bad people, if he had lived in Avraham's time, he would have been a greater tzaddik.

Others say it means that Noach was special only because he was better than his generation, where everyone was evil. But had he lived in the time of Avraham, he would not have been so special.

Fascinating Facts

The generation of the Mabul sinned against Hashem in many ways. But once they started stealing from each other, Hashem decided to bring the Mabul. In a way stealing is worse than sinning against Hashem, because it hurts both Hashem and His own creations.

"Noach, what are you doing? Why are you building such a large ship?"

"Because all the people are sinning, Hashem is going to send a Mabul that will cover the world with water and everyone will drown."

Pretty soon everyone had heard about Noach's building project, his Teivah, and how he claimed Hashem would bring a Mabul.

For 120 years Noach kept repeating Hashem's warning to whoever went by. Unfortunately, no one listened. They called Noach a crazy old man, and they continued with their evil ways.

So Hashem decided that the Mabul must come.

The Teivah

Noach finished building the Teivah. He followed Hashem's instructions on how to build it. It was big. It had to carry Noach and his wife, his three sons and their wives — and the biggest zoo the world had ever seen! The Teivah contained a male and female of every creature on earth, and 7 pairs of all kosher animals. The Teivah would also have to carry a year's supply of food to feed everyone, people and animals!

The Teivah was 300 amos long (almost 600 feet), fifty amos wide (almost 100 feet), and 30 amos high (almost 60 feet high). That's the height of a four-story building, and it was very long and wide!

Think about it. As big as it was, it wasn't big enough for every single animal! It was a miracle that everything fit in.

A Teivah Tour

From the outside the Teivah looked like a high, black, rectangular building, with a sloped roof that was only about two feet wide at the top. It had a window at the top. There was a door near one of the corners.

Why was it black? Because after the Teivah was built Noach covered it with black tar, both on the outside and the inside, to make it waterproof. He wanted to make sure it was strong and would not leak. It had to survive the powerful waters of the Mabul.

Let's take a tour of the three floors of the Teivah. We'll start on the ground floor. This is where Noach would throw all the dirt made by all the living creatures. The next floor up, the second floor, is for all the animals. The third, top floor is where Noach and his family stayed. Walking through the Teivah we see hundreds of rooms.

Once Noach and the animals move into the Teivah it will be their home ... for an entire year!

FASCINATING FACTS

Not only did the Mabul destroy every living thing, but it destroyed everything that grew from the ground as well. That's why Noach brought baby trees into the Teivah, to replant after the Mabul.

There were only ten generations between Adam and Noach.

QUESTIONS, ANYONE?

There were no refrigerators or freezers back then. How could the food Noach took with him in the Teivah last a whole year without going bad?

Hashem gave him a special blessing that the food wouldn't spoil.

FASCINATING FACTS

According to some opinions the light in the Teivah came not from the window, but from a precious, shining stone attached to the roof of the Teivah.

The Death of a Tzaddik

Finally, Noach finished the Teivah. It was time for the Mabul to start. But it didn't! Hashem spoke to Noach and told him that the Mabul wouldn't start for another seven days. After that, it would rain for forty days and nights.

In seven days? Why not right away?

To give the world time to give honor and mourn for the great tzaddik, Mesushelach, who had just died. He was 969 years old, the oldest man who ever lived.

Two and Seven

Hashem gave Noach instructions about the animals that were going to go into the Teivah. He had to take seven males and seven females from all the different kinds of kosher animals, and one pair of male and female non-kosher animals.

Why should there be more kosher animals than non-kosher animals?

Actually, only one pair of every creature on earth would survive the Mabul. Noach would use the other six pairs of kosher animals and birds as korbanos after the Mabul. That was how he would thank Hashem for saving him and his family from the Mabul.

"Am I a Hunter?"

When Hashem told Noach to gather all the animals, Noach said, "Am I a hunter?" Imagine having to go and hunt for every creature on earth!

"Don't worry about it," said Hashem.

Hashem sent a parade of animals to gather around the Teivah and march in. There were wild beasts like lions and tigers, large animals like elephants and hippos. There were cows, sheep, and goats. Grasshoppers, snakes, mosquitoes, and bees. Cats and dogs. Birds of all types: eagles, ravens, and doves. Either a pair or seven pairs of every creature on earth came from near and far to the Teivah.

They all came on their own, sent by Hashem.

The End Begins

It was time. The Mabul was coming! Hashem told Noach to enter the Teivah with his family.

But Noach didn't do it. He just couldn't believe Hashem would

Questions, Anyone?

How old was Noach when the Mabul started?

Six hundred years old!

Torah in our Lives

When Hashem tells Noach about how many kosher and non- kosher animals he should take, the Torah calls the kosher ones "tehorim," which means "clean," and the non-kosher ones "lo tehorim," which means "not clean."

The Torah could have used the word "temei'im," which is a shorter way of saying "not clean." There are no extra words in the Torah. Why did it say "that are not tehorim," rather than "temei'im" — which would have saved an extra word?

This teaches us not to say bad words. The Torah went out of its way and used extra words, just not to use the word "temei'im."

Using bad words is not the Torah way! A mouth should be used for holy things, like Torah, prayer, and making other people feel good. Not for bad words.

Questions, Anyone?

Were there fish in the Teivah?

No. The Mabul didn't kill the fish.

destroy all life on earth. Then it started to rain. Finally, Noach went into the Teivah, and Hashem closed the door behind him.

The Mabul began on the seventeenth day of Cheshvan.

The Mabul started as a gentle rain. Hashem did not want to have to kill all the people. He gave them one last chance to do teshuvah. There would have been a gentle rain, but no Mabul. The world would have been saved.

Sadly, no one repented.

The Teivah Is in Danger!

The rains came down hard. Suddenly, powerful fountains of water began shooting out of the earth. The land began to flood, and people were surrounded by deep, rushing flood waters.

An angry mob gathered around the Teivah. "Destroy it, break it into small pieces!" they shouted. Noach and the animals in the Teivah were in terrible danger!

Hashem sent vicious bears and lions to surround the Teivah and protect it from the mob. They killed anyone who tried to get near the Teivah. The Teivah was saved!

The End

Boiling hot rain began to fall. For forty days and nights it rained, and rained non-stop. Hashem opened up the ground and streams of boiling hot water shot out of the ground.

There was so much rain that the rivers and seas overflowed. The water level over the earth got higher and higher. People watched as everything they owned was destroyed by the waters of the Mabul. Their homes came crashing down as a result of the force of the flood, then crumbled to dust in the Mabul's hot water. Even their gold burst into flames and burned to nothing.

People and animals ran to higher ground, to the hills and mountains, hoping to escape the rising waters. It was no use. The water rose higher and higher, until even the mountaintops were covered with water. The people died first, then the animals.

At the end of the 40 days and 40 nights, the rain stopped. For another 150 days the water level kept rising, until the highest mountaintops were covered by 15 amah (approximately 30 feet) of water.

It was 1,656 years after Hashem created the world. Human civilization was gone. Not a building or tree was left standing. Not a bird, animal, or human was left (except for those in the Teivah, and the fish).

People's evil behavior had brought about their end.

The entire surface of the earth was covered with water.

The world needed a reboot.

Questions, Anyone?

How do we know that Noach learned Torah?

Hashem told him to take seven pairs of all kosher animals into the Teivah. If Noach hadn't studied Torah, how would he know which animals are kosher and which are not?

Fascinating Facts

When a lion roared or a bird chirped, Noach knew exactly what it was saying.
He understood all the animal languages.

Noach's faith in Hashem was less than perfect. When Hashem commanded him to go into the Teivah, he should have gone in right away. He still thought Hashem would cancel the Mabul.

When Noach was building the Teivah, people said to each other, "If we see Noach going into his Teivah to save himself, we'll kill him and break his Teivah." Yet when the time came for Noach to go into the Teivah and people wanted to stop him, miraculously, no one was able to do it.

QUESTIONS, ANYONE?

Who was Noach's wife?

Her name was Naamah. She was a tzaddeikes.

TORAH IN OUR LIVES

Before punishing the generation of the Mabul, Hashem waited so patiently for them to do teshuvah. First, He gave them 120 years (!) of warning. Then, another seven days, and even in the last minute, it began with a gentle rain.

Though the generation of the Mabul was horribly evil, Hashem was very patient with them. Hashem is patient with us, too, waiting for us to stop doing bad things. He waits and waits for us to do teshuvah for things we did that were wrong.

Remember, if you didn't listen to your mom, or if you forgot to daven, Hashem is Erech Apayim. That means He waits a long time before punishing. He gives us plenty of time to become better.

Feeding the Animals

Noach and his family did not have an easy time in the Teivah. It wasn't a luxury cruise. They had to feed and care for all the thousands and thousands of birds and animals in the Teivah. Hard work.

The family never slept! By day they fed the animals that sleep at night. At night they fed the ones, like bats, that sleep by day! They were feeding animals both day and night!

Awesome Chessed

Hashem saw how hard Noach was working. Feeding the animals was an awesome act of kindness. Noach deserved to be released from being imprisoned in the Teivah, so he could once again walk the surface of the earth and bring the world back to life.

Noach deserved to be released only because he fed the animals? Wait a minute! The Chumash says he was a tzaddik! Wasn't that enough of a reason for him to be allowed to leave the Teivah?

Not exactly.

Though Noach was a tzaddik, there was something missing in his kindness. After all, when Hashem told him He was going to destroy the world, Noach said nothing! He should have prayed and begged Hashem not to bring the Mabul. He should have been like Avraham, who we will meet in the next parashah. Avraham begged Hashem not to destroy S'dom, even though they were very bad, very cruel people.

By staying up day and night feeding the animals, Noach proved that he had learned to be kind. Now, he could leave the Teivah.

Dry Land!

The time had come for dry land to once again appear on earth. It was the first of Sivan, and the time for punishment was over. The level of the waters covering the earth began to get lower and lower. On the seventeenth day of Sivan, the bottom of the Teivah gently landed on the top of Mount Ararat. The mountain was still covered with water, but the Teivah was heavy and it just sat on top of the mountain.

Finally, on the first of Av, the mountaintops reappeared once again, rising above the water-covered earth.

Noach waited forty days. He then opened the Teivah's window and sent a raven out on a mission to see if there was still water covering the earth.

The raven just flew around the Teivah, refusing to leave. Finally, at Hashem's command, Noach pulled the raven back into the Teivah.

FASCINATING FACTS

When Hashem created the world, man was created after the animals. But during the Mabul, the opposite happened. People died first, then the animals, because it was the sins of the people that brought the Mabul.

The generation of the Mabul is one of the very few whose punishment was so severe that they have no share in the World to Come.

Once, Noach came late to feed the lion, and the lion bit him! From then on Noach walked with a limp.

A giant named Og held onto the outside of the Teivah, sitting on a wooden board. He promised to serve Noach forever if he would save him. Noach let him hold onto the the Teivah until the earth became dry again. He drilled a hole in the Teivah and passed food to Og through it.

QUESTIONS, ANYONE?

Why did the raven refuse to fly away?

There were only two ravens left in the world, a male and a female. The raven was afraid that while flying around he might get into an accident and be killed. If that happened there would be no way for more ravens to be born.

Flights of the Dove

Seven days later, Noach sent a dove out the Teivah window to see if the world was ready to be settled yet. After flying far and wide the dove couldn't find any dry land, and he returned to the Teivah.

Another week went by and Noach sent the dove out again. This time it came back holding an olive leaf in its mouth.

Seven days later Noach sent the dove out again. This time it didn't return. It had found a dry place to land and build a nest.

Free at Last!

This was the sign Noach was waiting for. He opened the Teivah and took his first breath of fresh air in almost a year. He looked around. As far as the eye could see, the land was dry! All the waters of the Mabul were gone!

This happened on the first day of Tishrei — Rosh Hashanah. What a wonderful way to celebrate the new year! Finally, Noach and his family could inhale the fresh air of a new, dry world.

Though the land was dry, it was still muddy. A dove could hop around on the earth, but elephants and humans would get stuck in the mud. It took more time until the earth was dry enough for animals and humans to leave the Teivah.

But Noach and the animals didn't jump out of the Teivah even when the mud was all dry. Hashem had commanded Noach to enter the Teivah. He couldn't leave until Hashem gave him permission to do so.

On the twenty-seventh day of Cheshvan, 365 days after Noach entered the Teivah, Hashem told Noach, "Go out of the Teivah. You and your wife, your children and their wives, all the animals, birds, and creeping creatures, they will be fruitful and multiply on earth." This was a blessing that they would have many children and many descendants.

They had spent an entire year in the Teivah. Now, finally, they were free!

A Promise Kept

Think about it. Every man, woman, and child you see walking around comes from Noach and his wife Naamah. Every lion in the world comes from the pair of lions that were in the Teivah. The same goes for every giraffe, parrot, and every single creature you see. Everything comes from one pair that was saved from destruction in the Teivah.

Our world is filled with so many living things. When Hashem promises something, it happens. The creatures that came out of the Teivah have been fruitful and multiplied. Just take a look around you and you will see the miracle.

Thanks!

The first thing Noach did on the freshly washed world that had been cleaned of evil was to thank Hashem for saving him.

To do so, he took six pairs of every kind of kosher animal and bird that had been in the Teivah to the place where the future Beis HaMikdash would stand, in Yerushalayim. He built a Mizbei'ach there.

In Hashem's honor he put on his most valuable and beautiful clothes. These were the clothes Hashem made for Adam after the sin. They had been passed down to Noach.

Noach brought the animals to the Mizbei'ach as a korban. As a reward for thanking Him, Hashem decided to never again destroy all life on earth.

Hashem also blessed and commanded Noach and his sons to have many children.

Meat

It's so good to eat delicious meat. But for us to have meat for supper, an animal has to be killed though a kosher shechitah. What gives us the right to take life away from another creature? To kill so we can eat?

Hashem gave us the right, in this parashah.

Hashem told Noach and his sons, "Every moving thing that lives shall be yours for food."

Hashem allowed Noach and his descendants to take an animal's life as a reward for Noach's hard work taking care of the animals for an entire year in the Teivah. Also, because all the animals survived and owed their lives to Noach, who had saved them from the Mabul!

Even though we can eat meat, Hashem allowed it only after the animal is dead. We are not allowed to cut a piece of meat from a living animal and eat it. This is called "eiver min hachai." It is the seventh and last mitzvah Hashem gave the non-Jews.

Don't Kill

Noach and his sons were warned not to commit murder. People are not even allowed to kill themselves. Our lives belong to Hashem. Only He has the right to put an end to a life.

Hashem warned Noach and his sons that anyone committing murder would be punished with death.

Questions, Anyone?

If the Mabul destroyed everything, where did the dove get the olive leaf from?

The leaf came from an olive tree that grew in Eretz Yisrael. The Mabul's rain didn't fall on Eretz Yisrael, but it was still under water. Flood waters from the surrounding countries poured into Eretz Yisrael, covering it. Because the hot rain didn't fall in Eretz Yisrael, the flood waters weren't strong enough to destroy the trees. That's how the dove found an olive tree there.

Fascinating Facts

Noach's evil son Cham stole the clothes Hashem had made for Adam, and gave it to his eldest son Cush. Cush gave them to his son Nimrod, who became a king and pretended that he was a god.

Hashem closed up the springs of hot water that He had opened during the Mabul. But He did leave a few for people to enjoy. A few examples: the hot springs in Teveria in Israel, and the Old Faithful geyser in Yellowstone National Park in America.

FASCINATING FACTS

There were times in history in which people were so good that Hashem never considered destroying the world. When that happened there were no rainbows!

For example, in the time of King Chizkiyahu and in the time of Rabbi Shimon bar Yochai, no rainbow ever appeared in the sky.

The Promise of the Rainbow

Noach was afraid to start working to rebuild the world. What if his descendants sinned and Hashem destroyed it again?

So Hashem said to Noach and his sons, "I am making an unbreakable agreement with you and all your descendants, and with all animals, birds, wild beasts, and every living thing on earth. Never again will there be a Mabul to destroy the world."

Then across the sky a dazzling rainbow appeared.

"This rainbow is a sign of the agreement we made."

When we see a rainbow, we say a blessing, to thank Hashem for promising not to flood the world again.

Drunk!

Noach was a man of the earth. He was a farmer who worked the land. After the Mabul he planted a vineyard, using the small grapevines he had brought with him to the Teivah. Miraculously, the same day he planted the grapevines, they grew grapes. Noach then made wine out of the grapes the same day.

He drank one cup, then another and another. Pretty soon he was drunk! It was hard for him to stand so he went into his tent, got undressed, and went to sleep.

Canaan, Cham's son, saw his grandfather lying drunk, and he told his father. Cham came into Noach's tent and saw his father undressed. He went out to his brothers and made fun of their father.

Shem was horrified at the way his brother was making fun of their father. He told Yefes, "Let's go and cover our father with some clothing."

In order not to see their father without clothing they walked in backward. Then, without looking, they dropped a garment over him.

Blessings and Curses

When he realized what had happened, Noach cursed Cham's sons:

- Canaan would forever be a slave to Shem and Yefes.
- Cush, Cham's oldest son, became dark and ugly.

Noach blessed Shem and Yefes for treating him with respect:

- Shem was blessed that his descendants, the Jews, would get the Torah and Eretz Yisrael.
- The Jews would have the great honor of having the Presence of Hashem in the Beis HaMikdash, which they built.

Yefes was blessed that his descendants:

- Would be very good at art and music.
- Would give the command that the Second Beis HaMikdash be built.
- Some of his descendants would convert and learn in the "tents of Shem"— that is, in yeshivah.

The three sons of Noach split up the world. The descendants of Shem took Asia, Cham got Africa, and Yefes took Europe.

Noach's three sons and their wives were the founders of the world's seventy nations.

Noach Passes Away

Noach died at the age of 950! He didn't learn about the Creation of the world out of a history book. Adam, who had been created by Hashem, had told Lemech about the Torah and the Creation of the world, and Lemech told Noach.

That means Noach knew someone who had met Adam, the first man. Avraham didn't just read a story about Creation and the Mabul. He actually knew Noach, who experienced the Mabul. Noach told him all about the Mabul and the Creation of the world.

Fascinating Facts

Noach drank too much. Warning! Drinking leads to troubles. Do not drink too much! To make the point, the verses that talk about how Noach got drunk include a combination of two letters fourteen times.
Which letters? The letters "vav" and "yud." Together they are pronounced "vay." That's Aramaic for "oy vey"! Oy vey — if someone drinks too much!!!

It was Shem's idea to cover Noach. As a reward, his descendants, the Jews, were given the mitzvah of tzitzis on their clothing.

The First King

For a while after the Mabul, there were no rulers. Everyone was equal and free. Until Nimrod.

Nimrod was a grandson of Cham. Cham stole the clothing that Hashem made for Adam, and he gave them to Nimrod. These clothes had great power. They attracted animals. Because he had these clothes, Nimrod became a great hunter. As a result he was known as a powerful man, and people began to follow him. Nimrod was also a fantastic speaker. He convinced people with his speeches to go against Hashem. These people made Nimrod a king.

Nimrod then went to war. He defeated whoever he fought, until finally there was no one else to conquer. He had conquered everyone! He was the first man to become a king. The capital of his empire was Shinar.

The world then was much different from today. Nowadays, people live all over the planet and speak many different languages. Then, the world was united as one empire under Nimrod. There weren't so many people living in the world back then, so everyone lived in what is today Iraq. There was one language spoken by everyone, Lashon HaKodesh, the holy language of Creation and the Torah.

Evil Again

But being the ruler of a big empire wasn't enough for Nimrod. He wanted to be a god. He persuaded people to stop serving Hashem and to bow down to statues made of wood and stone. He even made himself into an idol, announcing that he is a god.

Noach and Shem tried to stop it. They told people to believe in Hashem, but nothing helped. Nimrod was too powerful. The world had turned evil again!

The Tower

All the people on earth knew about the Mabul, and they were afraid. What if there would be another Mabul? They decided to build a tower. They thought that their tower would reach so high in the sky that they could fight Hashem in heaven. They would stop Him from sending another Mabul. And if the Mabul came anyway, they could use the tower to escape the water by climbing to the top of the tower.

QUESTIONS, ANYONE?

Why didn't Noach curse Cham, the one who made fun of him?

When Noach and his family came out of the Teivah, Hashem blessed all of them, including Cham. If Hashem had already blessed someone, he could not be cursed.

FASCINATING FACTS

Both the Jews and the Arabs are descendants of Shem.

He was called Nimrod because he caused the world to rebel against Hashem. The word for rebellion in Hebrew is "mered."

QUESTIONS, ANYONE?

How many years after the Mabul did they build the tower?

Three hundred and forty. The world had celebrated its 1996th birthday since Creation.

FASCINATING FACTS

Everyone was so devoted to the project that when a brick dropped, they cried, because a brick had been lost from the tower. But if a person fell from the tower and died, no one cared. They just kept on working.

The place where this all happened was named Bavel because Hashem replaced the world's one language with a mixture of seventy different languages. (The word "balal," which means "mixed up," sounds like Bavel.)

TORAH IN OUR LIVES

Why did the generation that built the tower get a lighter punishment than the generation of the Mabul?

Because in the generation of the Mabul, besides bowing down to idols, they were mean people. They stole from each other and hurt each other. But the generation of the tower worked together and got along with each other. That's why their punishment was light.

Of course, it's important to say berachos properly and dress modestly. But from the generation of the tower we see how important it is to Hashem that we are nice to each other.

To be mean to kids in our class, to say nasty things to friends and relatives with our speech – or to be good to others. It's your choice!

Ovens, Bricks, and Clay

They found a large place near Shinar, the capital of the empire, to build the tower. It was an enormous project and everyone was involved.

Today skyscrapers and high-rise buildings are built from steel and cement. In those days, mud was shaped into square bricks and baked in large hot ovens. The bricks were then cemented together and plastered over with clay.

Brick by brick the tower began to rise into the sky. On the ground, thousands of workers made bricks. Thousands of others would carry the bricks up to the top of the tower, where they cemented them to the top. Then the people came down the tower to pick up more bricks. The tower was HUGE.

Hashem was not happy with what He saw. On one hand, everyone was together, humanity was united. That was good! But they stopped believing in Him as the all-powerful one G-d. That was very, very bad!

They had to be punished, so they would learn you can't fight Hashem, and to teach them to believe in Him once again.

"Anata wa nan to iimashita ka?"

Compared to the generation wiped out in the Mabul, the generation that built the tower was given a light punishment. All of a sudden people spoke different languages!

Imagine what happened. A man building the tower asks for a brick from the person working next to him. But when he spoke, he was speaking Chinese!

"Gěi wǒ yīkuài zhuāntóu" ("Give me a brick" in Chinese).

But the worker he asked doesn't understand Chinese. Hashem made him speak Japanese. The Japanese guy doesn't understand what the Chinese speaker asked for.

So he asks, "Anata wa nan to iimashita ka?" ("What did you say?" in Japanese).

The Chinese guy doesn't understand the question, and he asks for a brick again. He doesn't get one, because the Japanese speaker hasn't a clue what he wants. Neither one understands the other. They get upset and start fighting.

This was happening up and down the entire tower!

People who don't speak the same language and don't understand each other can't work together to build anything.

That's how Hashem stopped everyone from building a tower.

Monkeys

But that was only the beginning of their punishment. Hashem scattered groups of people all over the world, each with their own language.

That's why until today there are people living all over the world, speaking different languages!

There were some people who were so wicked that they died. Hashem turned others into monkeys.

World Changer

Probably the most important person who ever lived is also the originator of the Jewish people. He is our father, Avraham Avinu. At that time his name was Avram.

Avram discovered Hashem all on his own, even though everyone around him didn't believe in Hashem. After discovering Hashem he spent the rest of his life teaching the world to believe in Him.

Of all those who lived in the world then, Avram was the one that Hashem picked to change the world from evil to good. He chose not only Avram, but He also chose all his descendants — the Jewish people — to finish Avram's mission.

What is that mission? To let the world know there is a Creator Who is One and all-powerful. He is a loving G-d Who can't be seen. He wants people to be good and kind to each other.

Avram's strong will and determination saved the world and made it better.

The Torah now begins the spectacular story of the man who changed the world. Avraham's story. We'll start at the beginning, before Hashem changed his name to Avraham, when his name was still Avram.

Birth

Avram's parents were Terach and Amaslai. Terach made and sold idol statues. He sold big ones and small ones, stone and wood ones, all types. He also served as a priest of the idols.

When Terach was seventy years old, Avram was born. He was a child genius. He was the firstborn. After him his parents had two more boys, the middle son, Nachor, and the youngest brother, Haran.

Very early in life Avram looked at the wonders of the world, at the sky above him and at nature. He knew all of this had to have come from somewhere. He began to search for who had made it. This question bothered him day and night. He was desperate to find an answer.

The Search Is On

He said to himself, "Someone must have made all this. Who did it? Who is the true king of the world?"

Avram looked at the sunrise and said, "The sun is powerful.

Questions, Anyone?

What happened to the tower?

Hashem sunk one-third of it into the ground, and burned a third in fire. What was left, Hashem left standing.

Fascinating Facts

Because Hashem scattered humanity all over the world, the generation in which this story happened is called the Dor Haflagah — The Generation of the Scattering.

Questions, Anyone?

Which of Noach's sons was Terach's ancestor?

Shem.

Fascinating Facts

Sarai was the daughter of Avram's brother Haran, so Avram married his niece! One day Avraham's son Yitzchak would marry Nachor's granddaughter, Rivkah. Yitzchak and Rivkah were cousins!

QUESTIONS, ANYONE?

How old was the world when Avraham was born?

1948 years old.

It must be the king who created me." So Avram prayed to the sun all day.

When the sun set Avram realized the sun wasn't the creator. It must be the moon that started to shine. He prayed to the moon.

When the sun rose again he said, "There must be a ruler and king that tells the sun and moon what to do!"

Hashem saw that Avram truly wanted to know Him and was searching for Him desperately.

That's when Hashem revealed Himself to Avram and spoke to him. Avram finally had his answer. His search was over!

Return Home

By the time he was three years old Avram knew that there was one Hashem who runs the world. The rest of the world was making a big mistake. They thought that idols and statues ran the world. Avram was determined to change their minds!

At age ten he went to the house of Noach and Shem. He learned Torah in their yeshivah for 39 years. Then he went back home.

Idol Smash-Up

Terach was going away on a trip. He asked Avram to take care of the idol store while he was away.

The first customer of the day came in to buy an idol. "How old are you?" Avram asked.

"Sixty."

"You are sixty years old, and you want to buy an idol that was made yesterday? It's only one day old!" The customer, embarrassed by Avram's words, left the store.

The next visitor to the store was a woman. She didn't want to buy anything. Instead she asked Avram to take a bowl of flour she had brought and give it to the idols as a sacrifice. She handed the bowl to Avram and left.

That's when Avram decided to take some real action. He took a big stick and went through his father's entire store, breaking and smashing all the idols to bits. BOOM! He destroyed all of them except for the biggest statue in the store.

Avram put the stick into the fat hands of the remaining statue and waited for his father to return.

Fighting Idols

When Terach came back and saw the destruction, he was in shock.

"What happened here!?" he asked Avram.

Avram told him about the bowl of flour that a woman had brought.

"I put the bowl in front of the idols and they got into a fight. Each one wanted to eat first. That's when the big idol took a stick and broke all the others."

"Why are you fooling me?" Terach said. "Idols don't understand anything. They can't do this."

"Listen to what you are saying!" Avram told Terach. "Don't you see that idols have no power! Why do you believe in them!"

Avram Argues with Nimrod

Instead of admitting his son was right, Terach was furious. He brought Avram to King Nimrod to be punished. In a country where everyone believes in idols, anyone who doesn't believe like everyone else does is a criminal.

Nimrod ordered Avram, "Bow down to the fire."

"Should we bow to water because water puts out fire?" Avram answered.

"Then bow to the water."

"Maybe we should bow to the clouds that carry the water."

That got Nimrod really angry. "Enough already! I bow down to fire. I will throw you into it. Let your G-d come and save you!"

Fiery Furnace

Now Avram had to make a decision. Should he bow to an idol and save his life, or give up his life for Hashem's honor?

Avram chose death rather than giving up his belief in Hashem.

His brother Haran was watching the argument. He said to himself, "If Avram is saved, I'm with him and will believe in Hashem. If he isn't saved, then I'm with Nimrod."

They prepared lots of wood for the furnace. Avram was tied up and thrown in. The wood was set on fire and it became a fiery furnace.

In Shamayim there was a great commotion. Would this tzaddik be killed?

The angel Gavriel rushed to come before Hashem. He begged Him for permission to go down and save Avram from the fire.

Hashem said, "No! I will do it Myself."

Imagine everyone's surprise when Avram walked out of the fire. Alive and not burned at all!

Into the Fire!

But still Nimrod didn't believe! Sometimes people are so blinded by what they believe that they simply can't see the truth.

Nimrod turned to Avram's brother Haran and

MAASEH AVOS

Like Avraham Avinu, the Jews often found themselves in places where everyone had a different religious belief, while we believed in Hashem. Like Avraham, we were treated like criminals and sometimes forced to choose between being killed for believing in Hashem or becoming like everyone else.

Our strength to believe in Hashem, even though everyone around us tells us we are wrong, comes from Avraham. He stood up to King Nimrod, and to anyone else who told him to bow to idols. He continued to believe in Hashem. And so do we!

FASCINATING FACTS

This was the first of the ten tests Hashem would test Avraham with during his life. Would Avraham give up his own life for Hashem? Or would he bow to idols?

Avraham passed all of Hashem's tests!

QUESTIONS, ANYONE?

Do we know the name of the place where Avram was thrown into the fire?

It was called Ur Kasdim.

said, "Who are you with?"

"I'm with Avram!"

"Then throw him into the fire!" screamed Nimrod.

How sad. Unlike Avram, Haran died in the fire.

Haran was the first person in the world to die al Kiddush Hashem — to show honor to Hashem.

Expecting a Miracle

Why wasn't Haran saved? Avram went into the fire even though he thought he would die. He was ready to give up his life for Hashem. Haran went into the fire expecting a miracle, he didn't want to die. He didn't really believe in Hashem, so a miracle didn't happen to save him.

Mazel Tov!

Avram married a beautiful woman, who was just as great as him. People called her Yiscah, from the word "socheh," which means to "look at," because people would stop and look at her extraordinary beauty. Her real name was Sarai. Later on Hashem would change her name to Sarah.

Sarah was the mother of the Jewish people. She and Avraham spent their lives teaching the world that Hashem exists. She is an inspiration for all Jewish girls and women, all through history. She was the first woman ever to light Shabbos candles.

Goodbye, Terach

Avram and Sarai had to say goodbye to Terach. They really should have stayed with Avram's old father and taken care of him. But as we will see in the next parashah, Hashem commanded Avram to leave Charan and move to Eretz Yisrael. Of course, Avram listened to Hashem.

Terach stayed in Charan until his death. He died many years after Avram and Sarai moved to Eretz Yisrael.

One Family

From the next parashah, Parashas Lech Lecha, until the very end of the Torah, we will learn about what happened to one family, out of all the families in the world: the family of Avraham and Sarah.

Why? Because it is to this family that the Torah would be given. The most important thing for the benefit of the world is for the Jews to learn Torah and do mitzvos. And that's why we're happy we are Jewish. It is what makes us special!

Questions, Anyone?

What was Haran's reward?

King David and Mashiach are his descendants!

Fascinating Facts

A woman has two missions in life. Her first mission begins from the time she is born until she gets married. After marriage her new mission is as part of a team, her and her husband.

We see this from the two names of Sarah. When she was single, the Torah called her Yiscah. After she married she is called Sarai/Sarah, because of her new mission, to tell the world about Hashem.

When Terach died, his grandson Yitzchak was 35 years old and Avraham was 135.

פָּרָשַׁת לֶךְ לְךָ

Parashas Lech Lecha

Lech Lecha • לֶךְ לְךָ

Parashah Pointers

- Hashem tells Avram to leave the country of his birth. Hashem will show Avram where he should go and He will bless him.
- Avram and his family arrive in Eretz Yisrael.
- Hashem promises Avram that Eretz Yisrael will belong to his descendants.
- There is a hunger in Eretz Yisrael, so Avram goes to Egypt, where there is food available.
- Pharaoh kidnaps Sarai and plans to marry her. Hashem stops Pharaoh and punishes him. Sarai goes free. She and Avram leave Egypt, and Pharaoh gives them great wealth.
- Lot was Avram's nephew. He had been living and traveling with Avram and Sarai. Now Lot leaves Avram and moves to S'dom, an evil city.
- Hashem tells Avram he will have a lot of descendants. They will be as many as grains of sand on the earth. Hashem promises to give Eretz Yisrael to Avram's descendants.
- There is a war between the armies of four kings against five kings. The four kings win and they capture Lot.
- Avram hears that Lot is a prisoner. He defeats the four kings and saves Lot.
- Hashem promises Avram that his descendants will be like the stars in heaven.
- Hashem tells Avram that his descendants will go into exile and be slaves, but in the end Hashem will save them.
- Sarai has no children. She asks Avram to marry her servant, Hagar, so that they will have children. Avram listens to Sarai and marries Hagar.
- When Avram is 86, Hagar has a child. Avram names the baby Yishmael.
- When Avram is 99 years old, Hashem changes his name to Avraham and Sarai's name to Sarah. He then gives Avraham the mitzvah of bris milah.

Maaseh Avos – It's in the Genes

In the rest of Sefer Bereishis the Torah tells us stories about our "Avos and Imahos" — the first Jewish "Fathers and Mothers" — and the twelve shevatim (Tribes).

The Torah is not just a storybook. What should we learn from the stories about our ancestors? Here are a few things.

We should learn how to behave. From Avraham we will learn how to be kind and hospitable. From Yitzchak we will learn to be courageous and ready to do anything for Hashem. From Yaakov we will learn to be honest. From our Mothers — Sarah, Rivkah, Rachel, and Leah — we will learn to have faith in Hashem and pray to Him, and to raise families to serve Hashem.

There is another thing we learn from these stories. There is an important rule: "Maaseh Avos Siman La'banim" — What happens to the Fathers will happen to the children.

Our first Fathers and Mothers are the genetic code of the Jewish nation — they are in our DNA. What happened to them in Sefer Bereishis were hints of what would happen later to their children. Here are some examples.

- Avraham went down to Egypt because of hunger, and when he left he was wealthy. Many years later, Yaakov's family went down to Egypt because of hunger, and when they finally left, during Yetziyas Mitzrayim, they too became very wealthy.
- Eisav wanted to destroy Yaakov, and he didn't succeed. This happened to the Jews so many times in our history! We suffered under the Romans, the Nazis, Spain, the Russian czars, and Communists, and so many other countries of exile. But they did not succeed in destroying us!

When you see this icon MAASEH AVOS it will explain how an event that happened to our Founding Fathers and Mothers also happened to the children. Check it out as we go through Bereishis.

FASCINATING FACTS

The Chumash calls Avram's followers "the people he made." But only Hashem can make people! This teaches us that when you teach people to believe in Hashem, it's as if you made them.

QUESTIONS, ANYONE?

Why did Avram take Lot with him?

Lot was Avram's nephew and an orphan. Avram felt responsible for him. Also, Lot would have a descendant named Ruth. She would become the mother of King David. Even Mashiach would be a descendant of Lot!

Where Are We Going?

Hashem told Avram to leave his country, his hometown, and his family.

Imagine going on a trip with your family. You don't know how long it is going to take. You don't even know where you are going. Exhausted, you stop and wonder: Are we staying here? Is this the last stop? The answer is: No. Keep going.

Another week of travel. You arrive at a beautiful town. This must be the place! Again, the answer is: No. Keep going.

How long would it take before you refuse to go any further and decide to go back home?

Something like this happened to Avram. Hashem told him: "Go, leave your home in Charan and move to a new country. I will let you know where to stop when you get there." Avram, his wife Sarai, his nephew Lot, and his many followers (whom he had taught to believe in Hashem) started to travel. They had no idea where they were heading. Yet Avram didn't get upset about wandering around the area, not knowing where he was going. He didn't even ask Hashem, "Where do You want me to go?"

Why didn't Hashem tell Avram where he was going? This way, Avram would be rewarded for every single step he took. It's so hard to travel when you don't know where you are going and how long the trip will take!

Why did Hashem tell Avram to leave his home in the first place and go? There are a few reasons.

The Test

Hashem commanded Avram to leave his country, his hometown, and his family.

Hashem's command to Avram to leave everything to travel to an unknown place was a very hard test. Would Avram leave his home, his family, his country? The people he knew? Everything he was used to? Would he be willing to start over in a strange new place? Would Avram complain to Hashem and say, "I'm 75 years old and You want me to move to a new country? Maybe You could let me serve You here"? Or would he accept Hashem's command without questions, as hard as that would be?

Avram passed the test! He didn't ask any questions. Hashem wanted him to go, so he just packed everything up and left!

A Great Smell

Hashem wanted Avram to travel so his influence and fame would spread throughout the world. Avram would be like a great-smelling air freshener, that has a beautiful smell, but if it is sitting in a bottle no one can smell it! A person must take it out of the pantry, open the bottle, and spray it all over. Ahhh, now the whole room smells better. By traveling, Avram would bring this "great smell" — that is, understanding that Hashem created the world — to the world. How? Wherever Avram went he would convince people to believe in Hashem.

TORAH IN OUR LIVES

Getting close to Hashem is easier in Eretz Yisrael than anywhere else.

Eretz Yisrael

Also, Hashem told Avram to leave Charan because he wanted Avram to live in the greatest land in the world: Eretz Yisrael. It's the holiest land on earth! In Eretz Yisrael, Avram would become a greater tzaddik than if he lived anywhere else in the world.

FASCINATING FACTS

The air in Eretz Yisrael makes people wise.

Hashem's Blessings

Hashem told Avram of the many blessings he would get for leaving his country. Hashem said:

- I will make you a great nation.
- I will bless you with a lot of money.
- I will make your name famous.
- I will give you the power to bless others.
- When you bless someone, it will come true.
- I will bless those who bless you.
- I will curse those who curse you.
- I will bless the nations of the earth with rain and dew because of you.
- The nations will bless their children to be like you.

MAASEH AVOS

Shechem, the first city that Avram visited in Eretz Yisrael, was also the first city conquered by his descendants. When the prince of Shechem kidnapped Yaakov's daughter, Dinah, two of her brothers conquered the city to free their sister. (For the full story, see p. 171.) Avram prayed there that his descendants should win their war.

First City

When Avram arrived in Eretz Yisrael, he went to the city of Shechem. There, Hashem appeared to him and gave him wonderful news. All of Eretz Yisrael would be given to his descendants! Avram's children would be the owners of the greatest piece of real estate on earth.

To show his appreciation, Avram built a Mizbei'ach. He brought a korban to thank Hashem.

Defeat!

Avram traveled from place to place, staying about a month in each location. When he reached the city of Ai, he knew that in this city the Jews would be defeated in their war to conquer Eretz Yisrael, hundreds of years later. (The story is told in the Book of Yehoshua.) To pray for his descendants, he built a Mizbei'ach in Ai.

Whenever they decided to stay in a place, the first thing Avram did was put up his wife's tent, before his own, because a husband is supposed to respect his wife more than himself. He should take care of her needs first.

FASCINATING FACTS

Rava advised, "Honor your wife and you will become wealthy!"

Hunger

Soon after Avram arrived in Eretz Yisrael, there was no rain. No rain meant no food. Imagine feeling like you are fasting on Yom Kippur, but there's nothing to eat when Yom Kippur is over. And not enough to eat the day afterward either, day after day.

Strangely, there was no hunger anywhere else, only in Eretz Yisrael.

Avram and Sarai couldn't bear the suffering they saw, and they helped whoever they could. It wasn't long before Avram gave away all the wealth that he had brought with him from Charan. With no food, Avram had no choice. He left Eretz Yisrael to go to Egypt, where there was plenty to eat.

QUESTIONS, ANYONE?

Why did Sarai have her own tent?

Avram and Sarai both worked hard to bring people to believe in Hashem rather than stone idols. For reasons of tznius, modesty, they split up the work. Avram taught the men, and Sarai taught the women. The men would go to Avram's tent that was like his yeshivah, while Sarai taught the women in her tent: her "seminary."

No Complaints!

Avram was absolutely amazing. Most people would have complained to Hashem. They would have said, "I was living comfortably in my home country, Charan, with my family. Because of Your command I picked myself up and came all the way to Canaan. Now You send a hunger only to this land, and I have to leave. How could You do this to me?"

Hashem did this because He was once again testing Avram's love for Him. When we love someone, we trust them. We love and trust our parents. Would Avram have bitachon, trust in Hashem, that He is doing the right thing?

Avram sure did. He did not complain, so he passed Hashem's test.

Evil in Egypt

Sarai was a beautiful woman, and Egypt was a bad and immoral place. Avram was afraid that when the Egyptians would see his wife, they would kill him so that one of them could marry her. To save his life and protect Sarai he did two things.

Hidden in a Box

When they got close to the Egyptian border, Avram hid Sarai in a box. He hoped that no one would see her. But just in case they were caught, Avram asked Sarai to say that she was his sister.

Border Police

When Avram came to the Egyptian border, the police asked Avram what was in the box so they would know how much tax they could charge him to bring it into the country.

They said, "Do you have gold in there?"

"Fine, I will pay the taxes for gold."

"Maybe it's more valuable than gold. What if it is a chest of expensive pearls? We would have to charge a lot more!"

"I'll pay it!"

Pharaoh Kidnaps Sarai

When they saw Avram was willing to pay anything rather than open the box — of course, the police opened the box anyway. Inside they found the most beautiful woman they had ever seen! The Midrash tells us that when the box was opened, all of Egypt shone with her beauty. All of Egypt began to talk about the beautiful woman who'd been hidden in the box.

They asked her who she was, and she said she was Avram's sister. They assumed she was not married.

When Pharaoh, the king of Egypt, heard about Sarai, he had her brought to his palace against her will. He was going to marry her!

As an "engagement gift" to Sarai's family, Pharaoh gave Avram gifts of cattle, donkeys, servants, and camels.

FASCINATING FACTS

When Sarai was considered the most beautiful woman in Egypt, she was over 65 years old!

A Seder-night prayer

That night was the 15th of Nissan, which in later years would be the Seder night. If we could peek into the room in the palace where Sarai was being held, we would see her crying and praying that Hashem save her from Pharaoh. She even told him that she was married, but he did not care. He still wanted to marry her.

Pharaoh Whipped

Hashem listened to Sarai's prayers. He sent an angel holding a whip to protect her. Every time Pharaoh would try to get near Sarai, she would say, "Beat him," and the angel would whip Pharaoh. The king couldn't see the angel, and he felt himself being hit with terrible blows coming out of nowhere! Terrified, he ran away. Then he came back, and it happened again!

All of a sudden, Pharaoh felt itchy all over. His whole body was covered with a horrible skin disease. Not only Pharaoh, but his entire family and the whole palace household had it too! This was another punishment from Hashem to Pharaoh, in order to protect Sarai.

Pharaoh gave up his plan to marry Sarai.

Honor Guard

Pharaoh was upset by all that happened to him. He ordered that Avram be brought to the palace. Pharaoh spoke to Avram in anger. "Look at the trouble you caused me! Why didn't you tell me she was your wife? Why did you tell me she was your sister? Take your wife back and leave my country!"

Pharaoh gave Avram, Sarai, and their followers an honor guard to escort them out of Egypt. Pharaoh himself escorted them for a short way as well.

Parting Gifts

When he let Sarai go, Pharaoh gave Avram expensive gifts and money, so he would forgive him for kidnapping his wife.

Pharaoh realized that Avram and Sarai were very special people. So besides the gifts to Avram, Pharaoh gave Sarai a maidservant — his own daughter, Hagar! Hagar was a princess of the Egyptian empire, but her father felt that she would be better being a servant of Sarai than the wife of a king of another country.

Pharaoh was right! As we shall see later in the parashah, becoming Sarai's maidservant was the best thing that ever happened to Hagar.

MAASEH AVOS

Avram went down to Egypt because of a hunger in Eretz Yisrael. Yaakov and his sons went down to Egypt for the same reason.

Pharaoh was punished for kidnapping Sarai. The Pharaoh of the Exodus was punished with ten Makkos for not letting the Jews go free.

Avram left Egypt a wealthy man from Pharaoh's gifts. The Jews left Egypt with great wealth given to them by the Egyptians.

FASCINATING FACTS

When Avram, Sarai, and their people went to Egypt during the hunger, they stayed overnight in inns. But because Avram had given all his wealth away to feed others, he had no money to pay. The innkeepers let them stay without paying, trusting that Avram would eventually pay his bills.

Traveling back to Eretz Yisrael, Avram stayed in the same inns that he had slept in when going to Egypt. Now he was wealthy again and repaid his bills.

It was the right thing to do for another reason as well.

Avram was famous. If he had not gone back to the same inns, people would hear about it. They would say he didn't go back because the service there was not good. Avram didn't want that to happen, because he was grateful to the inns that had been good to him on his way down to Egypt.

Back in Eretz Yisrael

Avram and Sarai were happy to leave the evil country of Egypt and return to live in the Holy Land, Eretz Yisrael. Though they were poor when they left Eretz Yisrael, they returned wealthy. Avram's nephew Lot also became very rich. This was because he lived with the great tzaddikim Avram and Sarai. In their merit Hashem made him rich too.

Nowadays if we want to know how rich someone is we ask, "How much money does he have?" In those days to know how rich someone was, you asked, "How many flocks of sheep and goats does he have?" Avram and Lot had many flocks and many shepherds to take care of the animals.

Fight!

To feed the animals, shepherds take them out to fields to graze. Avram's shepherds were very careful not to let the animals graze in fields that belonged to other people. But Lot's shepherds did not care and let his flocks graze in other people's fields.

That is stealing.

Avram's shepherds fought with Lot's shepherds over what they were doing. They said: "Why are you letting the animals eat there? It's not your field!"

Lot's shepherds argued back, "Everybody knows that Hashem promised the land to Avram's children. He doesn't have any children, so the land will belong to his nephew Lot. Since the land will belong to Lot later, why wait? We'll use it now!"

Lot's shepherds were wrong, of course. Until something is yours you can't use it, even if you are going to own it later.

And they were wrong in another way too: Eventually Avram did have children!

Left or Right?

Avram heard what was going on, and he wasn't happy about it. Here he was teaching people about Hashem, the G-d of kindness, truth, and justice — and his own nephew was stealing. Not only that, but because Lot looked very much like his Uncle Avram, people might think that Avram was stealing! Because of what Lot's shepherds were doing, people might stop coming to Avram to learn about Hashem.

Avram was very sad about this, but he knew there was no choice. He and Lot would have to go their separate ways. They could not live together any longer.

Avram spoke to Lot.

He told Lot about the fighting between the shepherds, and said, "Please, let's split up. If you go to the left to live, I will go to the right, and if you want to go to the right, I will go to the left." Avram also assured Lot that he would always be there for him if he needed protection or help.

"I Don't Want Avram"

Lot was not interested in staying with Avram. He loved money. He said to himself, "I don't want Avram or his G-d. I am going to move to one of the richest places in the country, the beautiful and fertile area around S'dom. That way I can become even richer than I already am."

Today, the area near S'dom is called the Dead Sea. Nothing grows there. But then it was the most beautiful place in Eretz Yisrael. It had huge grassy fields for the animals and large gardens with fruit trees. Lot was also attracted to S'dom because it was an evil place!

How evil were the S'domites?

They murdered, stole, bowed down to idols, and did many other terrible sins. They even did sins on purpose, just to anger Hashem. This was the place that Lot went to when he moved away from the holy home of Avram!

An Important Message

Now that the wicked Lot had left, Hashem once again spoke to Avram. He had a very important message for him. A message that affects us till today!

Hashem told Avram, "Look around you in all directions — north, south, east, and west. Everything you see will belong to you and your children forever."

How far can a person see? Twenty miles? Thirty miles? Miraculously, Avram saw all the borders of Eretz Yisrael, in all directions.

"Go," Hashem told him, "make the land yours by walking through it."

Dust

In addition, Hashem told Avram that he would have many children and descendants. His descendants would be like the dust of the earth. Just like there are millions and millions of pieces of dust,

TORAH IN OUR LIVES

Hashem promised Avram that the Jews would survive all the attempts by their enemies to destroy them. There is no better proof that Hashem loves us and watches over us than the fact that we are still here, over 3800 years after Avraham was born. Long after all our enemies — like the ancient Romans, Egyptians, and Greeks, and, in the modern world, the Nazis — are all gone, we are still here.

Just as Hashem promised, we are spread out all over the world. There are Jews in Chile, Alaska, New Zealand, and Australia. There is even a Jew at the North Pole. He lives on a weather research station and learns Daf Yomi!

Hashem keeps His promises. So when Hashem promised us through His prophets that Mashiach will come, we know he will. Let's hope it will be soon and we will be here!

there will be millions and millions of Jews coming from him! His children will be too many to count.

We will be like dust in other ways as well.

- Everyone steps on dust, but long after those people pass away, the dust is still around. Dust is not destroyed by being stepped on! Though the Jewish people will be stepped on and beaten down by anti-Semitic people and nations, we will survive those who make us suffer.
- Just like dust is found everywhere, Jews will be spread all over the world.
- Without the dust of the earth (that is, soil) the world would starve. No food would grow and that would be the end of the world. If there would be no Jews, the world would not be able to exist.

The Great War

One day, Avram got terrible news: Lot was taken prisoner!

In Eretz Yisrael there was a great war between two huge armies. The larger one was the combined armies of five kings. They were fighting fierce battles with the combined armies of four kings. Though outnumbered, the army of the four kings won the war. Now the four kings were the rulers over all the land, people, and property from the kingdoms of the five kings.

One of the conquered cities was the city of S'dom. When it was captured, everything in it was taken away by the victorious army, and the people were prisoners.

Since Lot lived in S'dom he was also a prisoner. He had made the choice to leave the holy home of Avram to move to an evil city, S'dom, to get richer. Now he didn't have a penny. All his wealth had been taken from him. He even lost his freedom!

Leaving Avram had been a big mistake. Now he was suffering for it.

Og

While all this was happening, Avram was busy preparing for Pesach. He was right in the middle of baking matzos on Erev Pesach when he saw a giant soldier coming toward him. The soldier's name was Og.

Og was in the army that lost the war. He had escaped and was running to Avram to tell him that Lot had been captured. He wasn't doing it because he cared about Lot. Og was wicked and wanted to marry Sarai. He was hoping Avram would hurry to save Lot and be killed in battle. Then Og would marry Sarai.

Who's Who in the Torah

Og

Og was a giant, and the only survivor of the great Mabul, other than Noach and his family. Og hung onto the Teivah and Noach fed him food through a hole in the Teivah.

Because Og arrived when Avram was baking "oo-gos," another word for matzah, he was nicknamed Og.

He lived a very long time — over 500 years. That was his reward for letting Avram know that Lot had been captured. But since he did this hoping Avram would be killed, he didn't die peacefully in his bed.

A great descendant of Avram killed him: Moshe Rabbeinu. Og was killed in a war with the Jews right before they entered Eretz Yisrael. How? Moshe jumped very high and reached up to Og's ankle. He struck it with an axe and Og fell over, dead.

Questions, Anyone?

Why was Avram baking matzos, if the story of the Exodus hadn't happened yet?!

Our first Fathers and Mothers kept the Torah, even though it hadn't been given yet. Avram wore tzitzis and Sarai lit Shabbos candles. Hashem gave them an instinct to know the mitzvos.

FASCINATING FACTS

The name of one of the four kings was Amrafel. His other name was Nimrod. He was the powerful king who had thrown Avram into the fiery furnace. Now Nimrod had been conquered by whom he had tried to destroy: Avram.

Malkitzedek was actually Shem, the son of Noach.

To War!

Avram made an announcement to his students. He wanted volunteers to go with him and fight the four kings. When they heard what Avram wanted, they turned white with fear and refused to go. Avram offered a reward for those who would go, and then 318 of his students volunteered.

Avram stood before his tiny army of 318 soldiers and made a speech. He told them that if anyone has sinned, he should go home. If anyone was afraid, he, too, should go home. After the speech only one lone soldier was left: Eliezer, Avram's faithful servant and student.

Dirt and Straw

With sword and spear Avram and Eliezer went out to chase after thousands of soldiers in the armies of the four kings. Two people with strong faith in Hashem — even though they were so outnumbered!

When they reached the enemy armies, Avram and Eliezer picked up handfuls of dirt and straw and threw them at the soldiers. Miraculously, the dirt and straw turned into thousands of arrows, swords, and spears, which came raining down on the soldiers of the four kings.

Terrified, the soldiers ran away. Avram and Eliezer chased them until midnight. What a sight: four armies running away from two people!

FASCINATING FACTS

The numerical value of Eliezer is 318. When Avram's 317 students left, Hashem said that he would give Eliezer the strength of 318 men.

When the Torah says Avram took 318 men with him, it means he took Eliezer, who had the strength of 318 men.

King of Kings

When the war was over the four kings had been conquered by Avram. He took back everything they had looted, including his nephew Lot and all of S'dom's people and possessions.

After the victory the kings and their people came together and built a high platform. They placed Avram on it, raising him over all of them. They made him the king of kings, emperor of the world, calling out together, "You are our king, our prince, our god."

Avram's response? "Only Hashem is the true King and the true G-d!"

Yerushalayim

In the time when Avram lived in Eretz Yisrael, the city of Yerushalayim was called Shalem. Its king, Malkitzedek, was a tzaddik and a Kohen to Hashem.

After the war, on his way back to his home in Chevron, Avram passed by Shalem. Malkitzedek went out to greet the great man. He gave Avram a gift of bread and wine, assuming Avram was tired and hungry after fighting in battle. He also gave Avram a berachah: "Blessed is Avram and blessed is G-d Who gave you victory over your enemies."

Because Malkitzedek was a Kohen, Avram gave him ten percent of what he captured, as a way of saying thank you to Hashem for the miraculous victory.

Mistake!

Malkitzedek's blessing had a big mistake in it! He blessed Avram and Hashem. Who did he bless first? Avram — and not Hashem. Because he should have put Hashem first, Hashem took away the Kehunah from Malkitzedek's family. Though he remained a Kohen, his children did not become Kohanim. Instead, Hashem gave the honor of Kehunah to Avram and his descendant, Aharon.

The King's Chutzpah

By conquering the four kings, Avram had captured the people of S'dom and all their possessions. The king of S'dom came to Avram and demanded: "Give me the people, and you keep the money."

By all the rules of war, Avram owned everything in S'dom — including its people. Yet the king of S'dom was bargaining with Avram, and telling him what he would let Avram keep, as if it still belonged to him!

Shoelaces and Threads

Avram answered the king of S'dom: "I swear that I won't keep anything! Not even something as small as a string or a shoelace. Because I don't want you to say, 'It is I who made Avram rich.' "

With these words, Avram gave up a large amount of money and possessions for the sake of Hashem. Hashem had promised Avram that He would make him rich. Avram wanted people to know Hashem kept His word, and that all of Avram's wealth came only from Hashem, not from the king of S'dom.

Avram then told Eliezer to take what was coming to him because he'd fought in the battle. Avram also gave a part of the wealth to his close friends Aner, Eshkol, and Mamrei. They deserved something for protecting and caring for Avram's household while he was away fighting the kings.

All the rest Avram returned to the king of S'dom.

FASCINATING FACTS

Avram was rewarded for saying he wouldn't even take a string or shoe straps, giving up a fortune. What was his reward? Because he said he wouldn't even take a string, Hashem gave Avram's descendants the mitzvah of putting tzitzis on a four-cornered garment. And because he wouldn't take a shoe strap, Hashem also gave Avram's children the mitzvah of tefillin straps.

Avram Is Worried and Afraid

When Avram got home after the war, he began to worry. With all the miracles that had happened to him, he now wondered if perhaps he had used up all his merits in Shamayim. Perhaps he had no merits left and he wouldn't be allowed into Gan Eden after he died.

He was also afraid of being punished because he had been forced to kill people in the war. And he also feared that the people he had defeated would come back some day and take revenge.

Hashem came to Avram in a vision and spoke to him. And Avram spoke to Hashem as well. This was their conversation:

Like Stars

Avram, don't be afraid! I am your shield. Your reward is very great!

With these words Hashem told Avram he would get into Gan Eden, and that he had plenty of reward coming to him, both in this world and the next. Avram shouldn't be afraid. There would be no punishment for having killed the enemy. Hashem promised to be Avram's shield, protecting him against enemy attack.

"My master, Hashem, what can You give me? I have no children."

"You will have children."

To answer Avram's question, Hashem took him outside his tent to show him the stars.

Suddenly Avram felt himself rising off the Earth, flying up to the heavens into space. Hashem lifted him above the stars, where he could look down on the stars. He told him:

"Look at the heavens. See if you can count the stars. It's impossible. Your descendants will be like that."

Hashem was telling Avram that there will be as many Jews as there are stars in heaven. When we keep the Torah we will be like stars. Stars are way up high, out of the reach of people. The Jews will be out of the reach of our enemies, who will not be able to hurt us.

Lifting Avram above the stars, Hashem was showing him that Avram would be above the laws of nature. Though by the laws of nature Avram and Sarai were too old to have children, they would most definitely have a child.

Cut Them in Half

The conversation continues ...

G-d said to Avram, *"I am Hashem Who took you out of Ur Kasdim to give you this land for you and your descendants."*

"How will I know that it will happen?" Avram asked.

Hashem answered: *"Take three young bulls, three goats, and three rams. Cut them in half. Also take a turtledove and a young dove."*

Why did Avram ask, "How will I know it will happen?" Didn't he know that if Hashem says it will happen, IT WILL HAPPEN!

Avram was actually asking: "How do I know that my children will inherit Eretz Yisrael even if they sin and no longer deserve it?"

Hashem answered by telling Avram to take some animals and cut them in half. How does that answer the question?

These animals were symbols of the korbanos the Jews would one day bring in the Beis HaMikdash. Hashem's answer was, "Because of the korbanos, the Jews will be forgiven for their sins and deserve to keep Eretz Yisrael."

Avram then asked, "But what happens when the Beis HaMikdash is destroyed and there will be no korbanos? What will happen then?"

"Don't worry," said Hashem. "Their sins will be forgiven through their prayers."

Questions, Anyone?

Why do we say the prayer Adon Olam only at Shacharis, the morning prayer? Why not at Minchah and Maariv, in the afternoon and evening, as well?

Avraham was the first person to call Hashem, Adon — Master. He also was the one who established the Shacharis prayers. That's why Adon Olam is said only at Shacharis — because Avraham called Hashem "Adon."

Torah in Our Lives

Not only would the laws of nature not apply to Avram, but they won't apply to us, the Jewish people, either. Here are some examples.

No other nation on earth could have survived all the many times so many enemies tried to destroy them. Only the Jews are still here, because the laws of nature don't apply to us!

The Jews were exiled twice from our land. We were spread all over, exiled again and again. And yet we are here. Not lost.

Why cut the animals in half? Today, when two people make an agreement, they sign a contract. In those days people making an agreement cut an animal in half and walked between the pieces.

Hashem was now going to make an unbreakable agreement with Avram about the future of the Jewish people. In Hebrew this agreement is called the "Bris Bein HaBesarim," the Agreement Between the Pieces. Hashem showed Avram the future, and what would happen to the Jewish people throughout time.

FASCINATING FACTS

The darkness and fear Avram felt in his sleep was Hashem telling him that the Jews would suffer in exile under the Babylonians, Persians, Syrian-Greeks, and Romans.

Animals represent the nations of the world. Jews are symbolized by birds. Avram cutting up the animals meant that Hashem would punish all the nations that made the Jews suffer. Hashem did not tell Avram to cut the birds. This meant that when Mashiach comes, the Jews will have outlived all their enemies and stayed whole, in one piece.

Darkness

It was sunset by the time Avram completed doing what Hashem had asked. Avram fell into a deep sleep, in which he suddenly felt very, very afraid. There was a deep darkness: blackness everywhere. The fear and darkness were hinting at the terrible suffering of the Jews when they would be in exile.

A Column of Fire

In his sleep Avram heard Hashem say,

"For four hundred years your descendants will not live in their own land and they will be slaves. Afterward they will be freed and leave with great wealth. I will punish the nation that made them slaves. But this will happen to your descendants, not to you. You will die in a good old age."

The sun set. Avram saw smoke and a column of fire passing between the pieces of the animals he had cut in half. He heard Hashem say:

"To your descendants I will give this land."

The smoke and fire showed that Hashem was sealing His agreement by going through the pieces.

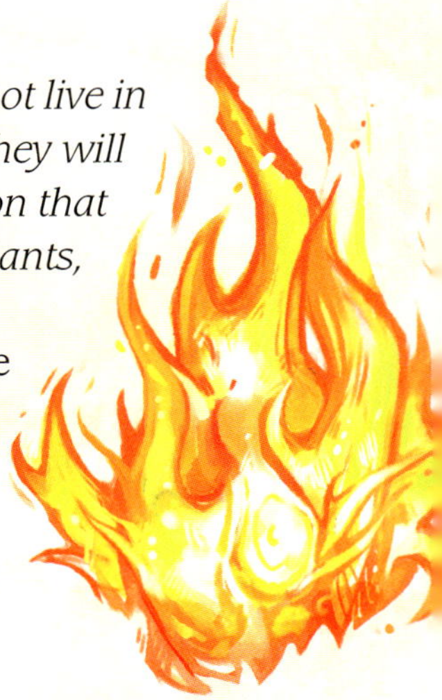

The Agreement

This was the agreement made between Hashem and Avram at the Bris Bein HaBesarim:

- For four hundred years, beginning when Yitzchak would be born, the Jews would live like strangers in a foreign country. They would wander from place to place.
- Things would get worse until finally they would become slaves in Egypt.
- At the end of the four hundred years, Hashem will punish the Egyptians

with ten Makkos. The Jews will be freed and leave Egypt, taking great wealth with them.

- Then Hashem will bring them to Eretz Yisrael to live.
- Avram will die in a good old age, knowing that his father, Terach, died as a believer in Hashem. Avram will live to see his wicked son, Yishmael, repent, but Avram will die before his grandson, Eisav, becomes wicked.

Sarai's Plan

Ten years had passed since Avram and Sarai had moved to Eretz Yisrael, and she still had no children. This made them very sad. Sarai thought of a plan.

She thought to herself, "Maybe Avram can't have children with me, but he could with a different wife. I will tell him to marry my maid, Hagar, the Egyptian princess whom Pharaoh gave me. [In those days men could have more than one wife.] I will be doing a great kindness for my husband, who will become a father when he marries Hagar. It will be hard for me. I will now have to share my husband with another wife. But I'll do it! Perhaps as a reward for doing this kindness, Hashem will give me children also."

Avram listened to Sarai's advice and married Hagar. Soon after the wedding Hagar realized she was going to have a baby. Of course everyone was so happy!

No Respect

But something happened that spoiled it all. Hagar began telling people that she was greater than Sarai! "After all, I will have a baby, while Sarai has no children even though she was married to Avram for so many years." Hagar thought, "Obviously, my prayers are greater than Sarai's." Hagar stopped treating Sarai with respect, even in front of Avram!

Of course, Hagar was wrong. Sarai was much greater than Hagar. When someone doesn't have children, or other tough things happen to them, it doesn't mean the person is bad. Hashem has reasons, we just don't know what they are.

Sarai went to Avram and complained, "Why don't you defend my honor? Why are you quiet when Hagar shows disrespect?"

Avram answered, "Take Hagar and do to her what you think is right."

A Lesson

Sarai was actually Hagar's teacher, just like she was for all the women in Avram's household. Sarai wanted to teach Hagar that despite what she thought, she must respect Sarai. To get that message across, Sarai told Hagar to prepare her a bath. She told her to fill up the tub with water and bring her towels. This was teaching her to act respectfully toward her teacher.

Hagar missed the point of Sarai's lesson. She was terribly insulted by what Sarai asked her to do, so insulted that she ran away, into the desert.

Angels with a Message

After traveling for a while, Hagar stopped at a spring of water and took a drink. When she finished drinking, she looked up and saw an awesome, holy light. Standing before her was an angel from heaven! He brought a message from Hashem.

The angel asked, "Where are you coming from and where are you going?"

Hagar answered, "I am running away from Sarai."

Another angel appeared and said, "Go back to her!"

Hashem sent still another angel with a promise. "You will have so many descendants that it will be impossible to count them."

A fourth angel flew down from heaven. "When your child is born, call him Yishmael," he said, "which means 'Hashem heard,' because Hashem heard your prayers. That son will grow up to be a wild man. He will live in the desert and trap animals. He will fight everyone and everyone will hate him."

No more angels appeared. It was the end of Hashem's message.

Hagar was used to seeing angels in the house of Avram, but she was amazed that even in the desert she had seen angels. In honor of being worthy of having a message sent to her from Hashem, Hagar called the spring where it happened "Be'er Lachai Ro'i — The Well of the Living One that Appeared to Me."

Mazel Tov!

Hagar got the message and returned to Sarai and Avram, to continue to learn from Sarai.

Mazel Tov! Hagar gave birth to a baby boy. When Avram was 86 years old he became a father for the first time.

The baby's name? Yishmael, of course.

National Treasure

Every country has its national treasures. In the USA, it's the Declaration of Independence and the Constitution. In England, it's the Magna Carta and the queen's crown jewels. For the Jews, our national treasures are the Torah and mitzvos.

One of our most precious treasures is the mitzvah that Avram was given in this parashah: the mitzvah of bris milah. The mitzvah is done on a baby's eighth day, even if it's Shabbos.

At a bris, Jewish men, women, and children gather together and celebrate with great joy. Why?

Because a bris is the sign of Hashem's promise to Avram, Hashem's promise is still with us. And it has not been easy! There were many times our enemies tried to stop us from doing this mitzvah, because it shows our special relationship with Hashem. But with courage, even when it was dangerous, we kept doing it.

With every bris, we are continuing our commitment to Hashem, which started in the year 2047, with Avram's bris.

This is the story of that very first bris.

Name Change

When Avram was 99 years old and Sarai was 89, Hashem appeared to Avram and told him that from now on he and Sarai would have different names. Avram would now be called Avraham, and Sarai would be Sarah. These new names described their new mission in the world. Avraham means "Father of many nations," and Sarah means "Princess of all the nations."

Questions, Anyone?

What happened to the blessing that Hagar would have so many descendants that they can't be counted?

Her son Yishmael is the father of the Arab nations. There are today over 400 million Arabs!

Everything that Hashem says will happen, happens!

Fascinating Facts

Hashem took the last letter from Sarai's name — י (numerical value = 10). He split it into two הs (each ה = 5). Hashem added one ה to Avram's name, changing his name to Avraham. Sarai got the other ה, and she was now called Sarah.

The י was upset that it had been taken away from Sarai's name, and it complained to Hashem. Hashem told the י that it would have the honor of being added to the name of Moshe Rabbeinu's closest student. So many years later Hoshea became Yehoshua. Yehoshua became the leader of Israel after Moshe died.

Bris Milah

Hashem told Avraham that He is making an agreement with him. The word for agreement is "bris." He promised Avraham that he would have many more descendants, and nations will come from him. Hashem said that he will have a special relationship with the Jews who accept Him as their G-d, and Eretz Yisrael will be their country.

But there is a condition to all these promises! All this will happen only as long as Avraham and his descendants keep the mitzvah of bris milah.

Hashem commanded Avraham, "All the males in your home should get a bris. It will be a sign between us."

The halachah is that a father gives a bris to his baby boy eight days after he is born.

Fascinating Facts

There is another reason why the baby was named Yitzchak. Each letter of his name represents something else.

י = 10, is for the ten tests that Hashem gave Avraham.

צ = 90, Sarah's age when Yitzchak was born.

ח = 8, Yitzchak was the first baby to get a bris milah on the eighth day.

ק = 100, Avraham's age when Yitzchak was born.

Laughter

Hashem also gave Sarah a blessing. He told Avraham that she would have a son, and she will be the mother of nations and kings.

When Avraham heard that he would have a son from his beloved wife, Sarah, he was so happy! What great news! A 100-year-old man and his 90-year-old wife would have a baby! Avraham's joy was so great that he laughed out loud.

The word in Hebrew for laughter is "Yitzchak." Hashem said, "When Sarah will have her boy, call him Yitzchak, because you laughed when you heard the news."

99, 13

Getting a bris at age 99 is a very painful and difficult operation. Yet Avraham didn't put it off. He did what Hashem wanted right away. On the same day that Hashem spoke to him, Avraham gave himself a bris milah. He also gave a bris to all the men in his home, including his son Yishmael, who was 13 at the time.

Passed the Test

Commanding Avraham to do the bris milah was another test for him. How?

Let's answer a question with a question. What did Avraham want more than anything else in the world? To convince people to believe in Hashem and know that He runs the world, and to teach people not to believe in the sun or stone statues!

Now Hashem came and told him to do a bris, at a time when nobody in the world had a bris! People would say, "I don't want to join Avraham. He's strange and different from everyone else. I don't want to be like that." Or they might say, "You mean if I believe in Hashem I'll have to have a bris also? No thanks!"

So when Hashem told Avraham to do the bris, he might have said, "People will stop coming to me! They will think I'm crazy. I won't be able to teach them to believe in Hashem!"

Avraham did not even dream of arguing. If Hashem wanted him to do something, he did it right away! Avraham passed Hashem's test!

In the end Hashem made sure that people came to Avraham, even though he had a bris. Until the end of his life, Avraham continued to do what he loved most: teaching people to believe in Hashem.

TORAH IN OUR LIVES

Sometimes kids feel strange and different because of the Jewish clothes they wear. Boys and men wear yarmulkes, girls and women wear long sleeves even in the heat of the summer. Like Avraham, though, we shouldn't care about what others think. We should have the courage to do what Hashem wants. And we should do it proudly!

Because we look different and people can tell we are Jews, when we act properly we bring honor to Hashem. People see us and say, "They are Hashem's people. Aren't they wonderful?" What a Kiddush Hashem that is!

פָּרָשַׁת וַיֵּרָא

Parashas Vayeira

Vayeira • וַיֵּרָא

Parashah Pointers

- Avraham is sitting outside his tent, hoping to see guests.
- Hashem visits Avraham because he isn't feeling well after the bris.
- Avraham sees three travelers and invites them to rest and eat. The travelers are really angels.
- One of these guests/angels tells Avraham that he and Sarah will have a baby boy in a year.
- Sarah thinks she's too old to have a baby, but Avraham tells her Hashem can do anything.
- Hashem tells Avraham that He is going to destroy S'dom because the people there are evil.
- Avraham argues that if there are tzaddikim living in S'dom it shouldn't be destroyed.
- But because there weren't even ten tzaddikim there, it had to be destroyed.
- S'dom is destroyed by a rain of fire.
- Avraham's nephew, Lot, and Lot's wife and their two daughters escape the destruction, with the help of the angels.
- Lot and his family were warned not to look at S'dom while it was being destroyed, but Lot's wife turns around and looks anyway. She turns into a pillar of salt.
- Lot's two daughters have sons.
- Avraham moves to Gerar. Avimelech, the king of Gerar, kidnaps Sarah. Hashem comes to Avimelech in a dream and warns him to return Sarah to Avraham. Avimelech sends her back and gives gifts to Avraham and Sarah.

- When Avraham is 100 years old, and Sarah is 90, she gives birth to a boy. They name him Yitzchak. He is the first baby ever to be given a bris when he is 8 days old.
- Sarah sees Yishmael trying to kill Yitzchak. Avraham sends Yishmael and his mother, Hagar, away.
- Yishmael and Hagar wander in the desert and run out of water. Yishmael is dying. Hashem miraculously makes a well appear. Hagar gives Yishmael water and he recovers.
- Avimelech and his general make a treaty with Avraham, swearing that they won't harm each other or their descendants. The place they make the treaty is called Beersheva.
- Hashem gives Avraham one final test, the Akeidas Yitzchak. He tells Avraham to take his son Yitzchak and sacrifice him.
- Yitzchak and Avraham arrive at the mountain and build a Mizbei'ach. Avraham ties Yitzchak up on the Mizbei'ach, takes out his knife, and prepares to sacrifice Yitzchak.
- Suddenly Avraham hears an angel telling him not to kill Yitzchak. Avraham puts down his knife. He finds a ram and brings it as a korban to Hashem in place of his son Yitzchak.
- Hashem blesses Avraham, telling him that the Jews will be as many as the stars in heaven and the sand on earth.
- Rivkah is born. She will become Yitzchak's wife.

The Visit

Hashem came to visit Avraham on the third day after his bris. Why? Because of his bris, Avraham wasn't feeling well. He was very weak. Hashem came to do bikur cholim. That's the mitzvah to visit the sick.

Good Meals and Drinks

Sick people usually lie in bed. Not Avraham. He was sitting at the entrance of his tent when Hashem visited him. Why was he there instead of in bed? He was looking for travelers whom he could invite in as guests.

In those days, there were no rest stops on the highways where you could buy food and drinks. Avraham was always busy doing chessed, an act of kindness, by inviting guests. He gave travelers good meals, drinks, and a place to rest during their journey. All free of charge!

Hachnasas orchim is the mitzvah of giving people a place to eat or sleep. It was a mitzvah that Avraham and Sarah were always doing. They did it perfectly.

While they were taking care of their guests, Avraham and Sarah would talk to them about Hashem. Avraham would talk to the men, and Sarah would talk to the women. Some of their guests even stopped bowing to idols because of what they heard in the tents of Avraham and Sarah.

Three Guests in Disguise

Hashem knew that Avraham would want to do the mitzvah of hachnasas orchim even though he wasn't well. Hashem made it a very, very hot day, so that no one would pass by, and Avraham would be able to rest and get well. It was like an oven outside. People stayed home and didn't travel.

But then Hashem saw that Avraham was suffering because he had no guests. It bothered Avraham so much not to do hachnasas orchim! So Hashem sent Avraham very special guests. These travelers wouldn't be bothered by the heat ... because they were angels!

Their names were Micha'el, Refael, and Gavriel. Hashem sent each one on his own special mission. Micha'el's job was to tell Avraham and Sarah that she would have a baby boy in a year. Refael's mission was to heal Avraham. Gavriel's mission was to destroy the evil city of S'dom.

The angels disguised themselves as Arabs. They appeared down the road from Avraham's tent. When he saw them he was delighted! Finally, there were people he could invite to his home and feed!

TORAH IN OUR LIVES

We see from Hashem's visit to Avraham how important it is to visit the sick. Next time someone in your class or a relative is not well, be like Hashem Himself and go visit them or call them!

Avraham wanted to do the mitzvah of hachnasas orchim even when he was in terrible pain. This teaches us how hard we should try to do this wonderful mitzvah.

Your uncle, aunt, and cousins are coming for Shabbos. Your parents want to put a cousin in your room. But there is only one bed. Who should sleep on the bed and who should sleep on a mattress or sleeping bag on the floor? What do you think Avraham or Sarah would have done?

QUESTIONS, ANYONE?

How many doorways did Avraham and Sarah's tent have?

Four, one on each side. That way, no matter what direction travelers were coming from, it would be easy for them to come in.

FASCINATING FACTS

Hashem didn't send one angel to do all three missions, because an angel can only do one mission at a time.

QUESTIONS, ANYONE?

Why did Avraham ask them to wash their feet?

To Avraham, the travelers looked like Arabs. In those days the Arabs prayed to the dust of their feet. Not wanting to have "idols" on his property, Avraham made sure they washed the dust off their feet.

FASCINATING FACTS

The cave that Avraham found is known today as Me'aras HaMachpeilah. It is where Adam and Chavah, Avraham and Sarah, Yitzchak and Rivkah, and Yaakov and Leah are buried.

The cakes that Avraham asked Sarah to make were actually matzos. The angels arrived Pesach time.

Three Tongues

Avraham ran toward them. He bowed and invited them to stay with him before continuing on their journey. He told them he would send for some water so they could wash their feet, and invited them to sit under his tree, where he would bring them some bread to eat. They would be cooler, sitting in the shade of a tree. The three travelers agreed.

Avraham went to share the good news about the guests with his wife, Sarah. He asked her to hurry and make cakes for them. Then he went to his flocks. He chose a juicy calf to serve. But it ran away. He chased after it, and the calf led him to a cave. In the cave he saw a shining light, and he heard angels saying, "Adam and Chavah are buried here."

Avraham finally caught the calf and returned to his tent. He chose two other tasty and juicy calves. He gave them to Yishmael and told him to slaughter them quickly. He wanted to serve each of his guests a delicious dish of tongues in mustard.

While the guests were waiting for their main dish to be ready, Avraham served them cream and milk. When the main dish arrived, Avraham served platters of three tongues, one for each guest.

The angels had a problem. Since they have no stomachs, angels can't eat! What should they do? Since they were among humans, they made believe they were eating the food. We can learn from this that it is a good idea to follow the customs of the place you are visiting.

Small Actions, Huge Rewards

- As a reward for Avraham feeding these three angels, years later Hashem fed and took care of the millions of Jews who wandered in the desert for forty years! When we do even small favors for other people, Hashem pays us back many times over.
- Avraham gave the angels water. The Jews in the desert had water that flowed miraculously from a rock.
- To protect his guests from the sun, Avraham let them sit under his tree. In the desert, the Jews were protected from the sun by Clouds of Glory.
- Avraham gave the angels food. In the desert, Hashem sent food from heaven, the mahn.
- Avraham served the angels meat. Hashem gave the Jews meat in the desert.

Great News!

One of the angels gave Avraham wonderful news. He said, "At this time next year, Sarah will have a son!"

Wow! Avraham was 99 years old, and Sarah was 89. What a miracle it would be for them to have a child after so many years!

Sarah was standing in the entrance of her tent behind the guests. When she heard what the guest said, she laughed. How could two old people have a child!?

Hashem was not happy at how Sarah reacted. Instead of laughing, she should have said "Amein" to the good news. Sarah, who was such a great and holy woman, should have known that Hashem can make anything happen.

Hashem spoke to Avraham. "Why did Sarah laugh and say, 'How can I give birth? I'm so old!' Is there anything Hashem can't do?! This time next year you will have a son!"

The meal was over and it was time to go. Avraham didn't just show them the door. He walked them out the door and continued along with them for a bit as they began their journey.

Where were they going? Micha'el returned to heaven, since he finished his task of telling them about the baby that would be born. Gavriel and Refael were going to S'dom. They had work to do there. Gavriel would destroy S'dom and Refael would save Lot and his family.

FASCINATING FACTS

When Avraham invited the guests he told them he would serve them bread. What a surprise when Avraham served them such a big meal!

Tzaddikim promise to do a little, but in the end they do a lot. Much more than they promised!

When guests leave our house we should walk them out the door for a few steps.

The Five Evil Cities

Unlike Avraham and Sarah, who were kind and giving, the five evil cities of the S'dom area were just the opposite. Even though they were wealthy, they didn't want to share what they had with anyone! The entire area in which these cities were located was called S'dom, which was also the name of the area's most important city.

The law in S'dom was that no one was allowed to help the poor. If someone came to S'dom and asked for a place to stay for the night, he would be sent to a hotel. If the guest was tall, they would give him a room with a short bed. The S'domites would grab him and cut off his legs, so that the bed would fit him just right!

Short guests got the same treatment in reverse. They were given a room with a very long bed. Three strong S'domites grabbed the guest's feet, and another three grabbed his hands, and they would pull in opposite directions, stretching the guest till he screamed in pain.

People heard how S'dom treated guests, and everyone stopped coming. That was exactly what the cruel and stingy S'domites wanted.

The S'domites murdered, stole, bowed to idols, and did many other terrible sins. They even did sins on purpose, just to make Hashem angry.

QUESTIONS, ANYONE?

What were the names of the five cities?

S'dom, Amora, Adma, Tzvoyim, Tzoar

Destroy S'dom!

One day, a young woman gave a poor man food! That was a terrible crime in S'dom.

The S'domites killed her in a cruel way. They smeared her with honey, tied her up, and left her on top of the city wall. Bees attracted to the honey stung her until she died.

When Hashem saw what they did to this girl, He made the final decision. S'dom must be destroyed!

Before destroying S'dom, Hashem told Avraham what He was about to do.

50? 45? 40? 30? 20? 10?

When Avraham heard that Hashem was about to destroy so many human beings, he tried to save their lives. Avraham said to Hashem that if there were at least ten good people in each of the five cities, Hashem shouldn't destroy the cities. Perhaps these good people would be able to influence S'dom to change and stop being so mean.

Avraham said to Hashem, "Will you destroy the tzaddikim together with the wicked? Maybe there are fifty tzaddikim living in these cities? Save the cities because of them!"

Hashem agreed and said, "If I find fifty tzaddikim, I'll save the cities."

But there weren't fifty!

Avraham didn't give up. He humbly asked Hashem for mercy, and to save the city if there were only forty-five good people. That would make nine in each city, and Hashem could be counted as the tenth in each city.

"I am dust and ashes. If only five are missing from the fifty would you destroy them?" Avraham asked, hoping for mercy.

Hashem said He was willing to save S'dom if there were forty-five tzaddikim.

But there weren't forty-five.

Avraham kept trying. Maybe he could persuade Hashem to save some of the cities. He asked Hashem to save four cities, if there were forty good people. Three cities for thirty? Twenty to save two cities? And, finally, he said, "Are there ten tzaddikim, so one city will be saved?"

But S'dom didn't even have ten tzaddikim. Avraham had done all he could. S'dom was doomed to destruction!

A Secret

The angels arrived in S'dom. Lot saw them and ran over to invite them to come to his house and to spend the night. Even though it was against the law, hachnasas orchim was something he had learned from living with Avraham. He couldn't give it up.

FASCINATING FACTS

The young woman who gave food to the poor man was Lot's daughter. Her name was Plutis.

QUESTIONS, ANYONE?

Why did Avraham call himself dust and ashes?

Avraham went to war against four armies. He should have been killed, and his body turned to dust! But Hashem had mercy on him and let him miraculously win the war.

When King Nimrod threw him into the fiery furnace, Avraham would have been turned into ashes, but Hashem had mercy and saved him.

Telling Hashem he was dust and ashes was Avraham's way of saying that Hashem had been merciful to him, and He should now show mercy to the S'domites as well.

Why didn't Avraham ask S'dom to be saved for the sake of 8 tzaddikim?

Avraham didn't ask for less than ten, because he knew eight tzaddikim couldn't save S'dom. How did Avraham know that? Because Noach and his wife, his three sons and their wives, totaled eight people, and they couldn't save the world from being destroyed in the Mabul.

At first, the angels kept refusing Lot's invitation. They told him, "We will sleep in the streets." But Lot insisted, and they finally agreed.

Lot knew that bringing the guests into his house was dangerous, so he did it secretly. He had a plan. He told the angels not to go directly to his house. They should walk around in circles before coming, to make sure nobody was watching them.

Feeding the Angels

The angels arrived. Lot went to the kitchen to make them a meal. Since it was Pesach, he baked fresh hot matzos for them as well. Lot's wife, Edis, was furious at what was going on. There were guests siting in her living room! How awful. Lot had married a S'domite and S'domites didn't like strangers, especially when they were in their living room!

Lot sat down to eat with the guests and he asked Edis to bring some salt for the guests. That's when Edis and Lot got into a terrible fight. She screamed at him, "Do you want to bring this evil custom of having guests here to S'dom?" Lot screamed back, telling her to bring salt.

Edis decided to get her husband in trouble and teach him a lesson. She went to neighbors, knocked on the door, and asked, "Can I borrow salt for the guests in our home?"

The secret was out! It spread all over the city. Lot had guests in his house!

An Angry Mob

The citizens of S'dom took to the streets, forming an angry mob. The mob surrounded Lot's house. They were determined to treat Lot's guests like S'domites treated all visitors to their city. Terribly! They would teach Lot a lesson to never do such a disgusting thing in their city! Nobody argued with or stopped the protesters. Both young and old agreed to hurt Lot's guests. Everybody in the city was evil!

Who Are You?

Inside his house Lot heard noise coming from outside. It was the mob yelling and chanting. Lot heard the mob saying, "Where are the people who came to you tonight? Bring them out here. We want to meet them!"

Lot knew what they wanted. They meant they wanted to meet them to hurt them and make them suffer!

He stepped out of his house, closed the door behind him, and faced the

Questions, Anyone?

What exciting thing happened to Lot on the day the angels came?

He was appointed chief judge of the city.

Fascinating Facts

The angels slowly made their way to S'dom after leaving Avraham. They didn't rush, to give Avraham time to pray for S'dom. By the time they got to S'dom, it was nighttime.

furious mob. He was going to protect his guests and persuade these angry people to go home and leave his guests alone.

Lot told the mob, "Don't be so wicked!"

This only made them even more angry. "Step aside. Get away from the door! Who are you to tell us what to do?" they yelled. They pushed forward to get past Lot and break through his door.

He said, "Hurt my daughters, but don't hurt my guests!" The crowd wouldn't stop. Lot was in terrible danger! He was saved when the door behind him opened, and the angels pulled him inside.

Then the angels did something miraculous. They blinded the entire mob. No one could see anymore!

Can you imagine if a group of people suddenly all go blind at the same time? They would panic, yell for help, and try to find a doctor to help them.

Not the wicked people of S'dom. They didn't panic. They didn't try to find a doctor to help them. Not one of them! They were so evil and single-minded that they just kept trying to find Lot's door, so they could break in and hurt his guests.

Escape

The angels told Lot astounding news. "We are going to destroy the city," they said. "Do you have other relatives in the city? Get them out of here!"

Lot had two married daughters. He ran to the homes of the sons-in-law and told them, "Get up and leave. Hashem is going to destroy the city!" Lot's sons-in-law thought he was joking. They ignored his warning.

Lot went home. The night was over and the sky was getting lighter. S'dom's last dawn was coming.

Inside the house, the angels were trying to get Lot to leave right away. Time was running out.

"Get up and go," they said. "Take your wife and your two daughters now or you will be destroyed with the city!"

Lot didn't hurry. He was looking through his treasure chests of money, gold, silver, diamonds, and expensive gems, trying to choose which to take with him. Money? Gold? He couldn't take them all; the chests were far too heavy.

It was time to destroy S'dom. If Lot would stay a moment longer trying to save his money, he and his family would be destroyed also. Hashem had mercy on Lot and didn't want that to happen.

The angels grabbed Lot, his wife, and his two unmarried daughters by the hand. In the next moment they found themselves outside the city. Lot didn't have the chance to save any of his treasures. He lost everything, but his life was saved.

QUESTIONS, ANYONE?

Why did Hashem have mercy on Lot?

In last week's parashah, Avraham told the Egyptians that Sarah was his sister. Lot was with them and didn't tell anyone Sarah was really Avraham's wife, even though he could have made a lot of money by telling the secret.

If the Egyptians would have found out Sarah was Avraham's wife, they would have killed him. By not revealing the secret, Lot had saved Avraham's life.

That's why Lot deserved to have his life saved.

Run for Your life

The angels led Lot and his family outside the city. "Run for your lives and don't look back!" they told him. "Run to the mountains."

The angels were telling Lot to escape to his uncle, Avraham, who lived on a mountain.

"No!" Lot said. "You did me a great favor by saving my life, but I can't go live with Avraham. If I do, I will die!"

Lot felt that he had been saved because compared to the people of S'dom, he was a good person. But if he lived near Avraham, Lot was afraid Hashem would compare him to Avraham and then he would die, because compared to Avraham, Lot was wicked.

WHO'S WHO IN THE TORAH

Lot's Descendants

After S'dom was destroyed, Lot's two daughters each had a son. One son was called Moav and the other Ammon. Each one of these sons eventually became a large nation. The nations of Moav and Ammon settled on the borders of Eretz Yisrael. They were often a source of trouble to the Jewish nation.

The fact that Lot's daughters survived the destruction was very important for our nation. Rus (Ruth) came from the nation of Moav. She converted, and was the great-grandmother of King David. We read all about her in Megillas Rus.

Naamah was a descendant of Ammon. She, too, converted, and she married King Shlomo, King David's son. Their child, Rechavam, was king after Shlomo.

Without these two righteous women, descendants of Lot's daughters, there would be no Mashiach, who is a descendant of David, Shlomo, and Rechavam!

On the Run

Lot told the angels that he would like to escape to the city of Tzoar. It was the last of the five cities to be built. He said that since it was younger than the others, it wasn't as evil. Lot begged the angels to save the city so he could go there.

The angels agreed, and the city of Tzoar was not destroyed.

Lot and his family began to run to Tzoar as fast as they could. They were afraid of being caught in the destruction going on behind them.

Fire and Smoke

Hashem had sent the angel Gavriel on a mission to destroy S'dom. Now it was time to do what he was sent to do. The sun rose over S'dom; it was daybreak. Rain started pouring down on S'dom. Then the rain from heaven turned into fire and sulfur. The city began to burn. People were terrified of the fire falling from heaven.

That was just the beginning.

The entire area of S'dom was built on an enormously large stone, the size of a large island. Gavriel used only one hand to lift the entire stone on which the cities were built up out of the ground. Then he turned the stone upside down and smashed it back in the earth.

All of S'dom, its people, its buildings, the trees and grass — everything in it — was buried under tons of rock. It was the end of S'dom and its evil. S'dom had been wiped off the face of the earth.

A huge pillar of smoke rose high up into the sky in the place where wicked S'dom used to be.

Salt

The angels had warned Lot and his family not to look back to see S'dom being destroyed. But Lot's wife didn't listen. As they were running to Tzoar she turned around for one last look at S'dom.

It was the last thing she ever did. When she looked back she was turned instantly into a pillar made of salt!

Lot and his two daughters made it to Tzoar, but they left soon after. Lot was afraid that Tzoar was not safe, because it was so near to S'dom.

Lot and his daughters went to live in a cave on a mountain. There they felt safe.

Kidnapped

Avraham lived near S'dom. With the whole area destroyed, there were very few travelers going by. This meant fewer people for Avraham to invite.

Avraham decided to move to a place where he would be able to do hachnasas orchim for many people. He packed everything up and moved to Gerar.

When he got to the entrance gate, the guards asked him, "Is Sarah your wife or sister?" A strange question! Afraid that if he said she was his wife they might kill him, he said, "She's my sister."

Sounds familiar? It was exactly what happened in Egypt all over again!

Word got back to Avimelech, the king of Gerar, that a beautiful single woman had arrived. Avimelech had her kidnapped and wanted to marry her. As a result of this evil deed Hashem made Avimelech and everyone in his palace very sick.

I'm Innocent!

Avimelech went to sleep and Hashem came to him in a dream. He told him he was going to be punished for kidnapping Sarah.

Avimelech said to Hashem, "How could I know she was Avraham's wife? Sarah, her servants, and Avraham's camel drivers all said she was his sister. Would you kill a tzaddik? I'm innocent!"

Hashem answered: "That's why I'm here, to stop you from sinning. Make sure you return her to Avraham, or you will die."

In the morning Avimelech called for Avraham to be brought to the palace.

Questions, Anyone?

Why did Hashem destroy S'dom in the early morning? Why not at night or the middle of the day?

Hashem wanted the S'domites to know that it was He Who was destroying them. Some S'domites worshiped the sun and some worshiped the moon. If Hashem had destroyed S'dom by day, the ones who worship the moon would have said it didn't happen at night because of the power of the moon god. If He had destroyed it by night, people who worship the sun would have said it didn't happen by day because of the power of the sun god.

So Hashem made it happen in early morning, when both the sun and moon are in the sky.

Why was Lot's wife turned into salt, and not something like pepper or cinnamon?

She turned into salt because she didn't want to give salt to the angels. And then she ran to borrow salt from neighbors, as a way of telling them that her husband was doing the big sin of having guests. Her sin was with salt so she was punished with salt.

Avimelech was angry. When Avraham arrived, Avimelech said, "Look what you have done to us! Everyone is sick. What did you see that made you tell us Sarah was your sister?"

Avraham said, "I saw there was no fear of Hashem here. I knew I would be killed because of my wife."

QUESTIONS, ANYONE?

What did Avraham "see" that made him realize the people of Gerar didn't fear Hashem?

It was what the guards asked him. Instead of asking if he has a place to stay and if he had enough food, all they asked was if Sarah was his wife or sister. That was a bad sign.

Gifts

Avimelech returned Sarah to Avraham. He also gave Avraham expensive gifts of many cattle and slaves. That's not all. The gift package included a thousand pieces of silver.

Avimelech said, "My land is before you. Go live wherever you want."

The Miracle Baby

Mazel tov! It's a boy! Not just any baby boy, but a miracle baby! His father, Avraham, was 100 years old, and his mother, Sarah, 90! By the laws of nature, people that old cannot have children! The baby was born exactly a year after the angels came to visit Avraham.

We Are a Miracle

Just as Yitzchak's birth was a miracle, the birth of the Jewish nation was also a miracle. We were a family of slaves in Egypt. Hashem freed us with the miracles of the ten Makkos, the splitting of the Sea of Reeds, and the astounding miracles at Har Sinai. Without these miracles there never would have been a Jewish nation.

And that was only the beginning. Time and time again our survival was miraculous.

After the Second Beis HaMikdash was destroyed, the Jews had no land and no government. How can a nation exist for more than 1900 years without its land? Who would have believed that our nation would continue to exist long after the Romans, who destroyed the Beis HaMikdash, were gone?

We are a miracle.

In modern times, it looked like Torah life was finished. The Holocaust had wiped out the great Torah centers of Europe. The yeshivos were destroyed. Yet now Torah learning has been reborn. There are more people learning in yeshivos and Bais Yaakovs today than there ever were in Europe!

We are a miracle! Don't forget it. Appreciate it. Thank Hashem for it.

Happiness and Joy

Imagine how happy Avraham and Sarah were when Hashem blessed them with a baby after waiting for so many years. Sarah said, "Hashem made me laugh with joy. Whoever hears about it will laugh and be happy about the miracle that happened to me."

The word in Hebrew for laughter is "tzchok." So they named him Yitzchak, for the laughter he brought them.

The Letters of Yitzchak's Name

The numerical value of the letters of Yitzchak's name stand for:

י Yud = 10: Avraham's tenth test was Akeidas Yitzchak. At that time Yitzchak was ready to die for Hashem.

צ Tzaddik = 90: Yitzchak's mother, Sarah, was 90 when he was born.

ח Ches = 8: The day Yitzchak had his bris.

ק Kuf = 100: Yitzchak's father, Avraham, was 100 when he was born.

After eight days passed Avraham took his precious baby and gave him a bris. He was the first baby ever to have a bris on the eighth day.

When Yitzchak was 2 years old, Avraham made a big party. Many important people were there. Shem and Eiver were there, and Avimelech, king of Gerar, also came. Most important of all, Hashem's Presence was there as well.

Idols and Grasshoppers

Unfortunately, Yishmael, the son of Avraham and Hagar, started to behave in bad ways. He was in his teens and had drifted away from what Avraham had taught him about being good. Sarah caught him building altars for idols and bringing them grasshoppers as gifts.

Avraham dedicated his life to teaching the world about Hashem. It was so awful that his own son was bowing to idols!

Attempted Murder

Once, Sarah watched Yishmael playing with his younger brother Yitzchak. She was horrified. They were playing a very dangerous game! Yishmael was practicing shooting

FASCINATING FACTS

Yitzchak's birth made many, many people happy. When he was born, other women who couldn't have children were also blessed with children. Sick people got better and people's prayers were answered.

The baby looked just like his father. That way, everyone knew he was Avraham's baby, born by a miracle. He wasn't someone else's baby that Avraham and Sarah adopted.

arrows in Yitzchak's direction! Of course, if during the "game" he missed and hit Yitzchak, he would say it wasn't his fault, right?

Sarah saw what Yishmael was up to. Attempted murder! Yishmael was trying to kill Yitzchak.

Why was Yishmael trying to kill Yitzchak? Yishmael had always expected that when Avraham would die he would get everything that belonged to his father. Then Yitzchak was born. Now he would have to share Avraham's wealth with his brother. He wouldn't be as rich as he thought he would be. He wasn't happy about that!

Out!

Sarah realized that Yishmael was getting worse and worse. What if he taught his bad ways to Yitzchak? Something had to be done. So she took action!

Sarah told Avraham to send Yishmael and his mother away, to go live somewhere else.

Avraham was very upset about the news that his son was doing evil things. He was also saddened about having to send his beloved son away. Maybe he could get Yishmael to do teshuvah?

Hashem told Avraham to listen to Sarah. He also let Avraham know that Yishmael would become a nation.

A Test

It wasn't easy for Avraham to send his son away. No parent wants to do that! Especially Avraham, who even let strangers stay at his home.

This was one of Avraham's ten tests. Would he listen to Hashem, or would he listen to his heart, which wanted to keep Yishmael at home?

Avraham passed his test.

Sick and Dying

Early the next morning, Avraham sent Hagar and Yishmael away. He put bread and a big bottle of water on Hagar's shoulder. He picked up Yishmael and put him over her shoulder as well.

Why did Avraham need to do that? Yishmael was 17, couldn't he walk? No, he couldn't. He was sick. Besides having fever, his bones and body had shrunk. He was now very small.

Hagar carried her son and walked out into the desert, where she got lost. She started praying to her old Egyptian gods.

Yishmael, burning with fever, kept asking her for more water, until the water in the bottle was gone. Lost in the desert, without water to drink, Hagar knew her child was going to die of thirst.

Questions, Anyone?

Who was a greater prophet, Avraham or Sarah?

Sarah. Hashem told Avraham to listen to Sarah and send Yishmael away, because she was the greater prophet and knew what had to be done. Yishmael had to go!

Avraham was a wealthy man, yet all he gave Hagar and Yishmael was bread and water. No gold or silver? Why?

Avraham didn't want to give him money, which he would use only to do evil things.

How did Yishmael become sick?

He made Sarah unhappy because of his terrible behavior. So Hashem made him very sick.

She stopped walking and dropped him under a tree. Then she walked away.

Not a Jewish Mother

Walked away? To leave her child to die by himself, all alone? Yes, that's exactly what she did. She didn't want to see her child suffer, so, selfishly, she left him to die. How unlike a Jewish mother! A Jewish mother would stay and try to make her sick child feel loved and comfortable.

Hagar found a place to sit and rest far from her dying son. Now that she was in such trouble, she returned once again to pray to Hashem.

Saved!

She cried out to Hashem, "At the well You said that my son would become a great nation. What happened to that promise? He is dying here!" she said to Hashem.

Yishmael, under his tree, was also crying and praying that Hashem should save him.

Meanwhile, up in Shamayim, the angels who saw what was happening tried to persuade Hashem to let Yishmael die. They argued that Yishmael's descendants, the Arab nations, would cause the Jews terrible suffering and death in the future. "Don't save him!" they pleaded.

Hashem answered, "I will judge Yishmael for the way he behaves right now. Right now he believes in Me, and he is praying to Me for help. I will save him."

Hashem sent an angel to Hagar with a message. "Don't be afraid. Hashem has heard the cry of your young man. I will make him a large nation."

Right in front of Hagar there was a well full of water. But she didn't deserve to see it until Yishmael had prayed for help. Once he did, Hashem opened Hagar's eyes and let her see the well. Hagar filled up her bottle, ran back to her son, and let him drink. Yishmael's life was saved!

Hagar and Yishmael continued their journey until they found a source of water in the Paran desert. They decided to stay and live there.

Champion

After leaving Avraham, Yishmael became very successful and wealthy because Hashem was with him. He became a champion shooter of bows and arrows, which in those days made him very important.

TORAH IN OUR LIVES

On Rosh Hashanah and Yom Kippur we pray a lot. We are very careful not to sin on those days.

Why does Hashem forgive our sins because we do the right thing on holidays? We all know that we will sin again the next day! It happens every year! Rosh Hashanah ends, and we go back to some of our old bad habits.

When we act this way Hashem judges us just like He judged Yishmael. When He sees us in shul, davening, He sees us the way we are right now, not how we might act in the future.

On Rosh Hashanah, we read in the Torah about Yishmael being answered. This is to remind us that Hashem wants to find ways to forgive us when we act properly.

Sometimes we may need help from Hashem desperately. We should believe that His help is right there, waiting for our prayers. Maybe just one more prayer or one more good deed is all we need. Then Hashem will open our eyes and we will see the help we are searching for.

Hashem's promises come true. Yishmael's descendants became the Arab nations. There are at least 366 million Arabs in the world now!

So let's remember: Hashem also made promises to us: Mashiach will come. The Beis HaMikdash will be built again. All Jews will live in Eretz Yisrael, and the dead will come back to life.

Believe it; it will happen! Hashem promised!

His mother, who had been born an Egyptian, found him an Egyptian wife.

Yishmael did teshuvah and returned to Hashem while Avraham was still alive.

Peace

King Avimelech and his general, whose name was Phichol, came to visit Avraham. The purpose of their visit? They wanted a promise from Avraham.

"Hashem is with you in everything you do," they said to Avraham. "Swear to us in the Name of Hashem that there will be peace between us, and between our children and our grandchildren. Do this because I was kind to you and let you live in my land."

Avraham said, "I swear."

On My Side

How did Avimelech know that Hashem was with Avraham?

Hashem had done so many miracles for Avraham! Though Avraham lived near S'dom, he hadn't been killed. He had also defeated the four kings in battle and had become a father when he was a very old man.

If Hashem does miracles for someone, you want that person on your side! Avimelech wanted Avraham to promise that they would not become enemies.

Seven Sheep

Way back in the days when Avraham lived, water did not come out of a faucet. It came from wells in the ground. A person finds a well by digging deep into the ground until he hits water. And the digging is done with shovels.

Imagine if someone did all that work, and someone else comes and uses up the water in his well. That is stealing!

Avimelech's shepherds were using Avraham's wells. They said the wells belonged to them. That was a lie.

Avimelech's visit was a good time for Avraham to complain about those shepherds. When Avraham told Avimelech about the stolen wells, the king said, "This is the first time I am hearing about this! Why didn't you tell me?"

The shepherds who worked for Avraham wanted to prove the wells belonged to him. They came up with an idea: they would let the wells themselves prove who was their true owner! They would do a test.

Avimelech's shepherds would come to a well. If the water in the well rose up to them to water their sheep, it was a sign that the well belonged to them. If Avraham's shepherds came to the well and the water rose for their sheep, it was a sign the well belonged to Avraham.

Avimelech's shepherds went to the well. Nothing happened. Avraham's sheep went to the well and the water immediately rose up to them! This was clear proof that the wells belonged to Avraham.

Avraham then gave Avimelech seven sheep. They made a treaty, a promise, that they wouldn't attack each other. The place where they met and made the treaty is called Beersheva.

Teaching His Guests

In Beersheva Avraham planted an orchard with many different kinds of fruit trees. This way he could offer his guests whatever fruit they liked.

When Avraham's guests finished their meals, he would say to them, "Please bless the One Whose food you have eaten." Then he would explain, "I don't mean that you should bless me. I mean you should bless Hashem Who created the world, because you ate His food."

Through the meals he served his guests, Avraham was able to teach them that Hashem created the world.

Code Word

The word the Torah uses for orchard is "eishel." That's a code word for what Avraham gave his guests. Let's break the code.

The Hebrew letters of the word are aleph (א), shin (ש), lamed (ל). These letters stand for אֲכִילָה, achilah (eating), שְׁתִיָּה, shesiah (drinking), and לִינָה, linah (sleeping). Avraham gave his guests food, drinks, and a comfortable place to sleep.

Satan Makes Problems

In Shamayim, the Satan accused Avraham of having done wrong at the party he made for Yitzchak.

Satan said to Hashem, "Avraham made a large celebration banquet, but he didn't bring even one korban to thank You for the happy event."

Hashem said to Satan, "The celebration was for his son, yet even if I asked him to bring Yitzchak as a korban, he would do it!"

After this discussion, Hashem tested Avraham to show what a great tzaddik he was.

MAASEH AVOS

The water rose out of the well in honor of Avraham. The same thing would happen to the Jews in the desert. When the Jews approached the well of Miriam, water rose up so they could drink and give water to their animals.

QUESTIONS, ANYONE?

Why was it called Beersheva?

"Beer" means "well" and "Sheva" has the same letters as the word that means to swear, which is what Avraham and Avimelech did when they made the treaty. "Sheva" also means seven, for the seven sheep Avraham gave Avimelech.

FASCINATING FACTS

Avraham put up a tent, a "hotel," where he gave out food, drink, and a place to sleep for free.

I Chose!

There was another reason for this difficult test.

Yitzchak and Yishmael had an argument. Yishmael told Yitzchak, "Hashem loves me more than He loves you. I chose to have a bris. I was already 13 years old, and I let our father do it. At your bris, you were a baby. You had no choice. My mitzvah is much greater than yours!"

"If Hashem asked me to give up my life for Him, I would do it!" Yitzchak answered.

Now Hashem would give Yitzchak a chance to prove that what he said was true.

The Tenth Test

Imagine if someone tells you to destroy an item that is most precious to you, something you worked hard for many years to get.

How would you feel? Would you argue and beg not to have to destroy it? Would you say, "It's not fair"? Would you try to hide it and not destroy it?

That's the challenge that Avraham had when Hashem tested him with Akeidas Yitzchak. It was his tenth and hardest test. But Avraham passed the test, and with no argument at all!

The Command

One night, Hashem spoke to Avraham. "Please, take your son."

"Which one?" Avraham answered. "I have two."

"Your only son."

"Each one is the only son of his mother."

"The one you love."

"I love them both."

"Take Yitzchak, go to the land of Moriah, and bring him up as a korban that is entirely burnt. I will tell you when you get there on which mountain to do it."

Hashem had commanded Avraham to kill his son. Did he argue with Hashem? No. Did he tell Hashem, "What about the promise You made that Yitzchak will become a great nation?" No.

Avraham was ready to do Hashem's command, even though it meant giving up his precious, beloved son. Why? Because doing Hashem's will is a mitzvah, it's what we live for. No wonder Hashem chose Avraham to create the Jewish people.

FASCINATING FACTS

The land of Moriah is Yerushalayim.

QUESTIONS, ANYONE?

Why didn't Hashem just say, "Take Yitzchak"? Why did He say all those things before telling him He meant Yitzchak?

To increase the reward Avraham would get for doing the mitzvah. Each separate piece of the command became another mitzvah. "Your son," is one, "Whom you love," is another, etc.

On Their Way

Avraham woke up early in the morning. He was in a hurry to do this mitzvah as quickly as possible.

He made preparations for the trip. He put a saddle on his donkey and cut wood for the fire he would need to burn the korban, his son. He did it all himself.

Why was Avraham doing all this himself? He had many servants. Why not tell them to do it? Because he loved Hashem so much, he wanted to do the mitzvos himself.

Avraham told Yitzchak that they were going, but he didn't tell him why. Avraham also took Yishmael and his trusted servant Eliezer with him.

The Journey

The four of them set out for the land of Moriah. After three days of travel, Avraham saw a cloud in the distance. It was hovering over a mountain. The cloud was a symbol that Hashem's Presence was over this mountain. There was also a pillar of fire rising to heaven from the top of the mountain. These were Hashem's signs, to show Avraham where to go. It was their final destination!

They were looking at the top of Mount Moriah. This was the place where the Beis HaMikdash would be built hundreds of years in the future.

Avraham asked Yitzchak, "Do you see what I see?"

"Yes."

Avraham asked Eliezer and Yishmael the same question. They answered no, they didn't see anything.

The cloud and pillar of fire were meant to be seen by holy people. Yishmael and Eliezer weren't holy enough to see what Avraham and Yitzchak saw.

Avraham told Eliezer and Yishmael, "Stay here with the donkey. I and Yitzchak will go up and pray, then we will return."

Avraham and Yitzchak walked up the mountain. Yitzchak carried the wood and Avraham carried the knife.

I'm Going!

It was almost time. Akeidas Yitzchak, tying Yitzchak onto the Mizbei'ach to bring him as a korban, was about to happen. It was one of the greatest mitzvos any person has ever done, because it would be so hard for Avraham to do this to the son he loved so much, and yet he would do it because Hashem asked him to. This mitzvah would be a powerful force for good in the world. That is why the Satan

MAASEH AVOS

As a reward for Avraham splitting the wood, Hashem "split" the Sea of Reeds when the Jews left Egypt.

WHO'S WHO IN THE TORAH

Avraham's Donkey

The donkey Avraham rode to the Akeidah wasn't just any donkey. It's the same donkey used by Moshe Rabbeinu when he went to take the Jews out of Egypt.

It is still alive today, somewhere! Waiting for Mashiach to ride on it when he comes to take us out of exile.

QUESTIONS, ANYONE?

How old were Avraham and Yitzchak when this happened?

Avraham was 137 and Yitzchak 37.

tried to do everything he could to stop it from happening!

First, the Satan appeared to Avraham as an old man. "Old man, old man, have you lost your mind?" he said. "Are you going to kill your son?"

Avraham answered, "Hashem told me to. I'm going to do what He says."

Seeing that Avraham would not listen to him, the Satan tried with Yitzchak.

He appeared to Yitzchak as a young man and told him, "You are going to be killed!"

"I'm going."

Failed again! But the Satan didn't give up.

He turned into a large river and put himself smack in the middle of the road where Avraham and Yitzchak had to pass.

Avraham and Yitzchak got to the river. They didn't say, "Hashem, we did our best. It wasn't our fault. The river was too big for us to pass, so we had to go home."

Not at all. Determined to fulfill Hashem's command, they walked right into the river and tried to cross it. They kept walking, further and further, until the water reached their necks.

If they went any further, they would drown!

Avraham called out to Hashem, "Take away the river so I can do what You want me to do!"

That's when Hashem told the Satan, "Enough!"

The river disappeared and the Satan stopped bothering them.

Where Is the Lamb?

Yitzchak asked his father, "We have the wood and the knife. Where is the lamb that we are going to bring as a korban?"

"Hashem will select the korban for us, my son," Avraham said.

From these words, Yitzchak realized what was happening: he was going to be a korban for Hashem.

It didn't make one bit of difference to Yitzchak! Avraham and his son continued their journey together. Their hearts shared the same feelings — excitement and enthusiasm to do Hashem's will.

The Akeidah

They arrived at the top of the mountain. Avraham and Yitzchak gathered stones to build the Mizbei'ach. Then they put the wood they had brought with them on it.

Avraham tied up Yitzchak. Tears flowed from his eyes as he put his son on the Mizbei'ach they had built.

Still crying, Avraham picked up the knife. The time had come.

Fascinating Facts

Avraham told Yishmael and Eliezer, "We will come back." This was a prophecy that both he and Yitzchak would return safely from the mountain. But Avraham didn't know that Hashem would tell him not to kill Yitzchak.

Angel's Tears

At that moment, there was a great commotion in Shamayim. The angels in Shamayim saw that Yitzchak was about to be killed.

Suddenly Shamayim was filled with the sound of angels crying and calling out to Hashem in prayer. Yitzchak, whose eyes were looking up at Shamayim, saw what was going on.

"Hashem, You are called merciful," they said. "Have mercy on Yitzchak! If Yitzchak dies there will be no Jewish people. There will be no Yerushalayim and no Beis HaMikdash."

The angels' tears fell to earth, where they dropped into the eyes of Yitzchak, who was looking up at heaven.

The time had come to stop Avraham from killing his son.

The Akeidah Lesson

During the years of the Holocaust, doing mitzvos was very hard. The Germans would often kill Jews who tried to follow the laws of the Torah. But Jews were clever and found ways to do the mitzvos anyway, even though they were risking their lives. In concentration camps and ghettos they put on tefillin, ate matzah, lit Chanukah candles, and did many other mitzvos.

Hundreds of years earlier, during the Spanish Expulsion, the Jews were told either to stop being Jews or they would have to leave the country. Thousands of Jews left their homes and everything they owned behind and became homeless refugees. Why? So they could continue to do the mitzvos.

In the early 1900's in America, if you didn't work on Shabbos it was almost impossible to get a job. Yet there were Jews who kept Shabbos anyway, even though it meant being very poor.

Where do the Jews get the strength to do mitzvos even when it's so difficult? The Akeidah.

Avraham and Yitzchak did what Hashem wanted. Even though it was incredibly hard to do. What they did was put into the genes of the Jewish people the power and inspiration to do mitzvos no matter how hard or dangerous it might be.

Because we come from Avraham and Yitzchak we too have the power to do mitzvos we find difficult. Getting out of bed to go to shul, though we would rather sleep. Not buying a really cool outfit we would love to wear because it is not modest. Apologizing to a friend who we hurt because of something we said, even if what we said was true!

We're children of Avraham and Yitzchak, and we do the mitzvos. No matter what. And that is the lesson of the Akeidah.

Fascinating Facts

The Mizbei'ach was built on the ruins of the Mizbei'ach Adam had built. Kayin and Hevel had used it as well. Adam's Mizbei'ach was destroyed in the Mabul but rebuilt and used by Noach. Later, it fell apart.

Questions, Anyone?

Why is this test called Akeidas Yitzchak? Wasn't it a test for Avraham?

Yitzchak told his father, "Tie me up tight. I am afraid that when I see the knife I will get scared, move, and ruin everything."

The special way Yitzchak was tied up is called "akeidah." It means tying a person's or animal's right hand to the right leg, and the left hand to the left leg, behind their back.

Fascinating Facts

The angels' tears that fell into his eyes eventually caused Yitzchak to become blind in his old age.

Who Are You?

Hashem sent an angel with a message.

"Avraham! Avraham!"

Avraham heard the angel calling him from heaven. He stopped and listened.

"Don't kill him or do anything to him. Now I know that you fear Hashem. You would even give up your most precious possession, your son, for Me."

Did Avraham immediately celebrate the good news that his son was saved? No! He was suspicious. Maybe this was another one of Satan's tricks?

Avraham asked the angel, "Who are you?"

"I am an angel."

Avraham answered: "When Hashem told me to take my son and bring him as a korban He personally came and told me. I won't stop unless He comes and tells me Himself to stop."

The heavens opened and Avraham heard Hashem tell him to stop.

How Can It Be?

Avraham was confused. He asked Hashem, "First You promised that the Jewish people would come from Yitzchak. Then You told me to bring him up as a korban, which means the Jews would not come from Yitzchak. Now You tell me to take him down from the Mizbei'ach. How can it be? Hashem doesn't change His mind!"

Hashem explained what happened. "I told you to put your son on a Mizbei'ach as a korban. But I never said you should actually kill him. Now that you've put him on the Mizbei'ach, you can take him down."

Hashem had wanted only to test Avraham, to show that he would actually put Yitzchak on the Mizbei'ach. Hashem never meant that Yitzchak should be killed.

The Ram

Avraham saw a ram whose horns were caught in the branches of a tree. He took the ram, put it on the Mizbei'ach as a korban, and burnt it to ashes.

QUESTIONS, ANYONE?

Why say, "Avraham, Avraham," twice? Wouldn't it have been enough to call his name once?

Calling someone's name twice is a way of showing that you love the person.

Hashem said: "Now I know you fear Hashem." What does this mean? After all, Hashem always knows what everyone is thinking! He always knew that Avraham feared Him. Why did He put Avraham through this difficult test?

What Hashem meant was: "Now I can answer the Satan and the non-Jewish nations when they want to know why I love you so much. I can point to the Akeidah, where you showed how you feared Me and would do anything for Me. I will tell them, 'That's why I love the Jews so much.'"

Why does it say, "don't kill him" and "don't do anything to him"? Wouldn't the words "don't kill him" have been enough?

When Avraham heard the words "don't kill him" he thought Hashem still wanted some of Yitzchak's blood sprinkled on the Mizbei'ach. So Avraham said, "I'll make a small cut in Yitzchak and take some blood from him." That's why Hashem told him, "Don't do anything!"

What is a ram?

A male sheep.

Why is the holiest city on earth called Yerushalayim?

Avraham called the place Yireh (He will see). Noach's son, Shem, called it Shalem (peace). Hashem combined both names and called it Yerushalayim. Since Avraham was a greater tzaddik than Shem, Hashem put the name that Avraham called it first. "Yireh-Shalem" became "Yerushalayim"!

The Ram

The ram Avraham burnt on the Mizbei'ach was amazing!

It was created on the sixth day of Creation, right before Shabbos.

Hashem made a shofar out of its left horn and blew it when the Torah was given at Mount Sinai.

Hashem made a shofar out of its right horn. He is saving it in Heaven. It will be blown to announce the coming of Mashiach.

The ten strings of King David's harp were made out of its veins.

The leather belt the prophet Eliyahu wore was made from its skin.

He Will See

Avraham called the place where the Akeidah happened, "Hashem Yireh," which means "Hashem will see."

What will He see?

He will always see the Akeidah, and He will forgive the Jews for their sins. He will judge us with mercy, rather than with strict judgment.

Avraham then said, "On this mountain Hashem will appear." He meant that the Presence of Hashem will always be on Mount Moriah. It will be the place where the Presence of Hashem will be.

Until today Jews come from all over the world to get as close as they can to Mount Moriah — to the Kosel. The Presence of Hashem is still there today, just like Avraham said it would be, thousands of years ago!

Stars and Sand

Once again an angel called out from heaven with a message for Avraham from Hashem.

"I swear that because of what you did, I will bless you. Your descendants will be as many as the stars in heaven and the sand on the beach. And they will defeat their enemies."

Hashem told Avraham that when we follow the Torah and mitzvos we will be a great nation. We will be like stars high in the sky. Our enemies will not be able to reach us, just as they can't reach the stars.

But when we don't follow the Torah we will be like sand on the beach. We will be hit by the waves: our enemies, who try to destroy us. However, like the sand, no matter how many times the waves hit the beach, the beach survives. We will always survive attempts by our enemies to destroy us.

A Baby Is Born

When he was returning from the Akeidah, Avraham thought: If Yitzchak had died at the Akeidah, he wouldn't have left over any children! Avraham decided that he must find the right wife for Yitzchak. Avraham was thinking of marrying Yitzchak to a Canaanite woman, because there were no Jewish women in the world.

Then Hashem told Avraham good news. Yitzchak would not have to marry a Canaanite. "Yitzchak's future wife has just been born. Her name is Rivkah."

Mazel tov!

QUESTIONS, ANYONE?

On what day of the year did the Akeidah happen?

On Rosh Hashanah. That's why the Torah reading on the second day of Rosh Hashanah is about the Akeidah.

TORAH IN OUR LIVES

On Rosh Hashanah we blow the shofar. When Hashem hears the sound of the shofar, He remembers the Akeidah, and forgives us.

When we pray at the Kosel, it's meaningful and exciting to remember all that happened right behind it. It's where the Akeidah happened. It's also where Yaakov had his dream of angels climbing up and down the ladder. And it's where the First and Second Batei Mikdash (Holy Temples) were built.

What makes it such a holy place? It's where a Jew, Yitzchak Avinu, was willing to give up his life. It's where a Jew, Avraham Avinu, was ready to sacrifice what was most dear to him ... all for Hashem!

FASCINATING FACTS

Rivkah was Avraham's great-niece. Her father was Besuel and her grandfather was Avraham's brother, Nachor.

פָּרָשַׁת
חַיֵּי שָׂרָה

Parashas Chayei Sarah

Chayei Sarah • חַיֵּי שָׂרָה

Parashah Pointers

- Sarah passes away at the age of 127, and Avraham speaks about her.
- Avraham buys a field and buries Sarah in a cave on the land. It is called Me'aras HaMachpeilah.
- Avraham sends his servant Eliezer to Charan, where his relatives live, to find a wife for Yitzchak.
- Eliezer travels to Charan, with a caravan of camels. He arrives just as the girls of the village are drawing water from the village well.
- Eliezer prays for a sign that will help him choose the right girl for Yitzchak. The sign will be that when he asks a girl for a drink of water, she will offer to give water to his camels as well. The girl who does this will be the one Yitzchak should marry.
- Eliezer goes over to a girl at the well and asks her for water. She answers, "I will give water to you and all your camels."
- Eliezer is very excited. This is the sign! This is the girl he was looking for. He discovers that her name is Rivkah, and she is the daughter of Avraham's nephew, Besuel.
- Eliezer gives her expensive jewelry as a gift and asks if he can stay overnight in her parents' home.
- When Eliezer arrives at Rivkah's home, he tells the family his story and asks: Would they agree to let their daughter Rivkah marry Yitzchak? They agree. Later, they say they want to ask the girl if she agrees to go with Eliezer. Rivkah agrees.
- The next morning Rivkah and Eliezer leave for Eretz Yisrael.
- Rivkah comes to Eretz Yisrael and marries Yitzchak.
- Avraham marries a woman called Keturah and has many children with her.
- Avraham passes away at the age of 175 and is buried by Yitzchak and Yishmael in Me'aras HaMachpeilah.
- The parashah ends with a list of Yishmael's descendants.

Chayei Sarah

We can't meet Avraham and Sarah. But we can go to where they are buried: Me'aras HaMachpeilah (the Cave of Machpeilah), in the city of Chevron.

Hundreds of thousands of Jews go there every year. They stand near the graves of Avraham and Sarah, Yitzchak and Rivkah, Yaakov and Leah. They pray there, pouring out their hearts, knowing that we are their children and they will hear our prayers and ask Hashem to answer us.

Me'aras HaMachpeilah

- It's the oldest Jewish cemetery in the world — over 3700 years old!
- The first man and woman to be created, Adam and Chavah, are buried there as well.
- Eisav's head is buried there.
- For 700 years the Arabs did not allow Jews to enter Me'aras HaMachpeilah. In 1967 the Jews conquered Chevron — including Me'aras HaMachpeilah — in the Six Day War with the Arabs. We are fortunate that our generation can go and pray inside.
- The big building where people pray is actually built over the cave where the Founding Fathers and Mothers are buried. The entrance to the cave has been sealed for many centuries and is below ground.
- It's one of our holiest places.
- All souls pass through this cave on the way to heaven.

Tragedy

When Avraham and Yitzchak returned home from the Akeidas Yitzchak there was sad news waiting for them. While they were away, Avraham's dearly beloved wife, Sarah, had passed away in the city of Chevron.

The Torah doesn't simply tell us she died at the age of 127. It writes that the life of Sarah was "100 years, and 20 years, and 7 years," to teach us what kind of person she was. She had as few sins at 100 as she had at 20 — that is, none. No sins at all throughout her life. And at 20 she was so beautiful that she didn't need to wear makeup, like a girl of seven, whose beauty is natural and who doesn't use makeup.

Sarah was one of the holiest women to walk the earth. She was a

QUESTIONS, ANYONE?

What did Sarah die from?

Sarah didn't die from sickness or old age. The angel of death came and told Sarah that Avraham had taken her one and only son to kill him as a korban. She died from the shock of hearing that Yitzchak had been killed (which, of course, was not true).

FASCINATING FACTS

The city of Chevron has another name: Kiryas Arba, which means "the city of four." It was called that because four pairs of holy people are buried in the city: Adam and Chavah, Avraham and Sarah, Yitzchak and Rivkah, Yaakov and Leah. Also, because of four giants that lived in Chevron.

The Jewish city today that is built near the Arab city of Chevron is called Kiryat Arba.

partner with Avraham, teaching the world about the existence of Hashem, connecting the world back to their Creator. Avraham taught the men and Sarah taught the women.

Funeral

In honor of Sarah's death, the whole city of Chevron closed their stores, left their homes, and came to her funeral. The tzaddikim that lived then came as well. Noach's son, Shem, and Noach's grandson, Eiver, were also there. Avimelech, Aner, Eshkol, and Mamrei came as well.

Eishes Chayil

Avraham got up in front of the crowd and spoke about his wife. The speech he gave described everything about her that made her such an amazing Jewish woman.

Every Friday night we sing Avraham's speech. It's called Eishes Chayil!

We praise our mothers and our wives with the same words that Avraham used to praise Sarah. When women want to know how a Jewish mother and wife should act, they look to Sarah Imeinu.

After his speech, Avraham cried over the loss of his dear wife. He didn't cry too much because Sarah had lived a long life and hadn't died young. Also, because he knew she was a wonderful woman who was going straight to Gan Eden.

The Cave

Avraham knew exactly where he wanted to bury Sarah. It was in the cave he had discovered when the angels came to visit him after he had a bris. (For the full story of the angels' visit, see p. 72.) This was the amazing cave where Adam and Chavah were buried.

But there was a problem. Avraham didn't own the property. It belonged to a man named Ephron, who was from the Hittite nation. Even a bigger problem: The Hittites ruled Chevron at that time, and the law was that land for burial could be bought only by another Hittite. It was illegal to sell land to a foreigner. Avraham had to get permission from the Hittites to buy a grave, and then he had to persuade Ephron to sell the cave to him.

Permission

After the funeral, Avraham spoke to the Hittites in Chevron and asked if they would let him have a grave for his wife. They answered with great respect that since he was a prince of Hashem he could have one for free. He could have any land that he wanted, even if it was owned by someone else. They told him they would be happy to give it to him.

Avraham then asked them to speak to Ephron and convince him to sell the cave of Machpeilah to Avraham. Avraham told them to let Ephron know that he would pay him and that he was not asking for a gift.

Making a Deal

Ephron was in the crowd when Avraham spoke. In front of everyone, he called out to Avraham, "I'll give you the field and the cave."

Avraham was very wise. He realized from what Ephron said that he would not give away anything for free. Ephron wanted to make a lot of money.

How did Avraham know this?

Ephron said, "I'll give you the field and the cave." Did Avraham ask for a field? He only wanted the cave. This was code talk for, "You want the cave, you will have to buy the field as well." Ephron wanted everyone to think he was a big tzaddik who would give Avraham whatever he wanted.

QUESTIONS, ANYONE?

In a Sefer Torah, why is the letter "kaf" in the word "v'livkosah" ("to cry for her") written smaller than all the other letters?

To show us that Avraham cried only a little at his wife's funeral.

Where else in Tanach do we find the number 127?

In Megillas Esther. 127 is the number of countries that King Achashveirosh ruled over. Which means that Esther, a descendant of Sarah, was the queen of 127 countries. Having such a descendant was Sarah's reward for her 127 years of living a good life and serving Hashem.

FASCINATING FACTS

Because the cave had two levels it was called the "Double Cave – Me'aras (Cave) HaMachpeilah (Double)."

QUESTIONS, ANYONE?

The Torah repeats ten times that Avraham was dealing with the Hittites! Why?

To teach us that if someone makes it easy for a tzaddik to do business and make a good deal, it's as if they kept all Aseres HaDibros.

But Avraham understood what Ephron really meant.

Avraham told Ephron, "I'll pay for the field."

Now Ephron got down to business. He let Avraham know how much money he wanted for the cave and field. He told Avraham, and the crowd, "400 silver shekels. Between two good friends like me and you, what is 400 silver shekels? Practically nothing!"

The truth was 400 shekels was a lot of money — and they weren't friends!

Avraham opened his coin purse and started counting out silver shekels. Ephron stopped him. "Hold on, I didn't mean these regular shekels. I want 400 Centenaria silver shekels." What a swindler! One Centenaria shekel equaled 2,500 regular shekels. Ephron made Avraham pay 400 Centenaria shekels — which meant that Avraham paid for Me'aras HaMachpeilah one million regular shekels!

But the price didn't matter. The important thing was: Now the cave was Avraham's, and it would belong to the Jewish people forever.

Burial

When Avraham entered Me'aras HaMachpeilah with Sarah's body, something very unusual happened. Adam and Chavah came back to life and got out of their graves!

They wouldn't let Avraham bury Sarah. They said, "Sarah did so much good in her life. If she is buried here we will be so embarrassed. We weren't like her. We sinned and brought death to the world."

It wasn't until Avraham promised to pray for them and ask that Hashem should forgive them that they let Avraham bury his beloved wife, Sarah Imeinu.

Face Change

The first time the Torah says someone grew old was when it talks about Avraham. Does that mean that before Avraham no one got old? Of course not! Adam died at 930, Sarah died at 127 — that's pretty old!

Avraham was the first person to look old. Until Avraham's time people's hair didn't turn gray, and their faces didn't get wrinkled.

It was Avraham's idea that people should look old.

Avraham told Hashem, "If a person meets a father and a son in the street, who do they say hello to first? Out of respect, to the father, of course. But if the father doesn't look older than his son, no one knows who to say hello to first. Please, Hashem, make it so old people look different from young people."

Fascinating Facts

Ephron had become one of the city leaders that day. He didn't know it, but he had become a leader because Hashem wanted Avraham to deal with someone important, not just anybody.

Ephron was a perfect example of how wicked people act. They promise everything, but when it comes to action, they do nothing. Ephron had said he would give Avraham the field and cave for free. In the end, he sold it for a very high price.

In the words of the Talmud: "The wicked say a lot, but even a little they don't do!"

Questions, Anyone?

In what month and year did Sarah die?

Cheshvan, 2085

Hashem agreed, and Avraham's hair turned gray! From then on when people got old, they looked old. Now people could tell the difference between fathers and sons, mothers and daughters, old and young.

Blessed with Everything

By the time Avraham reached old age, Hashem had blessed him "bakol" — with everything. Besides enormous wealth, he had defeated his yetzer hara and had no desire to sin! He couldn't sin. Avraham had passed all his ten tests, and now Hashem let him live the rest of his life in peace.

Avraham's greatest blessing was his "ben," his son, which has the same numerical value as "bakol" (the gematria [numerical value] of both "ben" and "bakol" is 52).

According to one opinion "bakol" means he was blessed with a daughter, and her name was "Bakol."

The First Shidduch

Avraham realized that if things would have turned out differently at the Akeidah, Yitzchak would have been killed and he would have no children! Who would have carried on Avraham's mission? Avraham realized it was time for Yitzchak to get married. After all, Yitzchak was forty years old.

This is the story of the first Jewish shidduch.

The "shadchan" was Avraham's trusted servant and student, Eliezer. Avraham gave him careful instructions on how to go about finding a wife for Yitzchak, and he described the kind of girl Eliezer should be looking for.

No Canaanim!

Avraham told Eliezer, "Swear to Hashem by the holiness of the mitzvah of bris milah not to bring a Canaanite girl to marry Yitzchak. Go to the country where I was born and bring back a girl for Yitzchak from my family."

"What happens if she doesn't want to come?" Eliezer asked. "Should I take Yitzchak there?

"Absolutely not!" Avraham answered. "Hashem will send an angel to go with you, and you will bring a wife back for my son.

WHO'S WHO IN THE TORAH

Eliezer

When Avraham left to Eretz Yisrael, King Nimrod gave him a going-away gift: his servant Eliezer. Avraham trusted Eliezer so much that he let Eliezer manage his household.

Eliezer learned all the teachings of Avraham and taught them to others.

When Avraham went to fight the five kings, Eliezer was the only one who went with him to the battle.

FASCINATING FACTS

Eliezer hoped that his daughter would marry Yitzchak. However, Eliezer was a Canaanite. Avraham would not allow Yitzchak to marry her, because the children of Canaan had been cursed by Noach. Avraham and Yitzchak were descendants of Shem, whom Noach had blessed. A match between someone cursed and someone blessed would not work.

QUESTIONS, ANYONE?

Which angel did Hashem send with Eliezer?

Avraham's special angel — Metatron.

If you can't find a match from my family who is willing to come back, then you can choose a wife for Yitzchak from the families of Aner, Eshkol, or Mamrei."

Ten Camels

Eliezer wanted to make a good impression on Avraham's family when he got to Charan. That way it would be easier for them to let their daughter go to Eretz Yisrael to marry Yitzchak.

He put together a grand caravan of ten of Avraham's camels. They were loaded with bags and chests overflowing with great wealth. When Avraham's family would see that, they would know that Avraham was very rich and important.

Avraham also gave Eliezer a contract that said he was giving all his wealth to Yitzchak. Whoever would be marrying Yitzchak would be the wife of a rich man! Eliezer would show the contract to Avraham's family. Their daughter would live in luxury.

Speed

Eliezer packed his bags for a long trip. From Chevron where Avraham lived till Charan, where his brother Nachor's family lived, was a seventeen-day trip by camel.

But a miracle happened! Three hours later he was there!

Eliezer arrived toward evening and stopped near the city well. The girls of the village were coming to the well to draw water for cooking and drinking. In those times, there was no running water in their houses or tents. People had to get water from the well, and then carry the heavy pitchers of water back home.

One Girl Not Like the Others

Eliezer thought about what a hard job it would be to pick a girl to marry Yitzchak. He decided to pray for help.

"Hashem, please help me for the sake of Avraham. Please make it happen that I will ask a girl for a drink, and she will say, 'Drink, and I will give your camels water to drink also.' She will be the right girl You chose for Yitzchak."

Now the question was: Which of all the girls coming to the well should he ask for a drink?

Hashem made it easy for him. One girl was different from the others. When her turn came to fill her pitcher with water, water suddenly rose up out of the well into her pitcher.

Questions, Anyone?

How were Avraham's camels different from everyone else's?

Avraham's camels were the only ones that traveled with muzzles over their mouths. That prevented them from munching on food in fields that belonged to others. That would be stealing!

Fascinating Facts

This was the first time Rivkah went to the well. Her father Besuel was a king, and she was a princess. Princesses don't go to wells. The servants are sent to bring water.

But this time Hashem arranged that Rivkah should go for the water that day, so she would meet Eliezer.

A camel can drink 53 gallons of water in just three minutes. Eliezer had 10 camels. Imagine how many gallons and gallons of water Rivkah must have carried that day!

Eliezer realized that a girl for whom miracles happen was probably the girl for Yitzchak. But would she offer to give water to his camels?

Bracelets and Nose Rings

Eliezer quickly ran toward the girl and asked her for a drink from her pitcher. She gave him water, and then when he finished drinking she told him, "I'll give your camels water too." Again and again, she ran to the well to bring water for all ten thirsty camels to drink.

The girl lowered the pitcher into the well, pulled it up again and again until all the camels had finished drinking. A pitcher of water is heavy, and what she did wasn't easy. Yet this girl did it for all ten camels, for someone she didn't even know!

Eliezer watched all this chessed. Hashem had answered his prayers so quickly! Surely, this was the perfect wife for Yitzchak.

Eliezer took out a golden nose ring, on which was a large and expensive jewel weighing a half silver shekel, and two bracelets weighing ten golden shekels. He gave them to the girl as a gift.

These gifts weren't just a way of saying thank you for giving the animals water. They were hints about the future of Rivkah's descendants. Two bracelets weighing ten golden shekels were for the Aseres HaDibros, which were given on two stone blocks. The jewel in the nose ring weighing a half shekel was for the half shekel the Jews would give to the Beis HaMikdash every year, to bring the korbanos.

Who Are You?

All this time Eliezer didn't know who she was. Now, he asked her who she was and if there was any room at home for him to stay overnight as a guest. She answered, "I am the daughter of Besuel, the son of Nachor, and we have room for guests." She added that they had food for his animals, as well. Once again Rivkah was ready to do more for a stranger than he asked for.

Hearing that this girl came from Avraham's family, Eliezer knew that he'd found Yitzchak's kallah. He bowed down to Hashem and thanked Him for answering his prayers. He said, "Blessed is Hashem, Who was kind to me and to my master, and Who led me straight to my master's family."

He's Rich!

Rivkah's trip to get water had turned out to be quite unusual. She ran home and told her mother all about her exciting experience. Lavan, Rivkah's evil brother, overheard Rivkah telling the story and saw the expensive bracelets she was wearing.

? Questions, Anyone?

How great was Rivkah's chessed?

Here she was, running back and forth, back and forth, between the well and the camels. Eliezer just stood by, watching.

Yet she didn't get angry at Eliezer. She didn't say: "These are YOUR camels — why are you letting me do all the work? Why aren't you helping me?"

Why didn't Eliezer or his servants help her?

They certainly wanted to, but they couldn't. Eliezer had asked Hashem for a sign. The wife for Yitzchak had to be someone who was so kind that she would do everything herself.

Torah in Our Lives

Eliezer prayed to Hashem to succeed, even though Avraham had sent an angel with him. That's a good lesson for all of us. Always ask Hashem to help us succeed.

Even though we work hard to win a game, or study hard to do well on a test, we still need to pray to Hashem for His help.

When Eliezer's prayers were answered he thanked Hashem. We pray to Hashem for so many things. Let's not forget to thank Him when He gives us what we asked for!

He got very excited. The man Rivkah met must be very rich if he gave such gifts! He ran out to Eliezer. Not to invite him or be kind to him. He ran out to kill him!

Why? The traveling stranger had ten camels that were carrying a fortune. Lavan figured he could kill him and take all his money! Who would care?

Camels in the Air

What Lavan saw when he got to the well made him change his mind about murdering the stranger. There, hovering in the air above the well, were Eliezer and his camels!

How did that happen?

When Eliezer saw Lavan running toward him, he could tell Lavan was up to no good. To protect himself, Eliezer said Hashem's powerful Name. That made it possible for him to float in the air, where Lavan would not be able to get to him.

Since he couldn't overpower and kill Eliezer, Lavan instead pretended to be friendly. "Come. Stay with us," he said. "Why stay out here? I even made room for the camels." Knowing that Eliezer wouldn't enter a house that had idols, Lavan told him that they had removed all the idols from the house.

Eliezer floated back down to earth and followed Lavan home.

TORAH IN OUR LIVES

The Torah teaches us how important it is to treat animals properly. Even if a person is hungry, he shouldn't eat until his animals have been fed!

Animals First

When they got to the house, the first thing Eliezer did was feed his camels. Why? Because when someone is invited as a guest they are usually given something to eat. But Eliezer would not eat until he had fed his animals. A person is not allowed to eat until he feeds his animals.

FASCINATING FACTS

One of the ways we know that Lavan was wicked is that he spoke up before his father to answer Eliezer's question. He did not show respect for his father.

Eliezer Speaks

Having fed the animals, Eliezer went to meet the family and settle in. His hosts brought him food, but he didn't touch it. This wasn't a pleasure trip, he had a job to do! Before eating he wanted to finalize the shidduch.

He began to speak.

"I won't eat until I finish telling you my story," he said. "I am Avraham's servant. Because of Hashem's blessing, Avraham is a very rich man. He gave all of his wealth to his son. I was sent here to find a wife for him."

He then told them the whole story of what happened between him and Rivkah at the well. How she had given him and his camels to drink, which was the sign from Hashem that she was the right match for Yitzchak.

Eliezer finished his story and asked the family, "Now tell me if you agree. Otherwise, I will look for a wife for Yitzchak elsewhere, finding a wife for him either from the daughters of Lot or Yishmael."

FASCINATING FACTS

Since Rivkah's grandfather, Nachor, was Avraham's brother, she was Avraham's great-niece, and Yitzchak was her cousin.

Gifts

The family listened to Eliezer's fascinating story. It was so obvious that Hashem had chosen Rivkah for Yitzchak.

Rivkah's brother, Lavan, and her father, Besuel, said, "This is clearly what Hashem wants. We can't say no. Take Rivkah to be Yitzchak's wife."

When Eliezer heard this, he bowed low and thanked Hashem for the good news. Rivkah's parents had agreed to the marriage. Mazel tov!

Eliezer then gave the kallah gifts made of gold and silver, and expensive clothing. Her mother and brother got luscious and tasty fruit from Eretz Yisrael.

Now that his mission was completed, Eliezer allowed the meal to begin. Everyone was eating, drinking, and celebrating.

Poison!

In the middle of the meal Besuel, who had just taken a spoonful of food, suddenly began to choke. He was having trouble breathing and fell unconscious over the table. A few moments later he was dead! What a terrible tragedy. Everyone was in shock.

What happened? How did he die?

Poison.

Lavan and Besuel wanted Eliezer to die, so they could steal the fortune he had with him. They decided to poison his food. Eliezer was in great danger! But an angel came and switched the dishes. Eliezer got Besuel's food and Besuel got Eliezer's. Besuel ate the poisoned food and died.*

Let's Go

Eliezer stayed overnight with Rivkah's family. In the morning, he told the family that he wanted to take Rivkah and leave immediately. They

** There is another opinion that an angel killed Besuel in middle of the night because he would have stopped Rivkah from leaving right away.*

FASCINATING FACTS

Yitzchak was the first person to daven Minchah. He taught us that people should pray in the afternoon. It's because of him that we daven Minchah.

asked if she could stay for about a year before going to get married.

Eliezer said, "No delays! We have to go."

They said, "Let's ask Rivkah if she wants to stay or go."

They asked Rivkah if she wanted to stay a while or leave right away.

She told her mother and Lavan, "I am going whether you want me to go or not."

That seems to be a strange way for a daughter to talk to her mother. It does not seem to be very respectful. How could a girl full of kindness like Rivkah behave like that?

Really, she wasn't being disrespectful. She was simply stating a fact: Hashem wants me to go, and He will make sure I go whether you like it or not.

Rivkah and Devorah, the nurse who had taken care of Rivkah since she was a baby, packed their things and were ready to leave.

Before Rivkah left, her brother and mother blessed her. They said she should have tens of millions of descendants, and her descendants should defeat their enemies.

Minchah

Rivkah and Devorah got on the camels and began their journey back to Eretz Yisrael. Once again Hashem stepped in. Instead of the trip taking 17 days, they made it in only three hours. They got back just in time to see Yitzchak going to daven Minchah.

He was davening in a field on Mount Moriah, the place where the Beis HaMikdash would one day stand. Rivkah and Eliezer passed and saw a holy man praying, wrapped in a tallis, with his hands outstretched to the heavens. It was an awesome sight, like looking at an angel. She didn't know who the man was.

If she had been standing up, she would have bowed out of respect for the tzaddik. But you can't bow while sitting on a camel! So instead, she leaned way over. It looked almost like she was going to fall off. She asked Eliezer who the man was. Eliezer told her it was Yitzchak. Out of modesty, she covered her face with her veil.

Clouds, Candles, and Dough

When Yitzchak finished davening Minchah, Eliezer told him about all the miracles that had happened to him and how his prayers had been answered so quickly.

All this didn't satisfy Yitzchak. Before he would marry Rivkah he wanted to know if she was a great woman, someone who would be as great as his mother.

When Sarah was alive, the Shabbos candles she lit never went out. They stayed lit all week. Her challah dough was blessed. And a cloud always hung over her tent, showing that the presence of Hashem rested there.

Would all these miracles happen for Rivkah? he wondered.

Yitzchak brought Rivkah into his mother's tent. The candles stayed lit, her dough was blessed, and the cloud came back.

So Yitzchak married Rivkah — and that's the story of the first Jewish shidduch.

What was Eliezer's reward for doing such a good job? Yitzchak gave him his freedom, and in addition, Eliezer never died. He was taken straight to Heaven without dying first.

The Last Years

The parashah now tells us what happened in the last years of

Questions, Anyone?

In what way was Sarah's dough blessed?

Whatever she made never burned and it always tasted fresh and wonderful.

Fascinating Facts

Just as Hashem was so involved in the match between Yitzchak and Rivkah, Hashem is involved in everyone's shidduch.

A camel isn't kosher. It has only one sign of a kosher animal; it chews its cud but its hoofs are not split. Yitzchak first met Rivkah riding on a camel. This was a hint that she would have two children. One would be "kosher" — Yaakov. The other would not be "kosher" — wicked Eisav.

We will read about Yaakov and Eisav in the next parashah, Parashas Toldos. Even though they were born before Avraham died, the Torah wants to finish telling us Avraham's story before going on to Yitzchak's family story in the next parashah, so this is said out of order.

Avraham's life.

Avraham lived to see his grandchildren Yaakov and Eisav. They were fifteen years old when he died. He should have lived longer, but Hashem didn't want Avraham to suffer by seeing his grandson Eisav become evil.

Remarriage

Right after Yitzchak married Rivkah, Avraham married Keturah. Her real name was Hagar. Hagar had gone back to Egypt with Yishmael many years before. But she had done teshuvah and had done many mitzvos and good deeds.

Because Hagar's actions had become sweet and beautiful, Hashem changed her name to Keturah. That name comes from the word "ketores," which means sweet-smelling incense.

Avraham had six more sons from this marriage!

Yitzchak Gets It All

Before Avraham passed away, he gave generous gifts to the children of Keturah. But he made it clear that all his wealth should go to Yitzchak. Eretz Yisrael belonged only to him and he would be the father of the Jewish people. Avraham also gave Yitzchak and Rivkah the right to be buried in Me'aras HaMachpeilah.

Avraham wanted to make sure that Yitzchak's brothers from his remarriage to Hagar did not give Yitzchak any trouble about who gets his inheritance after he passed away. So when they grew up, he gave all six sons many expensive gifts. Then he sent them away from Yitzchak — to the Far East.

A Tzaddik Passes Away

Avraham died when he was 175 years old. He was one of the greatest tzaddikim who ever walked the earth. He stubbornly stood up against the entire world and declared there is an All-Powerful, invisible, One and Only G-d in the universe. And that Hashem is kind. He cares about people, and He wants people to be good to each other. Thanks to Avraham, many people started to believe in Hashem.

He was the father of many nations that believe in one G-d. But most important: he was the father of the Jewish nation.

Avraham's Funeral

Yishmael traveled all the way from where he lived, far away in

FASCINATING FACTS

There is an opinion that many people in China are the descendants of these six children.

Who was at Avraham's funeral? All the people who had come to Sarah's funeral were also at Avraham's. Even though the funerals were 38 years apart, no one had died in that time! It was their reward for going to Sarah's funeral.

QUESTIONS, ANYONE?

What is the secret to long life?

The secret is found in the Midrash. It explains that the reason Avraham reached such an old age —175 — was because he spent so much time giving charity. It's a great way to live long!

the desert, to be at the funeral. When Avraham's body was being carried to the grave, Yishmael allowed Yitzchak to go first. By this time of his life, Yishmael had done teshuvah and he realized that Yitzchak was a great tzaddik.

Shem and Eiver brought Avraham's body into Me'aras HaMachpeilah and laid him down next to Sarah's grave.

Sitting Shivah

Yitzchak sat shivah (the week of mourning) for his father. The custom is for visitors to come and comfort the mourner. A special "visitor" came to comfort Yitzchak. Hashem Himself! He spoke to Yitzchak, giving him comfort, and He blessed him.

Yishmael

The parashah ends with a list of Yishmael's descendants and the death of Yishmael.

פָּרָשַׁת תּוֹלְדוֹת

Parashas Toldos

Toldos · תּוֹלְדוֹת

Parashah Pointers

- Yaakov and Eisav are born.
- Yaakov is a tzaddik who sits and learns. Eisav is a rasha, and he makes a living hunting animals.
- Eisav was the bechor, the firstborn, so he should have been given the Torah and its berachos. He didn't want them. Instead, he sold them to Yaakov.
- There is a hunger in Eretz Yisrael. Yitzchak plans to go to Egypt, where there is food.
- Hashem tells Yitzchak not to go, and He blesses him. He says that Yitzchak's descendants will be like the stars, and they will receive Eretz Yisrael.
- Yitzchak stays in the Philistine city of Gerar, which is in Eretz Yisrael.
- The Philistines are jealous of Yitzchak. Avimelech, the Philistine king, kidnaps Rivkah to be his wife, but Hashem saves her.
- Avimelech tells Yitzchak to leave the country. Yitzchak moves to Beersheva. Avimelech comes to Beersheva and makes a peace treaty with Yitzchak.
- Eisav marries two idol-worshiping Hittite wives.
- Yitzchak wants to bless Eisav. Rivkah tells Yaakov to pretend he is Eisav and get the blessing. Yaakov does so.
- Eisav wants to kill Yaakov for taking the blessing away from him.
- Yitzchak blesses Yaakov once again. He sends Yaakov to Rivkah's family, to find a good wife there.
- Eisav marries Machalas, the daughter of Yishmael.

A Rose

The parashah begins by letting us know what an awesome woman our mother Rivkah was. She grew up with wicked, wicked people — her father, Besuel, and her brother, Lavan. She grew up in a wicked place, a city of idol worship. Yet she refused to be influenced by their evil ways. On her own, she came to believe in Hashem, And on her own, she learned to be kind. Without anyone's help, she grew up a tzaddeikes (righteous woman).

She was like a beautiful red rose, surrounded by ugly, pointy, painful thorns — her family. Hashem removed Rivkah from among the thorns, and brought her into the family of Avraham and Yitzchak.

10, 15, 20!

Ten years had passed since Yitzchak married Rivkah, and yet they had no children. Fifteen years — still no children! All that time Yitzchak and Rivkah never gave up hope. They prayed and prayed that Hashem would send them children.

Rivkah would pray in one corner of the room and say: "Let all the children You give me be from this tzaddik."

And Yitzchak would pray opposite his wife, in the other corner, and say: "Let all the children You give me be from this tzaddeikes."

Yitzchak would even take trips to Mount Moriah, the future location of the Beis HaMikdash. It was also the place where the Akeidah happened. Yitzchak prayed there for children.

Finally, after twenty years, Hashem decided to give them children, because of Yitzchak's prayers. Why Yitzchak's prayers and not Rivkah's? Yitzchak was a tzaddik and the son of a tzaddik. Rivkah was a tzaddeikes, but she was the daughter of a wicked man. Because Yitzchak had his own merits and also those of his parents, his merits were greater, so it was his prayers that were answered.

Terrible Pains

Rivkah and Yitzchak knew they were going to have a child! They were so happy. But before the baby was born Rivkah began having horrible pains. The pains were especially bad when she would pass by Avraham's yeshivah or the yeshivah of Shem and Eiver. It felt like the baby was fighting to get out. Strangely, when she went past a place where people worshiped idols, the same thing happened.

Rivkah asked other women if this was normal. They told her, "No, it's not." Rivkah was suffering so much she actually thought, *Why did I pray to have a child? Why do I need all this pain?*

Torah in Our Lives

Did you ever meet a baal teshuvah? Before becoming religious, many of them lived a life very far from Torah. They were surrounded by people eating food that was not kosher, not keeping Shabbos, not ever having learned Torah.

Yet at some point in their lives, they decided to change. They searched for the truth and found the Torah.

They changed their lives and started eating kosher, keeping Shabbos and dressing modestly.

Absolutely amazing!

Like Rivkah, baalei teshuvah chose not to copy the world around them.

Baalei teshuvah should make us appreciate how lucky we are to be Torah Jews. And we should give baalei teshuvah loads of credit for having made such great choices.

Fascinating Facts

Avraham and Yitzchak looked exactly alike. Anyone who knew Avraham and saw Yitzchak knew that Yitzchak was Avraham's son.

Rivkah decided to go to the yeshivah of Shem and Eiver and ask Noach's son, Shem, to explain what was happening.

The Prophecy

Shem was a prophet. Hashem gave him a message for Rivkah. She was going to give birth to twins, he told her. One would be evil and one would be good. They would both become great nations. There would always be a struggle between them. Each one would try to overpower the other. Sometimes the evil son and his descendants would be in power over the good son and his descendants. At other times the good son's descendants would rule over the evil one's descendants. In the end, the younger, good son's descendants would win this battle!

The Rabbi and the Emperor

Shem also told Rivkah that each of her two sons would have a descendant who would be a rich and powerful ruler. Shem was talking about Antoninus, who was the emperor of Rome, and the Jewish leader Rabbi Yehudah HaNasi, whom we call Rebbi. Rebbi was the prince of the Jews. They were the wealthiest men of their time. Antoninus was a close friend of Rebbi and had great respect for him. When he came to visit Rebbi, the emperor would personally serve Rebbi his meals!

Now I Understand!

Now Rivkah understood why she was in such pain. Her children were fighting each other inside her! The evil son kept fighting with the good son and the good son was fighting back. When she would pass a yeshivah, the good child would be trying to get out to go and learn, and when she passed a place where idols were worshiped the evil son would try to jump out to the idols.

Happy Birth Day!

Right before they were born, the twins had a big fight. Each one wanted to come out first and be the firstborn. Finally, the evil baby overpowered his brother, and he was born first. His younger brother held onto the older one's heel, trying to stop him from being born first, but it was too late.

Ever see babies? They usually have very little hair, they have no teeth, and they're cute. But Rivkah's firstborn was different. His skin color was

QUESTIONS, ANYONE?

Why didn't Rivkah tell Yitzchak about Hashem's message?

Since Hashem had not told Yitzchak this prophecy, Rivkah realized that this message was only for her, not for him.

TORAH IN OUR LIVES

The Torah writes that Rivkah went to ask Hashem why she was suffering, when in fact she went to the yeshivah of Shem and Eiver. This teaches us that visiting a tzaddik is like visiting with Hashem, because Hashem's Presence is with the tzaddik.

QUESTIONS, ANYONE?

Every Jewish baby learns Torah from a malach (angel) before being born. Why did Rivkah's good son want to leave when his mother passed a yeshivah — isn't it better to learn from an angel?

He wanted to get away from the influence of his wicked brother!

reddish. He had hair all over — even on his face and hands — and he was born with teeth! Not cute at all.

They called him Eisav.

The younger twin was born with a bris! Hashem Himself named the baby Yaakov, and told Yitzchak the baby's name.

Why Yaakov? Because he came out holding his brother's heel, which is called "eikev" in Hebrew.

Yitzchak became a father for the first time at age 60! Mazel tov!

When Mashiach Comes

The day the twins were born was one of the most important ever! It marked the beginning of a struggle between the Jews and Eisav's nations. That struggle would last thousands of years ... and is still going on.

The Jews believe in kindness, peace, and holiness. The way of Eisav is the way of war, greed, and evil. Eisav's nations care about money and power, and live only to enjoy the pleasures of this world. They are greedy, and want more and more and more.

All through history Eisav's evil forces have tried to destroy the Jews. Some day there will be one last struggle, when the Jews will take Eisav's power away forever. This is hinted at by Yaakov's holding on to the "end" of Eisav's body, his heel.

When will this happen? Very soon, we hope — when Mashiach comes.

QUESTIONS, ANYONE?

Why was the older baby called Eisav?

Because he was hairy, like a grownup. The word Eisav has the letters of the Hebrew word "asui," which means "completely made." He was a baby who looked like he had been born already finished – like a grownup who already has hair.

FASCINATING FACTS

Eisav's red skin was a hint that he would grow up to be a killer who would spill blood.

The Twins Grow Up

Yaakov and Eisav grew up together. They behaved the same way. Both were good Jewish boys, doing the mitzvos, learning Torah, and loving Hashem.

Until their bar mitzvah. That's when everything changed. Eisav left his studies and became a hunter. He was an expert shot with his bow and arrow, and he wandered in the fields looking for animals and birds to kill. Yaakov stayed in his tent — that is, studying Torah.

As time went on Eisav began to sin more and more. His mother, Rivkah, who had grown up with evil people, caught on quickly that Eisav was becoming wicked. That is why, though she didn't stop loving Eisav, she loved Yaakov more.

But Yitzchak loved Eisav more. Eisav would serve him good-tasting food made from the animals he had caught, and give him wine. There was no one who ever honored his father like Eisav did. In this one mitzvah, he truly was a tzaddik.

Eisav was very clever in coming up with ways that would make him seem like the same good and innocent boy he used to be. He had a talent to speak in a way that fooled people. He asked Yitzchak all kinds of questions to show how religious he was. For example, he would ask him, "How do you take maaser* from salt? What about from straw?" Of course, we don't have to give maaser from salt or straw. Eisav was just trying to show that he was more religious than anyone else!

Murder!

When Eisav was fifteen he managed to do many serious sins all in one single day.

This is what happened.

Eisav committed murder. He killed King Nimrod, the king who had tried to kill Avraham by having him thrown into a fire. Eisav did other bad sins as well.

Running away from the scene of the crime as fast as he could, Eisav came home. Killing someone and running away had tired him out. He was exhausted and very hungry.

* *The mitzvah of maaser is to take ten percent of food that grows and give it to the Levi.*

Torah in Our Lives

Even though the Jews have done so much good for the world, still, in every time and place, there has been anti-Semitism. Hatred of the Jews has been around for thousands of years, and we still see it in so many places! Why is that?

Our Sages tell us that there is an unbroken rule: "Eisav sonei es Yaakov — Eisav hates Yaakov."

Anti-Semitism can't be wiped out until Mashiach comes.

Fascinating Facts

When he served his father, Eisav didn't wear his regular clothes. To show honor to his father, Eisav changed into royal robes before bringing Yitzchak his food.

Questions, Anyone?

Yitzchak knew that Eisav had stopped studying Torah, so how could Eisav fool him?

Even though Eisav had left yeshivah, Yitzchak thought that Eisav would become a tzaddik, a working man who supports the Torah learning of his brother Yaakov. But Eisav chose to follow his yetzer hara, rather than follow Hashem.

Yaakov Is Cooking

Going into the kitchen, Eisav found Yaakov cooking a pot of red lentil bean soup.

Why was Yaakov in the kitchen cooking beans? Why had he left his learning?

The answer has to do with a sad event that happened that day. Yaakov's grandfather, Avraham Avinu, had passed away. Yaakov had gone to the funeral along with his parents. When they got back home Yaakov went to the kitchen to prepare the traditional mourner's meal for his father. This is the first meal a mourner eats after coming back from a funeral. Round foods, like eggs or beans, are served. This comforts the mourner, reminding them that life is round, like a wheel. People die, their family mourns him, and then slowly the pain goes away, and the family goes on. This happens over and over, generation after generation.

FASCINATING FACTS

That Avraham died on the same day that Eisav murdered someone was no coincidence! Hashem didn't want Avraham to suffer the pain of having a grandchild who was so wicked. So Hashem took Avraham away before Eisav committed murder.

Eisav Sins Again!

Seeing the red soup, Eisav asked Yaakov what he was doing. Yaakov told him about their grandfather's death, and he explained that he was cooking the mourner's meal for their father.

Eisav was shocked. And then he said some terrible things. "You mean, after all of Avraham's good deeds and holy living, he died? Then I believe that Hashem does not reward people in this world. And I don't believe there is a next world of reward and punishment. And I don't believe the dead will ever come back to life again!"

With these words, Eisav committed two more major sins! He rejected some basics of Jewish belief: That after death a soul goes to the next world where Hashem gives reward for the mitzvos and punishment for sins. And Eisav also said that the dead will not come back to life.

Feeding Time

Then Eisav collapsed into a chair and roared at Yaakov, "I'm exhausted. I'm just going to open my mouth wide and you pour that very red soup down my throat!" He sat with his mouth open wide, like an animal in the zoo at feeding time, waiting for Yaakov to do what he had ordered.

"Just a minute," Yaakov said. "Let's make a deal. You want the food? I'll sell it to you for your rights as the firstborn."

What rights were those? Until Hashem appointed the Kohanim to serve him, only the firstborn son in a family had the right to bring korbanos to Hashem. Also, Yitzchak's firstborn would receive the Torah and mitzvos. Yaakov wanted Eisav to sell him this valuable and awesome responsibility — the opportunity to serve Hashem on a high level, and to be like the Kohanim.

"What do I need this right for?" Eisav answered. "I don't even believe in Hashem. (Another sin!) I'll sell you the birthright. I want to eat!"

Knowing that Eisav could not be trusted, Yaakov made him swear that he was agreeing to the deal — to trade his birthright for a pot of beans.

FASCINATING FACTS

The color red, the color of blood, comes up again and again in Eisav's life. You might say it was his color.

He was called Edom, which means red, and he was born with a reddish skin. The country that he and his descendants lived in, called Edom, has many red-colored mountains and the land, too, is reddish. Eisav's soldiers wore red uniforms, of course!

Eisav and Friends

Eisav had no problem swearing. His birthright wasn't worth anything to him. He thought he had made a great deal! Eisav quickly finished a bowl full of bean soup. Then he went out and brought over a few of his friends. They all sat around while Yaakov served them the rest of the bean soup Eisav had bought.

Eisav told his buddies the story of the sale. They made fun of Yaakov and laughed at him for being so dumb that he cared about something as worthless as the birthright.

Eisav had sinned again! He made fun of something so great and valuable.

So many sins, and all in one day!

Because Eisav sold the birthright for some red soup, people called him Edom, the Hebrew word for "red."

Hunger!

There was a famine in Eretz Yisrael. There was no food to be had. It was just like in the times of Avraham. People and animals walked the streets starving, searching for whatever scraps they could find.

Yitzchak decided to go to Egypt, where there was food. On the way, he traveled through Gerar, a city in Eretz Yisrael where Avimelech, king of the Philistines, lived.

Don't Go!

Hashem appeared in a vision to Yitzchak. He told him: "Don't go to Egypt. Stay here and farm the land of Eretz Yisrael. Your descendants will be as many as the stars in the heavens, and I will give them Eretz Yisrael, because Avraham obeyed My mitzvos and the Torah."

QUESTIONS, ANYONE?

Why didn't Hashem want Yitzchak to leave Eretz Yisrael?

Because at the Akeidah, Yitzchak had become holy, like a sacrifice. Someone so holy was not allowed to leave the holiness of Eretz Yisrael.

Life in Gerar

So Yitzchak canceled his plans to go to Egypt and stayed in Gerar with his family. His neighbors asked him very strange questions. They wanted to know all about Rivkah. Her age, where she was from, and how she was related to Yitzchak.

Yitzchak understood from their questions that he had moved into a city of bad people. If he would say Rivkah was his wife someone would kill him, and take Rivkah for himself.

So Yitzchak did what his father had done in Egypt years before (see Parashas Lech Lecha, page 49). He said Rivkah was his sister. At first Rivkah and Yitzchak were careful to act toward each other like brother and sister.

Caught!

But after a while they got careless, and King Avimelech saw them behaving like husband and wife. Avimelech got very angry. He had wanted to marry Rivkah himself, and he realized that if he hadn't found out that Yitzchak and Rivkah were married, he would have done a terrible sin.

He called in Yitzchak and spoke angrily to him.

"Rivkah is your wife. Why did you tell me she was your sister?!"

Yitzchak defended himself. "Otherwise I would have been killed!" he answered.

Avimelech was still angry. "I almost tried to marry her, and I would have committed a terrible sin!"

Avimelech then warned his people, "Leave Yitzchak and his wife alone! Don't harm them or bother them in any way! Anyone who does will be put to death!"

Now that they had Avimelech's protection, Yitzchak and Rivkah didn't have to act like brother and sister anymore, and they went back to living normally.

Jealousy

As Hashem had instructed, Yitzchak went into farming. He had his servants plant the land. Even though it was a year of very little rain, and the land was not good for farming, Yitzchak was very successful. His fields produced 100 times more than expected! Yitzchak's success was clearly because of Hashem's blessing.

Yitzchak gave ten percent of what he grew to the poor. The rest he sold, and he bought cattle. Very quickly he became the owner of many herds of animals, including donkeys and camels. He also had an army of servants.

Yitzchak was a wealthy man. He became even richer than the king. This made the king and all his people jealous.

Yitzchak's animals needed water, so his servants dug wells for them to drink from. To annoy Yitzchak, neighbors filled up his wells with earth so he couldn't get to the water. When Yitzchak spoke to them about it, they came up with a great excuse. "We did it because we are afraid that if we are attacked the enemy's soldiers will drink this water. We closed up your wells in self-defense." They pretended that it was not because they were jealous of Yitzchak.

Leave!

The jealousy and hatred for Yitzchak only got worse. Finally, the king himself came to Yitzchak and told him, "Leave! You are mightier than we are." They hated seeing a stranger becoming so rich.

With no choice, Yitzchak moved away, to a place called Nachal Gerar. There, his servants dug a well. But Philistine shepherds came and argued with them. "The water here belongs to us!" they said, and they took the well for themselves. Yitzchak's servants dug another well in a different place — and the same thing happened again. Finally, the third time Yitzchak's servants dug a well the Philistines left them alone.

Worry

Yitzchak moved to Beersheva. With all the problems he was having with the Philistines, he was worried that he was in danger. What if he would wake up one day and find himself surrounded by Philistines who wanted to kill him?

Hashem appeared to Yitzchak at night and told him, "Don't be afraid. I will bless you and you will have many descendants, because of Avraham, My servant."

Thieves and Scratching

Ever since he had told Yitzchak to leave his country, Avimelech was having a hard time. One day he came home and found thieves had broken into his palace. They had partied all night in his home, eating his food, drinking his wine, and breaking things. The palace was a

MAASEH AVOS

The first two wells Yitzchak dug were taken away by the Philistines. This was a hint that we would have two Batei Mikdash that our enemies would destroy. The Third Beis HaMikdash will remain forever, never to be taken away, just like Yitzchak's third well, which wasn't taken away by the Philistines.

wreck! On top of that aggravation, his skin was covered with boils, and he couldn't stop scratching himself.

He thought to himself: *I had better make friends with Yitzchak or who knows what else Hashem will do to me because I threw him out.*

Peace Talks

Avimelech set out to Beersheva to meet Yitzchak. He took along some important people, including Phichol, his general.

When they got there Yitzchak asked them, "Why are you coming to me? You hate me, and you threw me out of your country." He wasn't afraid of them because Hashem had promised to protect him.

They answered, "We saw that Hashem is with you. So let's make a treaty. You don't hurt us, just like we didn't hurt you."

What!? How could they say that? They treated him so badly, and they wouldn't let him stay in their country.

They thought they had been good to Yitzchak, because they only threw him out, they hadn't killed him!

Overnight Guests

Yitzchak agreed to make a peace treaty with them. To celebrate, they ate a meal together. Yitzchak put up his Philistine peace partners overnight. In the morning, Yitzchak and Avimelech made a promise to keep the peace between them. Yitzchak and Avimelech then parted on good terms.

Split Hooves

In order for an animal to be kosher it has to have two signs: its hooves (that is, its feet) have to be split, and it has to chew its cud. A chazir, a pig, has split hooves but it doesn't chew its cud, and so, of course, it's not a kosher animal.

There are animals that tuck their feet under their bodies when they lie down. Not the pig. It lies down with its feet sticking out in front of its body. It's as if it is showing everyone, "Hey, look, see my kosher sign! I'm really kosher." Though it is not!

Eisav was like the pig — he did things just for show, to give the impression that really he is a holy man. We already saw how he used to ask his father, Yitzchak, questions about taking maaser from salt, at the same time he was doing terrible sins.

FASCINATING FACTS

The city of Beersheva is very ancient, and still exists today. It's located in the southern part of Eretz Yisrael and is one of its largest cities, with over 200,000 people. There are two events in our Torah that the city is named for.* Avraham and Avimelech swore to each other in Beersheva that they would keep the peace between them. Later, Yitzchak and Avimelech also promised each other in Beersheva to keep the peace. The Hebrew word for swearing is "shavuah," which has the same letters as the Hebrew word "sheva," in the name Beersheva (just pronounced differently).

* *See Parashas Vayeira page xxx and Parashas Toldos p. xxx for more details.*

Here's another example. Eisav waited until he was 40 years old to get married. Why? It was like he was announcing: "Look at me! I'm just like my holy father, Yitzchak. He married at 40 and I'm marrying at 40. I am a tzaddik just like my father!"

Eisav was a show-off, like the non-kosher pig. Who did he marry at 40? Not a tzaddeikes like Rivkah, someone from Avraham's family. He married women from the tribe of the Hittites! They were idol worshipers.

Many years passed. As Yitzchak grew older his eyesight got weaker and weaker until he became blind.

Yitzchak's Blindness

There are many reasons given why Yitzchak turned blind.

- When Eisav's evil wives burned incense for their idols, the smoke drifted into Yitzchak's eyes and made him blind. Rivkah, who grew up with idol worship as a young girl, wasn't affected by the smoke, because she was used to it.
- During the Akeidah, Yitzchak was tied up on the Mizbei'ach, facing death. Seeing this, the angels in heaven began to cry that Yitzchak was going to die. Their tears fell into Yitzchak's eyes. Over time the angels' tears caused his blindness.
- Hashem wanted Yaakov to get Yitzchak's blessings. Hashem made Yitzchak blind so that Yaakov was able to pretend he was Eisav, and Yitzchak would not see who he really was.

Yaakov Takes the Blessings

We are about to read about how Yaakov tricked his father into thinking he was Eisav. How could Yaakov, who was a completely honest man, do such a thing? Where is his respect for his father?!

Actually, it was very hard for Yaakov to do this. It went against his truthful nature. But Yaakov was obeying his mother, who was a prophet. When a prophet tells you to do something, you have to obey, because it is Hashem's will.

Bow and Sword

Yitzchak thought, *I'm already 123 years old. I have to bless my sons before I pass away.*

He decided that the best time to bless his sons would be on Pesach. On Erev Pesach, Yitzchak called Eisav and told him, "I don't know when I will pass away, so I will bless you now. But before I do, take your sword and bow, and go out and hunt. Then make me a good meal out of what you trap. Make sure to sharpen your knife, so that you will shecht it the way the Torah commands. And you should hunt far from the city, so you don't accidentally capture an animal that belongs to someone else."

Eisav had no intention of listening to his father! If he wouldn't be able to capture an animal he would just steal one and bring it to Yitzchak.

FASCINATING FACTS

Yaakov and Eisav weren't children when Yitzchak blessed them. They were 63 years old.

QUESTIONS, ANYONE?

Why did Yitzchak ask Eisav to sharpen his knife?

In order for an animal to be kosher it has to be shechted with a knife that is very sharp. If the knife edge is not absolutely smooth, the animal will not be kosher. Yitzchak was worried that Eisav would do everything in a rush not to keep his father waiting. So Yitzchak told Eisav not to hurry. He should take his time and make sure the knife is sharpened correctly before shechting the animal.

A Good Mood for a Good Berachah

The best way to give a blessing is when the one who is giving it is in a happy mood. So before blessing his son, Yitzchak wanted to eat a good meal.

Yitzchak also planned to use Eisav's food for his Korban Pesach. Though the miracles of Yetziyas Mitzrayim were far in the future, Yitzchak knew that the 15th of Nissan would be a special day. That's why he chose it as the day he would bless his son.

I Will Be Cursed

Rivkah overheard Yitzchak's conversation with Eisav. She knew that Yitzchak was about to give the blessing to the wrong son. To stop that from happening, she jumped into action. She called Yaakov and explained the situation. Then she commanded him: "Go to our flocks and bring me the two best young goats you can find. From them I will prepare a meal that your father will enjoy. You will bring the food I prepared to your father, and he will bless you."

Yaakov told his mother, "How can I fool him? My brother is hairy, but I have smooth skin. If our father touches me he will realize I am trying to fool him. He will curse me!"

"Don't worry. The curse will be on me," Rivkah answered. "Because your father will know that it was I who told you to do this, and he will curse me and not you."

FASCINATING FACTS

You want to know what deer meat tastes like? Eat the meat of a young goat, which has the flavor of deer meat.

The Disguise

Rivkah prepared the two goats Yaakov brought her. Then she took out Eisav's special clothes.

What made them special?

Hashem had made them for the first man, Adam. This clothing had special powers. Pictures of animals and birds were woven on it. Animals were attracted to the pictures, so whoever wore the clothing was soon surrounded by animals.

For someone like Eisav, who was a hunter, having clothes that brought the animals to him would make his job a lot easier. He would be the greatest hunter in the world! Instead of having to find animals to kill, they would come to him!

There was only one problem. These clothes of Adam were owned by King Nimrod. Eisav wanted them, but they didn't belong to him.

For someone like Eisav, though, the answer to his problem was easy. He killed Nimrod and took the clothing.

If the clothing made hunting so easy, why didn't Eisav wear them when he went to hunt for meat for Yitzchak's meal? Because Eisav also used to wear the special clothing when he served his father, to show him respect. He left the clothing at home now, because he didn't want to serve his father in dirty clothing!

Eisav would leave the clothes with his mother for safekeeping. He wouldn't leave them in his own home, because he didn't trust his wives! He knew they were just as evil as he was. He might come back one day and find the valuable clothes were gone, stolen by his wives.

So Eisav gave the special clothes to his mother, Rivkah, since he knew he could trust her!

Now Rivkah began disguising Yaakov. She wanted him to smell like a hunter, not like someone who sat in a tent learning all day, so she gave him Eisav's special clothing to wear. To hide Yaakov's smooth skin, she took the hairy skin of the goats that she'd cooked, and put them on Yaakov's arms and on his neck. That way if Yitzchak would touch Yaakov he would feel as hairy as Eisav.

Yaakov's disguise was complete. He was ready to face his father.

Taking the dishes of food his mother had prepared, Yaakov walked into his father's tent.

Who's There?

Yitzchak heard someone entering his room, but he couldn't see who it was. Yaakov greeted his father and said, "Abba."

"Who are you?" Yitzchak asked. He couldn't tell from the voice which of his sons had come in.

Questions, Anyone?

Aren't two whole goats a lot of food for just one person? Why did Rivkah prepare two goats?

Since it was the Seder night, the two goats were symbolic of the two goats that the Jews would serve at their Seder table when the Batei Mikdash stood — the Korban Pesach and the Korban Chagigah.

Fascinating Facts

Adam's clothing ended up in Noach's Teivah. Noach's son Cham took them with him when the Teivah came onto dry land. Nimrod inherited them from his grandfather Cham.

"It is I, Eisav your firstborn," said Yaakov.

Yaakov had to lie because of Rivkah's prophetic command to take the berachos. But he did his best to say the lie in such a way that what he said was true.

Yaakov said, "It is I" — that's true, it was he — Yaakov.

Then he said, "Eisav your firstborn," and that was also true — Eisav was Yitzchak's firstborn.

Suspicion

Yaakov told his father, "Please, my father, come and eat from the food I brought, and bless me."

"So quickly? How did you manage to hunt down something so fast?" said Yitzchak.

"It was Hashem Who helped me find something quickly."

Hearing Yaakov's answer made Yitzchak suspicious. He thought to himself: *Whoever my guest is, he used Hashem's Name and he spoke politely. That doesn't sound like Eisav at all. I had better make sure it's Eisav.*

Yitzchak said, "Come closer, so I can touch you. Are you my son Eisav or not?"

Yaakov realized his father was suspicious. He became very afraid. What if his father found out who he was and cursed him!

His heart began to pound and his legs became so weak he couldn't move closer to his father. Suddenly, he felt himself being pushed forward.

What happened? Hashem sent two angels, who grabbed hold of Yaakov's arms and pushed him forward.

Yitzchak touched Yaakov's arms and felt that they were hairy. It was a good thing he was wearing the goat skins!

Yitzchak was still puzzled. The arms felt like Eisav, but he spoke like Yaakov. "The hands are the hands of Eisav, but the voice is the voice of Yaakov," he said. (See page 135 at the end of this parashah for the deeper meanings of these important words.)

Yitzchak was finally convinced that it was Eisav. "You are my son Eisav," he said.* "Bring me the food you brought so I can bless you."

Yaakov served his father the meal and gave him wine to drink.

After he ate, Yitzchak said, "Come closer so I can kiss you."

When Yitzchak hugged and kissed Yaakov, instead of smelling the awful smell of goat skins, Yitzchak smelled a very nice aroma. It was the smell of Gan Eden.

The Blessing

It was time for Yaakov to get the blessing. Yitzchak said:

"Hashem should always give you dew from the heavens and land that is fertile, with plenty of grain and wine. Nations will serve you and kingdoms will bow down to you. You will be a lord over your brother. Those who curse you will be cursed and those who bless you will be blessed."

In short, Yitzchak blessed Yaakov and his descendants, the Jews, with wealth and power. But by first saying the words "Hashem should always give you," Yitzchak meant it would happen only if the Jews listen to Hashem.

FASCINATING FACTS

Imagine eating something like this. The first spoonful tastes like sushi, the second like a barbecued steak, the third like chocolate cake. Every spoonful tastes like something different. It would be the best meal ever.

That was the kind of meal Yitzchak had when he ate Yaakov's food. The food was like the mahn. It tasted like any food that Yitzchak wanted to taste. It was the best meal he ever had!

QUESTIONS, ANYONE?

Where did Yaakov get the wine he served his father?

An angel brought the very special wine. It was more than 2,000 years old! It was made from grapes that Hashem created when He made the world.

* *There are opinions that this was a question, "Are you Eisav?"*

More than Wealth

Let's take a closer look at the words of the blessing. More than wealth and power, Yitzchak blessed Yaakov that Hashem should send the Jews extraordinary gifts.

When Yitzchak said:

- "Give you," he meant that Hashem will also give the Jews part of Eisav's blessing. What part? Like Eisav, they would be mighty warriors who would defeat their enemies. But this would only happen when they prayed for victory. Throughout history we have seen this blessing come true in people like Shimshon, King David and his soldiers, the Chashmonaim who defeated the Syrian-Greeks, and other victorious Jewish armies throughout history.
- "Dew from the heavens" is talking about the Torah, which came from heaven.
- "Land that is fertile" is the Mishnah, written by the Sages who live on land.
- "Grain," out of which is made our most basic foods like bread, pasta, and cake, is the Gemara, which contains the basic laws of all Torah life.
- "Wine," which is sweet and makes people happy, is the Midrash. Studying the Midrash, with its sweet stories and interesting teachings, brings joy to those who learn it.
- "Kingdoms will bow down to you" are the Yishmaelite nations — the Arabs.
- "A lord over your brother" are the European nations that come from Eisav, whom the Jews will rule.

Yaakov Hides

Yaakov had received the blessings and was about to step out the door of his father's tent. Suddenly he stopped short. Through the entrance of the tent Yaakov saw Eisav coming! It would be very dangerous if Eisav caught him disguised and taking the blessings for himself. Eisav might kill him!

Yaakov quickly hid behind the door. Once Eisav came in and had his back to the door, Yaakov saw his chance. He stepped very quietly out from behind the door and escaped, without Eisav realizing he was there!**

Walking away from Yitzchak's tent, Yaakov suddenly felt very strong. Hashem sent down a special dew from Heaven that made Yaakov extraordinarily powerful!

*** Another opinion is that Yitzchak's tent had two entrances. Just as Yaakov left one entrance, Eisav entered in the other. They missed each other by only seconds.*

FASCINATING FACTS

Have you ever seen wedding pictures? The chassan is smiling and glowing with joy. That's how Yaakov looked when he left his father's tent, after having received the blessings.

Eisav and the Dog

Where had Eisav been all this time? Hunting. But though he was a great and famous hunter, he wasn't having any luck. Whatever he caught would somehow get away.

This was Hashem's doing, of course. Hashem sent angels to free the animals Eisav had trapped. That gave Yaakov the time he needed to get the blessings before Eisav got back.

After failing again and again to trap anything, Eisav became very frustrated. He gave up trying to capture a wild animal to serve his father. Instead, he found a dog and killed it. After cooking and preparing it he brought it into his father. After all, he thought, Yitzchak was blind, and he wouldn't notice he was being served dog meat.

How wicked can a son get?

Eisav approached his father and said, "Get up and eat so you can bless me." Unlike Yaakov, Eisav didn't say "please" or mention Hashem's Name.

TORAH IN OUR LIVES

When we speak, we can speak politely, as Yaakov did. We can say "Please" when we ask for something from storekeepers. We can say "Thank you" to our bus driver, to the person who drives the car pool, and when we get presents from relatives. We can even say "Please" and "Thank you" to our parents, just like Yaakov did.

Or we can be like Eisav.

The choice is ours.

Yitzchak Is Terrified

"Who are you?" Yitzchak asked Eisav.

Eisav answered, "I'm your firstborn, Eisav."

Hearing this, Yitzchak began to shake with fright.

Why?

When Eisav entered, Yitzchak felt the gates of Gehinnom open under him, and the walls began to shake around him. Since he was now talking with Eisav, it meant he had given the blessing to the wrong son.

He wondered: *Who is Gehinnom opening for? For me, because I did not give the blessings to Eisav, my firstborn son, or for Yaakov, who tricked me?*

Hashem answered him. "They are opening for Eisav," He said.

Yitzchak now knew that he and Yaakov had done no wrong. He stopped shaking, calmed down, and said to Eisav, "Who is the one who served me a delicious meal and whom I blessed? He should still be blessed."

With those words — "He should still be blessed" — Yitzchak now gave Yaakov the blessing, knowing it was Yaakov. There was no more confusion. Now, no one could say that Yaakov did not deserve the blessings.

Eisav Cries and Begs

Eisav was very upset that he lost the blessings to his brother. He was furious. He let out a loud and bitter scream of pain and anger over what happened.

Then he asked his father, "Bless me too!"

Yitzchak answered, "Your brother took your blessing."

"That's why he is called Yaakov!" Eisav cried. "He tricked me twice. First he took my firstborn rights, and now he took my blessing!"

What was Eisav talking about? The letters "ayin," "kuf," and "beis" that appear in Yaakov's name spell the Hebrew word "eikev," which means trick. Eisav was saying that Yaakov had acted like his name — with trickery.

When Eisav said Yaakov had tricked him out of the rights of the firstborn, that was a lie. Eisav had sold Yaakov the rights of the firstborn for a pot of red beans.

Eisav would not take no for an answer from Yitzchak. "Did you leave me any blessing?" he asked his father.

"I have made him [Yaakov] your master," Yitzchak said. "You are his slave, and whatever a slave owns belongs to his master. There is nothing I can do."

"Do you have just one blessing, Father?" begged Eisav.

Eisav was so upset that he wouldn't get anything that he began to cry.

Eisav's tears awakened his father's mercy. Yitzchak thought it over and found a way to bless his son.

Eisav's Blessing

Yitzchak told him, "You will live on fertile land and have dew from heaven. You will live by the sword and serve your brother. But when your brother doesn't deserve his blessing because he's not listening to Hashem, then you will be freed from being his slave."

Eisav's Blessings Explained

- Yaakov was blessed with being under Hashem's direct protection, living on what Hashem would give him. Eisav, though, would just get whatever the laws of nature would give him.
- Yaakov's descendants will rule over Eisav's nations as long as the Jews keep the Torah. If they don't, they will suffer under the harsh rule of Eisav's nations, who will try to destroy them.
- Eisav will "live by the sword," which means that he and his nations will be powerful warriors and be the victors in war.

Escape!

Eisav already hated Yaakov, and because of the blessings, he hated him even more. Eisav swore he would kill his brother. But not right away. He would wait until his father, Yitzchak, died, so he would not cause his father the pain of losing a son. Then he would kill Yaakov!

Hashem told Rivkah that Eisav wanted to kill Yaakov. The news worried her. No one knew when Yitzchak will die. What if he died right away? Eisav would try to kill Yaakov, Yaakov would fight back, and they might kill each other! They were both in terrible danger! She could lose both her children!

Rivkah came up with a plan to save her children. She instructed Yaakov to escape.

She said, "Go! Run away to my brother Lavan who is living in Charan. Stay there until Eisav's anger passes. I'll let you know when it's safe to come back. Do it because I don't want to mourn for both of you on the same day!"

Send Yaakov Away

Rivkah didn't want to tell Yitzchak lashon hara about Eisav. Speaking badly about someone else, even if it's true, is wrong. Instead she told Yitzchak that she wanted to send Yaakov to Charan because she didn't want Yaakov to marry a Canaanite woman. She wanted Yaakov to go to Charan, where he could find someone from her family to marry.

Yitzchak agreed with his wife and sent for Yaakov. He told Yaakov, "Don't marry a Canaanite woman. Go to your uncle, Lavan, and marry one of his daughters. Hashem should bless you with many children and give Eretz Yisrael to you and your children."

Eisav Marries Again

Eisav heard that Yitzchak had told Yaakov not to marry a Canaanite woman. That made him realize that his parents were disappointed in his Canaanite wives. To show his father what a tzaddik he was, Eisav married Machalas, the daughter of Yitzchak's half-brother, Yishmael. But clearly he wasn't really sorry, because he did not divorce the Canaanite women he should never have married.

Fascinating Facts

What Rivkah said, "I don't want to mourn for both of you on the same day," this was actually a prophecy, though she didn't know what would happen in the future.

The day Yaakov was brought to be buried in the Me'aras HaMachpeilah was the same day that Eisav died. Both were buried on the same day. If Rivkah had been alive she would have begun sitting shivah for both of them on the same day.

Machalas's name was actually Bosmas. When she married Eisav the Torah calls her Machalas, which comes from the word mochel, which means to forgive.

Why did the Torah change her name? To let us know that on the day someone gets married they are given a "wedding present" from Hashem. He forgives their sins. Because it was Eisav's wedding day, he was forgiven for the evil he had done.

The custom is for the chassan and kallah to fast on their wedding day, because the wedding day is a time for forgiveness, just like Yom Kippur.

Voice of Yaakov, Hands of Eisav

When Yaakov came to Yitzchak for the blessing, Yitzchak was suspicious. The son who was talking to him didn't sound like Eisav. So Yitzchak touched him to see if his arms were hairy, like Eisav's hands.

Then Yitzchak said a few famous words: "The voice is the voice of Yaakov, and the hands are the hands of Eisav." Though Yitzchak didn't know it, these words were a prophecy about the future. Here are some of the things that these words were hinting at:

- The secret of Jewish power will be in their voice. They will defeat their enemies not through being expert soldiers, but through their voice — their prayers and Torah learning. But Eisav's nations will have their power in their hands — that is, the weapons they hold in their hands to kill their enemies.
- When the voices of Jewish children can be heard learning Torah, then Eisav's nations will have no power over them. When the Jews don't teach their children Torah, they will suffer at the hands of Eisav's nations.
- "The voice of Yaakov" hints at the sounds of the screams and cries of millions of Jews who were killed by Eisav's descendants in the cities of Beitar and Alexandria. "The hands of Eisav" is talking about when Eisav's descendants destroyed our Beis HaMikdash.

פָּרָשַׁת וַיֵּצֵא

Parashas Vayeitzei

Vayeitzei • וַיֵּצֵא

Parashah Pointers

- Yaakov leaves Beersheva and travels to Charan.
- On the way, Yaakov stops to daven Maariv on the mountain where the Beis HaMikdash will be built in the future.
- Yaakov falls asleep there and dreams about a huge ladder stretching from the earth to the sky. Angels are going up and down the ladder.
- Hashem speaks to Yaakov in the dream. Hashem promises to give Eretz Yisrael to him and his descendants. He also promises to protect Yaakov and that He will bring him back to Eretz Yisrael.
- Yaakov promises that if Hashem gives him food and clothing and brings him back safely to Eretz Yisrael, he will give Hashem ten percent of all he earns.
- Arriving in Charan, Yaakov meets Lavan's daughter, Rachel, at a well. He gives water to her sheep.
- Yaakov wants to marry Rachel. In order to get Lavan to agree he offers to work seven years as a shepherd for Lavan's sheep. Instead of paying Yaakov for his work, Lavan will give him permission to marry Rachel.
- Seven years pass. Lavan cheats Yaakov. Instead of letting him marry Rachel, Lavan tricks him into marrying Leah, Rachel's older sister.
- When Yaakov complains about being tricked, Lavan agrees to let him marry Rachel if he works for another seven years.
- Yaakov agrees. He marries Rachel a week after he married Leah, and goes to work for seven years.
- Leah gives birth to Reuven, Shimon, Levi, and Yehudah.

- Rachel has no children, so she asks Yaakov to marry her servant Bilhah. Bilhah has two children, Dan and Naphtali.
- Leah stops having children, so she has Yaakov marry her servant Zilpah. Zilpah has Gad and Asher.
- Leah then gives birth to Yissaschar, Zevulun, and Dinah.
- Finally, Rachel has a baby and names him Yosef.
- Yaakov wants to go home, but Lavan convinces him to continue working for him. This time he will be paid in sheep and goats.
- Hashem helps Yaakov become wealthy.
- Hashem tells Yaakov it's time to go home. His wives agree. Yaakov and his family begin their journey back to Eretz Yisrael. He is afraid Lavan might stop him so he leaves without saying goodbye.
- Before leaving, Rachel steals her father's idols, so that he will stop worshiping them.
- Lavan discovers that Yaakov and his family have left. Angry, Lavan chases after Yaakov.
- Hashem appears to Lavan and warns him not to harm Yaakov.
- When Lavan catches up with Yaakov, he accuses him of stealing his idols. Lavan searches all their tents but can't find them.
- Lavan and Yaakov build a pile of stones and make an agreement not to hurt each other. The next morning Lavan returns home.
- When they reach Eretz Yisrael, Yaakov sees two groups of six hundred thousand angels each. One group was with him in Charan. They will now leave him. The other group came flying toward him to greet him as he was about to enter Eretz Yisrael.

The Journey Begins

Yaakov left Beersheva. He was traveling to Charan, where his mother Rivkah's family lived. In Charan he would find a wife. To get there he would have to cross the Jordan River.

On the way to the Jordan River, Yaakov met his nephew Eliphaz, Eisav's son. Eliphaz wasn't there to say goodbye to his uncle. Eisav had sent him to kill Yaakov.

Eliphaz didn't know what to do. He loved his grandfather Yitzchak, who had taught him not to kill. But his father ordered him to kill Yaakov. Wasn't it a mitzvah to obey his father?*

Eliphaz asked Yaakov what to do. Yaakov had an idea. He had brought a huge amount of money and jewelry to give to his future bride and her family as gifts. He would use them to save his life.

He told Eliphaz, "It is said that a poor man is like a dead man. You can 'kill me' by taking my wealth, leaving me a poor man."

Eliphaz took Yaakov's wealth and let him live.

The River Splits

Yaakov continued on his journey. When he got to the rushing waters of the Jordan River he faced a problem. He had no money to pay someone to take him across in a boat.

Yaakov took the only thing he still owned, his walking stick, and stretched it over the Jordan. A miracle happened. The river waters split and made a dry path so Yaakov could walk across.

Yaakov Turns Back

Though it should have taken Yaakov over two weeks to go from Beersheva to Charan, he miraculously got there the same day. When he arrived, Yaakov realized he had passed Mount Moriah, where his father and grandfather had prayed, and he hadn't davened there! He decided to travel back to Eretz Yisrael to pray on the holy mountain.

Yaakov began to return to Mount Moriah. Hashem shrank the distance, moving the mountain to meet Yaakov! Yaakov soon found himself standing on the mountain.

Hashem wanted Yaakov to sleep over on Mount Moriah, in order to send him a dream about the future. But since it was still daylight, Yaakov would have prayed and then left to go to Charan. To make sure Yaakov

** Eliphaz was not thinking logically. Of course, it's not a mitzvah to obey a parent if it means going against Hashem's command not to kill!*

Fascinating Facts

When Yaakov left Beersheva the city lost its beauty and glory. That's because tzaddikim bring beauty and glory to the place where they live.

For example, why is the little village of Radin famous? Because the Chofetz Chaim lived there!

After getting the blessings from Yitzchak, Yaakov went to learn in the yeshivah of Eiver, Noach's great-grandson. He learned there for 14 years.

Yaakov did not want to interrupt his learning. So for 14 years he didn't take the time to go sleep in a bed. He would only take short naps while sitting up.

This was the same stick Moshe would use to split the Sea of Reeds when the Jews left Egypt.

Who's Who in the Torah

Mount Moriah

Hashem took the earth to make the first man, Adam HaRishon, from Mount Moriah.

Akeidas Yitzchak happened on Mount Moriah. (See Parashas Vayeira, page 87.)

Mount Moriah's other name is Har HaBayis (Mountain of the House) because it's where the Beis HaMikdash was built.

would stay on the holy mountain, Hashem made the sun go down early, so it would be too dark to travel and Yaakov would stay there.

Maariv and Sleep

When Yaakov saw that it was dark, he immediately davened Maariv. How do you get ready for bed out in the wild, when you don't have a tent or a sleeping bag? Yaakov collected rocks. One was his "pillow." He placed the others in piles around his head as a protective wall against wild animals. Then he lay down on the ground and fell asleep.

Talking Rocks

While he was asleep, the rocks began to argue. Each rock wanted to be Yaakov's pillow.

Each rock said, "Let this tzaddik rest his head on me."

Because they all wanted to be Yaakov's pillow, Hashem joined all the stones together, making them one stone. Now Yaakov's head rested on all of them. The rocks stopped arguing.

Yaakov took 12 stones.

Later, when Yaakov woke up and saw that the rocks had miraculously become one, he knew it was a sign from Hashem.

Yaakov would have 12 children who would become the 12 shevatim — and become one united Jewish nation.

Ladders and Angels

As Yaakov slept he dreamt. In his dream, he saw a very, very tall ladder reaching from earth to heaven. Angels were going up the ladder and other angels were going down.

The angels going up were the angels that were protecting Yaakov in Eretz Yisrael. They aren't allowed to leave Eretz Yisrael. So Hashem sent down other angels who would guard Yaakov while he would be living outside the Holy Land.

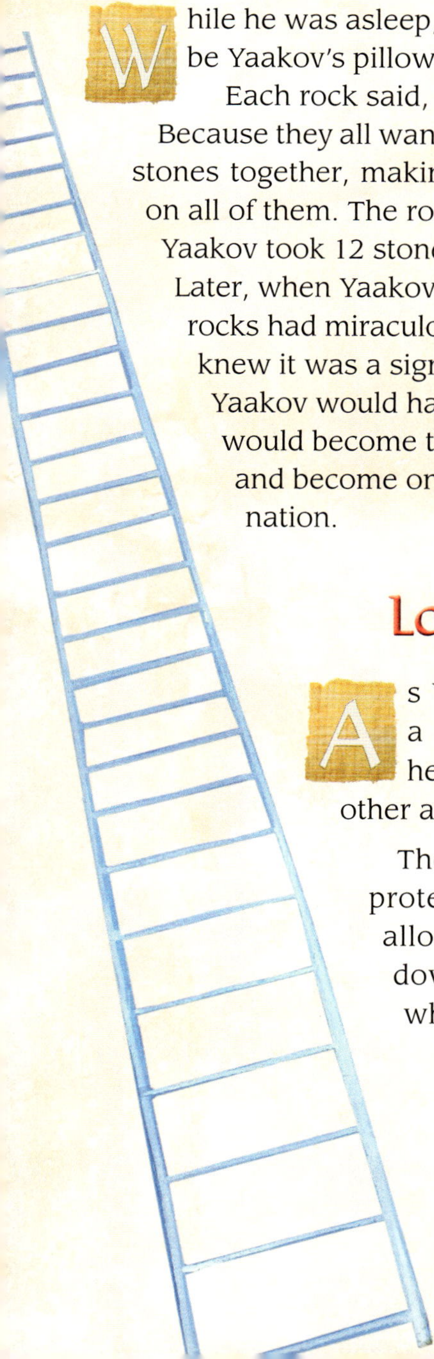

Questions, Anyone?

Who was the first person to establish that we should pray at night?

Yaakov. That is one of the reasons we daven Maariv every night.

Fascinating Facts

Yaakov slept on the spot that would become the Kadosh Kedoshim in the Beis HaMikdash, in the exact place where the Aron would rest in the future. When the Beis HaMikdash stood, no one was allowed into the Kadosh Kedoshim, except once a year. On Yom Kippur, the Kohen Gadol went in. It's the holiest spot on earth!

Ladders and Angels

What do they mean?

The vision of the ladder with angels going up and down was hinting to Yaakov about many future events.

- The numerical value of the Hebrew word "Sinai," where the Torah was given, is the same as the value of "sulam," the Hebrew word for ladder. Like an angel, Moshe would go up from Sinai to heaven and come down with the Torah.
- The Mizbei'ach, the Altar of the Beis HaMikdash, had a ramp on which Kohanim, almost like angels, would walk up and down as they brought korbanos. The merit of their service rose to Hashem in Heaven.
- Since the destruction of the First Beis HaMikdash, the Jews have suffered through four exiles, named for four nations: Bavel (Babylon), Paras (Persia), Yavan (Greece), and Edom (Rome — which is the exile we are still in today). The angels going up and down the ladder were the guardian angels of these four nations. Each angel went up the same number of steps as the number of years that their nation would be in power, and then came down. When the last exile, the one we are in now, will lose its power, Mashiach will come.

The Message

In his dream Yaakov saw the Presence of Hashem over him, guarding him.

Hashem spoke. "I am the G-d of Avraham and Yitzchak."

Hashem then folded up all of Eretz Yisrael into a small piece of land under Yaakov and said, "I will give the land you are lying on to you and your descendants. Your descendants will be as many as the dirt on the earth. You will spread out to the west, east, north, and south. All the nations on earth will bless themselves by you and your descendants. I am with you now and I will guard you wherever you go, and I will bring you back to Eretz Yisrael."

Hashem was telling Yaakov about the future. First, Eretz Yisrael would be given to his descendants. They will conquer the land easily, as if it were just a small piece of land that could fit under a person.

Yaakov will have many descendants, but they will go into exile, where they will be treated like the dust under people's feet. They will be stepped on and beaten down by the world's nations. Then, Mashiach will come and the Jews will return to Eretz Yisrael. Its borders will spread out in all directions so there will be room for everyone. It will be a large country.

MAASEH AVOS

Though we don't see them, all Jews have angels protecting them, just as Yaakov had. When someone visits Eretz Yisrael there is a changing of the guard. Eretz Yisrael's holier angels take over from the angels who are out of Eretz Yisrael.

TORAH IN OUR LIVES

It's amazing. Even though many nations tried to destroy the Jews, we are still here! There are no ancient Romans, Syrian-Greeks, or Babylonians. We have outlived them all.

The Jewish people has survived for over 3,300 years! How? Because Hashem is always there, with us, watching us, keeping the eternal promise He made to Yaakov.

FASCINATING FACTS

When someone davens in Yerushalayim, it's as if they are davening right in front of Hashem on His heavenly throne.

According to the Gemara, Yaakov actually promised to give a fifth, that's 20 percent. From this the Gemara learns that in general a person should not give more than 20 percent of their income to tzedakah.

Because Yaakov was afraid of what Lavan and Eisav would do to him, Hashem promised Yaakov that He would protect him from them and bring him back to Eretz Yisrael.

His descendants would also have Hashem's promise that He will be with us, protecting us even while we are in exile. We will never be destroyed, and the Jewish nation will return to live in Eretz Yisrael.

Gate of Heaven

Yaakov woke up from his dream. "This is a holy place," he said, "and Hashem's Presence is here. If I would have known, I wouldn't have slept here! It's the gate of heaven. All prayers from everywhere in the world pass through this place on their way up to the gate of heaven. This is where the Beis HaMikdash will one day be built." Yaakov then took the stone under his head and poured oil on it, using oil that Hashem had given him.

Ten Percent

Yaakov promised to take ten percent of his earnings and use it to bring korbanos to Hashem. He would give that ten percent if Hashem will

- Protect him on his journey.
- Give him food and clothing.
- Let him return to his father Yitzchak in peace, not having learned any bad behaviors from Lavan.

Why did Yaakov say, "If Hashem will do all these things," when Hashem had promised to take care of him? Of course, Yaakov knew that Hashem would keep His promises. But Yaakov was afraid that he might lose all these things if he sinned and didn't deserve Hashem's blessings anymore.

In addition to giving ten percent, Yaakov also promised that the stone on which he'd poured oil would be a place where he would pray and bring korbanos.

Yaakov named the place he had his dream Beis El, which means House of Hashem.

It was time to continue his journey. Destination: Charan. After what Hashem had just promised him, Yaakov traveled feeling very happy.

The Heavy Rock

Yaakov reached Charan and saw three flocks of sheep resting on the ground. Their shepherds were standing around a well, doing nothing. The top of the well was covered with a large, heavy rock.

Today, our water comes from a faucet. But in Yaakov's time water

came from wells. In places like Charan water was precious. People had to share whatever water there was.

That is why the well was covered with a heavy stone. It could be lifted only after all the shepherds arrived. No one could lift it by himself and take more than his share of water.

"My brothers, where are you from?" Yaakov asked the shepherds.

"Charan," they answered.

"Do you know Lavan?"

"We know him. Look," they pointed. "That's his daughter coming this way with her sheep."

Yaakov said, "It's still daylight, why don't you water the sheep and take them to graze in the fields?"

They explained that they were waiting for the other shepherds to come so there would be enough men to lift the rock, and they could water the sheep.

Meanwhile, Rachel had arrived at the well. She was Yaakov's cousin, and he wanted to help her. In an awesome show of strength, he lifted the heavy rock, rolling it off the well with only one hand! Yaakov did it easily, without effort.

Will You Marry Me?

Yaakov started to cry. He realized immediately that Rachel was going to be his wife, and he remembered how Eliezer had brought gifts when he came to find a wife for Yitzchak. Yaakov had no rings or bracelets to give Rachel, because Eliphaz had taken everything from him.

Yaakov asked Rachel, "Will you marry me?"

"Yes!" she answered. "But my father cheats people. He'll try to trick you."

"I can be as tricky as he is," Yaakov answered. "How can he trick me?"

"I have an older sister who isn't married yet. He won't let me marry before her."

The Secret Code

To solve the problem, Yaakov gave Rachel code words to use as a secret signal. When they got married, Yaakov would ask her for the code words. If she knew the code words, it would mean that the girl behind the wedding veil was Rachel and not someone else.

FASCINATING FACTS

That well was very, very ancient. Hashem created it on Erev Shabbos at twilight. It was one of the last things He made during the six days when He created the world.

Another reason Yaakov cried when he met Rachel was that he saw that she would not be buried next to him in the Me'aras HaMachpeilah.

QUESTIONS, ANYONE?

What were the code words of their secret signal?

Yaakov told Rivkah about the mitzvos that are usually done by women, like lighting candles and taking challah. Under the chupah, he would ask her to tell him what they were.

No Money!!??

After meeting Yaakov, Rachel ran home to tell her father. When Lavan heard that Avraham's grandson had arrived, he immediately remembered the time when Avraham's servant had arrived with ten camel loads of riches. Lavan's imagination ran wild thinking of the money he would get out of Yaakov. He'd be so rich!

Wasting no time, Lavan ran out to the well. Imagine his disappointment when he saw Yaakov standing alone. No camels loaded up with jewelry and riches.

Lavan thought to himself, *It can't be, he's from a rich family. He must be hiding gold coins.*

Making believe he was so excited at seeing his nephew for the first time, he gave Yaakov a big hug. While hugging him, he moved his hands over Yaakov's clothes, feeling for hidden coins.

Though Lavan found nothing, he was too greedy to give up. Maybe Yaakov was hiding expensive pearls in his mouth? So Lavan decided to give Yaakov a big kiss.

No, there were no pearls hidden there.

Finally, Lavan gave up and invited Yaakov to come back home with him.

Yaakov told him all about what happened when he met Eliphaz. Lavan was very disappointed. All the riches he imagined would be his were just empty dreams!

A Guest in Lavan's House

Imagine you have relatives visiting from Eretz Yisrael. Would your parents make them wash dishes, do the laundry, and wash the floors? Of course not. They are guests.

But Lavan didn't act that way. He told Yaakov that because they were related, he could stay for a month, but he put Yaakov to work taking care of the sheep.

Please, Not Eisav!

Lavan had two daughters, Leah and Rachel. Leah was the oldest, and her eyes were weak. Rachel was very beautiful.

People love talking about shidduchim! They used to say that since Yitzchak has two sons, and his brother-in-law Lavan has two daughters, Leah, the older daughter, would marry Eisav, the older son. Yaakov, the younger son, would marry Rachel, the younger daughter.

When Leah asked people what kind of man Eisav was, she was

QUESTIONS, ANYONE?

Why did Rachel run home and tell her father and not her mother about meeting Yaakov?

Rachel and her sister Leah were orphans. Their mother had died.

Why did Yaakov ask Lavan to marry "Rachel, your younger daughter"? Didn't Lavan know who Rachel was?

Yaakov was very careful with the words he used, so Lavan wouldn't be able to cheat him. If Yaakov had asked for only Rachel, Lavan could give him a different girl named Rachel. If he didn't say your younger daughter, Lavan could change Leah's name to Rachel, and give him Leah, now called Rachel! So Yaakov was very, very clear to say about who he was working for. Still, it didn't help. Lavan was dishonest and gave him Leah anyway.

horrified. People told her that he was an evil murderer. She did not want to marry him!

Leah sat in prayer, and she cried and cried to Hashem, "Please let it be Your will that I do not marry Eisav." All that crying made her eyes weak.

Prayers are powerful. As we shall see, not only did she not marry Eisav, she married Yaakov — and she married him even before Rachel did!

Seven Years

When the month was over Lavan asked Yaakov, "How much do you want to be paid to work as my shepherd?"

"I will work for you for seven years," Yaakov answered. "After those seven years, you will let me marry Rachel, your youngest daughter."

Lavan agreed.

Cheated!

The seven years passed and Yaakov told Lavan that it was time for the wedding.

But instead of marrying him to Rachel, Lavan married him off to Leah instead!

Lavan gave Leah a wedding present. A maid named Zilpah.

How was Yaakov tricked? Hadn't he had made up a secret signal with Rachel so it shouldn't happen! Why didn't Yaakov discover that he wasn't marrying Rachel when Leah didn't give him the code words?

Yaakov never discovered it was Leah until after the wedding because when he asked Leah for the code words she knew them! Rachel had given them to her.

Even though she loved Yaakov, and had waited seven years to marry him, Rachel gave her sister the signal. Why?

Rachel knew that if her sister Leah wouldn't know the signal, then under the chupah, in front of all the guests, Yaakov would refuse to marry her. Leah would be so ashamed!

Rachel decided to give up her wedding and the man she loved, just so her sister wouldn't be embarrassed.

Yaakov Marries Rachel

When Yaakov found out how Lavan had cheated him, he was angry. He told Lavan, "What did you do to me? I worked for Rachel! Why did you cheat me?"

Lavan had his answer ready. He sounded like a big tzaddik. "Here, the custom is that we don't marry off the younger daughter before the older one is married. If you work for another seven years, you can marry Rachel."

QUESTIONS, ANYONE?

How old was Yaakov when he got married?

84

TORAH IN OUR LIVES

Sometimes it may seem to be fun to make people look foolish. For example, Shmuel and Ari might give Moshe a cup that has a tiny hole in it. Then they can laugh at him when he is drinking and it is dripping all over his shirt. Leah may ask Adina to help her hide Malky's schoolbag. Then they can giggle while she looks all over for it.

Next time some of your friends want to get together to play a trick on someone, think of our mother Rachel and what she did just so her sister wouldn't be embarrassed.

FASCINATING FACTS

Giving Leah the secret signal was a very great thing for Rachel to do. When the First Beis HaMikdash was destroyed Hashem promised He would end the exile and bring the Jews back to Eretz Yisrael. Why? As a reward to Rachel for what she did.

Right after the week of sheva berachos celebrating his marriage to Leah, Yaakov married Rachel.

Lavan gave Rachel a wedding present, a maid named Bilhah.

Though Yaakov loved both his wives dearly, he loved Rachel more. This made Leah feel bad.

A Growing Family

Leah couldn't have children. But Hashem saw how much it hurt her that she wasn't as loved as her sister, so He gave Leah children. It was a miracle! And not just one child — she had four sons! They were named Reuven, Shimon, Levi, and Yehudah.

Meanwhile, Rachel didn't have even one child. She decided to ask Yaakov to marry her maid, Bilhah. Rachel was like Sarah, who had no children and gave her maid Hagar to Avraham. Rachel hoped that by doing this, she would be able to raise the children of Bilhah. Hashem would see how much she wanted children and He would listen to her prayers and give her a child too.

Bilhah was blessed with a child. Rachel named him Dan and she raised

QUESTIONS, ANYONE?

Why didn't Yaakov marry Rachel right away?

For one week after the wedding, Yaakov was celebrating his marriage to Leah. It wouldn't be right to celebrate marrying Rachel at the same time. That would be mixing two happy events with each other.

Of the sons of Yaakov, whose name contains all the letters of Hashem's Name?

Yehudah. His name — יְהוּדָה — is made up of the four letters of Hashem's Name, plus the letter dalet.

him. Bilhah had another child that Rachel called Naphtali.

Leah saw that she had stopped giving birth, so she did what Rachel had done, and she asked Yaakov to marry Zilpah, her maid.

Zilpah had two children. Both were named by Leah. The first was Gad, the second was Asher.

Then Leah had two more children after that, Yissaschar and Zevulun.

Mazel tov! After ten boys Yaakov finally had a daughter, when Leah gave birth to Dinah.

All this time Rachel hadn't had any children! She poured out her heart to Hashem to make a miracle and give her a child.

Hashem heard her prayers, and in the merit of giving the secret signal to Leah, she finally had a child. She named him Yosef.

Yaakov's family had grown to four wives and eleven children. His wives Rachel and Leah were holy women who were also prophetesses who knew the future.

For the meaning of the names of Yaakov's sons, see pages 252-257.

Time to Return

Yosef's birth was important to Yaakov. Until he was born Yaakov was afraid to return home and face Eisav. Yaakov knew through prophecy that Yosef had in him the power to destroy Eisav. Now it was safe to go home.

Out of "derech eretz," good manners, Yaakov met with his father-in-law to tell him that he was planning on leaving and to ask for his permission to go.

Yaakov Makes a Deal

When Lavan heard Yaakov's plans, he was not pleased. Lavan needed him to stay. Before Yaakov had arrived, Lavan had no sons. Now he did. From the time Yaakov came, the number of animals in his flock increased. A thousand more sheep, a thousand more goats and a thousand more rams ... every month! Lavan was now a very, very wealthy man. He wanted Yaakov to stay and continue working for him. He wanted the blessings Yaakov had brought to continue.

Lavan told Yaakov, "I know Hashem blessed me because of you. Tell me what you want to get paid and I'll give it to you."

Yaakov then made a deal with Lavan.

Fascinating Facts

Hashem decided on the Rosh Hashanah before Yosef was born that Rachel would have a baby. The same happened to Sarah Imeinu before Yitzchak was born, and to Chanah, mother of Shmuel HaNavi.

Torah in our Lives

Why did Yaakov treat Lavan with derech eretz ? Lavan had cheated him, making him work for fourteen years instead of seven by switching Leah for Rachel. Must you show respect to such a man?

The answer is – yes! When dealing with dishonest people you can do two things. You can behave like them – or you can be better than they are. Yaakov chose to be better than Lavan.

Questions, Anyone?

Why did Lavan do so much better when Yaakov came?

Our Sages say that wherever a tzaddik goes, Hashem sends blessings to that place.

Striped, Patched, and Spotted

Lavan removed all the animals in his flocks that weren't all black or all white, and put them in the care of his sons. Yaakov took care of the animals that were left, which were either all black or all white. His payment would be that all animals born that were brownish red, had colored spots or patches, were striped, or had rings around their ankles, would belong to him. This wasn't a very good deal for Yaakov, since all black and all white animals don't usually have multicolored kids!

To make things worse, although Lavan was supposed to leave all the white and black animals, he left him only the sick and weak ones.

It looked like Yaakov was going to be cheated by Lavan again. But then Yaakov had a dream. He saw an angel that showed him that Hashem was going to make a miracle, and Yaakov would get the best of the deal.

Because of this heavenly message, Yaakov came up with a plan. He took branches of trees and peeled off some of the bark. Now the pieces of wood had spots and patches on them. When he gave the animals water to drink, Yaakov put the sticks in front of them. Miraculously, the animals were influenced by looking at the spotted and patched sticks, and they had babies with spots and stripes. Yaakov's flock grew and grew.

Lavan was furious! He kept changing his agreement with Yaakov, hoping to stop him from being so successful.

How many times did Lavan change the conditions of the agreement?

One hundred times!

"You get only the spotted ones," said Lavan. It didn't help — only spotted animals were born. Then he said, "This time only the ringed ones are yours." Nothing helped! No matter how Lavan changed the deal, the animals had babies that were colored according to the new deal. Yaakov's flocks got larger and larger.

With Hashem's help, after six years went by Yaakov was very, very wealthy! He owned large flocks. From the sale of some of his flocks Yaakov bought many camels and donkeys, and he had lots of servants.

Lavan and his sons were very jealous of Yaakov's wealth.

Time to Go Home

Yaakov had been living with Lavan for twenty years when Hashem came to him and told him, "Go back to where you were born."

Yaakov called Rachel and Leah to meet him in the field, where he was taking care of the sheep. He wanted to know how they would feel about having to leave their home.

He told them, "I see that your father is jealous of me. He tried to cheat me many times."

He told them about the dream with the angel, who had told him that Hashem would miraculously make him successful anyway.

Then he gave them the important news: Hashem wanted him to go back to the land where he was born.

"Lavan treated us not like daughters, but like strangers," Rachel and Leah said. "He sold us to you as payment for the work you did for him. Do whatever Hashem told you to do."

Running Away

Yaakov packed up all his belongings, his wealth, and his flocks. He took his children and wives and left.

They couldn't move very fast. They were traveling with wagonloads of belongings and large flocks of animals, not to mention a lot of children.

Why didn't Lavan try to stop Yaakov and his family from leaving? He would have, but he didn't know they were going! Lavan wasn't home. He had taken a trip, which was three days away from his home, to take care of his sheep.

When he was told that they had left, Lavan took a group of his relatives and ran after them. His plan? To kill Yaakov!

FASCINATING FACTS

As soon as Yaakov left, the blessing that he brought to the city stopped. The wells, the city's water supply, all dried up.

Stolen Idols

Before they left, Rachel went into her father's home and stole his idols. This was her last hope to make her father give up his belief in idols. She hoped that when Lavan saw that his "mighty and powerful gods" had been stolen, he would realize that worshiping idols is silly. Why pray to idols for help when they can't even protect themselves from being stolen?!!

Angel and Sword

Lavan and his men caught up with Yaakov at Har Gilad. Yaakov was camped on top of the mountain, not realizing that he and his family were in danger. Lavan and his men reached the foot of the mountain before dark. They decided they would attack Yaakov the next morning. Lavan and his men made camp and went to sleep.

Lavan began to dream. He saw a frightening vision. The fiery angel, Micha'el, was standing over him holding a long, sharp sword, as if he were going to kill him.

The dream was a message. A warning from Hashem.

Lavan heard Hashem speaking to him, "Don't speak with Yaakov, either good or evil!"

Hashem also told Lavan not to try to convince Yaakov to go back to work for him.

Lavan woke up and knew he should not dare try to kill Yaakov. Also, he realized that Yaakov wasn't going to return.

But he was going to go meet Yaakov anyway. Why? He wanted his idols back.

Goodbye Party

In the morning, Lavan and his men climbed the mountain to where Yaakov was camped. Yaakov and Lavan met face to face.

Wicked people want people to think that they are good, and that it's the good and decent people who are evil. They twist facts and they lie. Lavan spoke in a way that made it seem that he was the innocent victim and Yaakov the wicked crook.

Lavan said, "Why did you run away in secret? You tricked me by not saying you were planning to leave. Had I known, I would have made a fancy goodbye party. You didn't even give me a chance to kiss my family goodbye. I have the power to hurt you, but I won't, because Hashem came to me last night in a dream and warned me not to."

And then he added, "You left, but why did you steal my gods?"

QUESTIONS, ANYONE?

Hashem told Lavan not to speak good things to Yaakov. Why not? What harm could speaking nicely do?

When wicked people speak to a tzaddik, even if they say good things, they don't really mean it. In their thoughts and hearts they really want to hurt the tzaddik.

Yaakov's Curse

Yaakov explained that he didn't tell Lavan they were leaving because he was afraid Lavan would find some way of stealing his wives from him and not letting them go with him.

As for the stolen idols, Yaakov invited Lavan to search all his tents. If he finds his idols, then the person who stole them should be cursed, and would not live long. Of course, Yaakov didn't know that Rachel had taken them.

Lavan searched through the tents of Yaakov and his wives. He couldn't find the idols.

Why didn't he find them in Rachel's tent? That's where they were! Before Lavan came to search her tent, Rachel hid the idols in a good place. She put them in a saddlebag and sat on it. When Lavan came into her tent she told her father she wasn't feeling well and couldn't stand up for him. Lavan searched the tent and though the idols were right there under Rachel, he never found them.

Prove It!

Lavan stood before Yaakov, empty-handed. He hadn't found a thing. Now Yaakov was angry. Being accused of stealing by this thief was too much!

"What did I do wrong that you came chasing after me!" Yaakov told Lavan. "You searched through everything I own. Did you find anything of yours? Prove it, show us what you found."

Lavan stood there, humiliated. He had found nothing, and he'd accused Yaakov for no reason.

Yaakov continued. "For twenty years I worked for you. If an animal was killed by a lion or wolves, I paid for it, even though by law I didn't have to. Whether it was stolen by day or by night, I paid for it. By day the heat was unbearable, at night it was bitterly cold. I hardly ever slept while working for you. You always changed my wages. Instead of working for Rachel for seven years I had to work for both daughters for fourteen years. Then while working for you the next six years you changed the terms of my payment one hundred times! If Hashem had not protected me, you would have succeeded in making me a poor man."

Lavan answered, "They are my daughters and my sons. All your flocks are mine. They come from me. How could I harm them?"

FASCINATING FACTS

Yaakov had cursed whoever had stolen the idols. Since Rachel stole them, she died young, before her older sister. When a holy tzaddik says something will happen, it does.

Treaty

Lavan then asked Yaakov to make a treaty with him. Hashem would be their witness.

What were the terms of the treaty?

Yaakov shouldn't mistreat his wives or marry anyone else. In addition,

Lavan and Yaakov would set up stones as a marker. It would be like a border. Neither Yaakov nor Lavan could pass those stones in order to attack or harm the other.

Yaakov agreed. They set up a large stone surrounded by a pile of stones. Lavan named the stone Yegar Sahadusa. Yaakov called it Galeid.

FASCINATING FACTS

The names Galeid and Yegar Sahadusa mean the same thing: a (stone) pile as a witness. Galeid is Hebrew, Yegar Sahadusa is Aramaic, the language Lavan spoke.

I've Been Robbed!

The next morning Lavan got up, kissed his daughters and grandchildren, blessed them, and returned home.

When Lavan got home there was a big surprise waiting for him. It wasn't a nice one!

While he was chasing after Yaakov, he'd been robbed. Thieves had broken into his house and stolen everything, including his flocks! Lavan went back to being the same poor person he was before Yaakov had come. All of Lavan's blessings had come to him because Yaakov was living with him, and Hashem took everything away when Yaakov left.

Dancing Angels

Yaakov was finally free of Lavan! He continued on his way toward Eretz Yisrael. As he got closer he had a wonderful vision. He saw more than a million angels dancing and singing! They were divided in two camps of six hundred thousand angels in each.

Who were these angels? The angels in one camp had protected him outside of Eretz Yisrael. Now their job was done. It was time for them to return to Shamayim. The other camp was made up of the angels of Eretz Yisrael. Now that Yaakov was coming home, they went out to greet him with joy, and to take over the job of protecting him.

Because of what he saw, Yaakov called the place Machanayim, which is Hebrew for a pair of camps.

MAASEH AVOS

Like Yaakov, the Jews will return to Eretz Yisrael from exile. There, they will be wealthy and there will be many, many Jews.
Once again we will be a nation of holy people!

Let's hope this will be soon!

From Beginning to End

When the parashah began, Yaakov had nothing but the clothes on his back and his walking stick. Eliphaz had taken everything else from him. Now, twenty years later, he had a large family and was a wealthy man.

Most important of all, in all those years he never changed. Even though he lived with evil people, he never behaved like them. He remained a holy tzaddik and a holy person who raised a fine Jewish family, even though everyone around him worshiped idols!

The message behind Yaakov's children's names

Leah's children: Six boys and one girl

Reuven

When Leah had her first child she said, "Hashem has seen my suffering, because my husband does not love me as much as he loves my sister, and He has given me a son. Now my husband will love me."

She named the baby Reuven because the name has the Hebrew word "reu" (see) in it, to show that Hashem had seen her pain.

Also, Leah was proud of how her son would act in the future. She said, "See, my son is not like Eisav. Eisav sold his birthright. In the future my son will have his birthright taken from him and it will be given to Yosef. Eisav hated his brother, but my son will not be jealous of Yosef. He will love him." This explains why she called him Reuven. The name can be split into two words, רְאוּ and בֵּן, which in Hebrew means "see my son."

Shimon

Shimon's name has the Hebrew word שְׁמַע (hear) in it. When he was born Leah said, "Hashem heard that I was unloved and gave me this child also."

Levi

When Levi was born Leah said, "This time my husband will go with me." The word לֵוִי means to go with someone.

Why will Yaakov go with her? A mother of two children can hold one child with each hand. But what does a mother of three do? Now that Leah had three children, Yaakov would have to walk with her, holding onto the older children while she carried the baby.

Unlike his brothers, Levi was named by Hashem Himself! Why? Moshe and Aharon descend from Levi, and the Kohanim would come from Levi's shevet.

Hashem sent the angel Gavriel to bring the baby to heaven. There, Hashem gave him the rights to the twenty-four gifts the Jewish people give the Kohanim. The baby returned to earth, accompanied by all these heavenly gifts. So Hashem named the baby Levi, from the Hebrew word לְוָּה, to accompany.

Yehudah

It was a big surprise when Leah had another son. She knew that Yaakov would have twelve sons, so she thought that each of his four wives would have three sons. She was now blessed with more than her share! She said, "Now I will give thanks to Hashem," and she named him Yehudah, from the Hebrew word הוֹדָאָה, thanks. The word also includes the letters of Hashem's Name. So Yehudah stands for "Thanks, Hashem."

Yissaschar

Before Yissaschar was born, Leah told Yaakov to marry her maid, Zilpah. Now that Leah had another child she said, "Hashem has rewarded me for giving my servant to my husband as a wife."

Yissaschar's name has the letters of the Hebrew word שְׂכַר, reward.

Zevulun

With the birth of her sixth son, Leah said, "Now my husband will make his permanent home with me (that is, he will spend most of his time in my tent) because I have six children."

She named him Zevulun, from the Hebrew word זְבוּל, home.

Dinah

When Leah realized she was going to have another baby, Yaakov already had ten sons — Leah had six and each of the former maids had two.

Leah knew that Yaakov would have twelve sons. She realized that if she would have another son, Rachel would have only one son. How sad for Rachel! So Leah prayed hard that Hashem give her a daughter, so her sister would not be embarrassed.

Hashem listened to her prayers and Leah had a daughter. She named the baby Dinah, from the Hebrew word דִין, judgment, because Leah had passed judgment on herself to have a girl.

Bilhah's two sons

Dan

When Bilhah's first child was born, Rachel said that at first Hashem had judged her not to have children. But then He judged her again, and gave her a child through Bilhah. Since Rachel would raise the child, it was considered as if he were her son also. She called him "Dan," the Hebrew word for judging, דָן, because Hashem had judged her.

Naphtali

Rachel called Bilhah's second son Naphtali, from the Hebrew word תְּפִלָּה, prayer, because Rachel's prayers had been accepted. She now had children like her sister.

Zilpah's two sons

Gad

Leah named Zilpah's first child Gad, because when he was born Leah saw that in the future his descendants would win their battles. So she said Hashem has sent good luck. The word for good luck is גָּד.

Asher

Leah felt that she was fortunate to have this child. She saw that in the future his descendants would be rich and have beautiful cities. Also, the women of his shevet would have the honor of being married to Kohanim Gedolim and to kings. The word for fortunate in Hebrew is אַשְׁרֵי.

Rachel's two sons

Yosef

When Rachel finally had a baby she said, "Hashem has removed my disgrace."

What disgrace was she talking about?

People were saying that since she had no children Yaakov might divorce her, and she would have to marry Eisav. Now that she had a son, no one would say that anymore.

Also, Rachel knew that Yaakov would have one more son. She very much wanted him to be hers, and she prayed for another son. She named her baby Yosef for what she said in her prayer, "May Hashem add another son to me." The word for "add" in Hebrew is יוֹסֵף.

(We'll talk about Binyamin's name when he's born, in Parashas Vayishlach.)

פָּרָשַׁת
וַיִּשְׁלַח

Parashas Vayishlach

Vayishlach • וַיִּשְׁלַח

Parashah Pointers

- Yaakov sends angels with a message to Eisav, telling him that Yaakov is returning to Eretz Yisrael and he would like there to be peace and love between them.

- The angels come back with bad news. Eisav is coming with 400 men to attack Yaakov!

- Yaakov splits his family into two groups. That way, if Eisav attacks one group, the other can run away and be saved.

- Yaakov prays to Hashem to save him from being destroyed by Eisav.

- Yaakov sends a large gift of animals to Eisav, hoping that the gifts would persuade Eisav to make peace with him.

- Yaakov crosses the Yabok River with his family and all his belongings.

- After the crossing, Yaakov returns in the middle of the night for some jars that had been left behind.

- Suddenly he is attacked by the angel of Eisav. They wrestle all night. Yaakov defeats the angel!

- Before Yaakov lets the angel return to heaven, he forces the angel to bless him.

- While they are fighting, the angel hits Yaakov, dislocating his hip. To remember how Yaakov was injured, Jews do not eat the part of the animal called the "gid hanasheh."*

** The gid hanasheh is the sciatic nerve. This nerve runs along the inside of the animal's leg, which is the place where the angel hit Yaakov.*

- The next morning, the brothers meet. Eisav runs to Yaakov and gives him a hug and a kiss. Yaakov is very happy that there will be no war between them. He introduces his family to Eisav, and Eisav returns home.
- Yaakov then settles in the city of Shechem. The prince of the city, who is also called Shechem, kidnaps Yaakov's daughter Dinah and wants to marry her.
- Shimon and Levi attack the city and free their sister.
- Yaakov's next stop in Eretz Yisrael is Beis El. There, Hashem appears to him and gives him a new name: Yisrael.
- Yaakov's mother Rivkah and her nurse Devorah die.
- Rachel gives birth to Binyamin and dies in childbirth. Yaakov buries her on the side of the road, not far from the city of Beis Lechem.
- Yaakov finally arrives home to his father Yitzchak.
- Yitzchak dies at the age of 180.
- Eisav's descendants and the rulers of his country are listed.

FASCINATING FACTS

Yaakov said, "I lived with Lavan." The Hebrew word for "I lived" is garti, גַּרְתִּי, which has the same letters as תרי״ג, taryag. There are "taryag" (613) mitzvos in the Torah. Yaakov was hinting that even though he had lived with Lavan, he had kept all 613 mitzvos. He was still a tzaddik and Hashem would help him.

Yaakov Sends a Message

Yaakov had finally left Lavan. But now he was facing an even more dangerous enemy: Eisav. They had not seen each other for 34 years. Did Eisav still hate him?

Yaakov sent angels to bring a message to Eisav.

This was the message: "Your servant, Yaakov, told me to tell my lord, Eisav: Until now I have lived with Lavan. I own oxen, donkeys, flocks, and servants. I am sending you this message to let you know I am coming, and I want you to love me."

It was a short message, but Yaakov knew that Eisav would understand its hidden meaning.

Yaakov was hinting to Eisav that he had no reason to be angry that Yaakov had taken the blessings from their father. After all, it seemed that the blessings had not come true. "Yitzchak said that I would be a lord, but I was just a worker for Lavan. Yitzchak also blessed me with good land that would grow a lot of food, but I have no land, only animals!"

So there was no reason for Eisav to hate him!

MAASEH AVOS

Jews in exile often face enemies who hate them. We should prepare ourselves in the same ways that Yaakov did.

Sometimes we give our enemies money and gifts so they will leave us alone. Sometimes we have to fight. But we always pray to Hashem to save us!

Bad News!

The angels delivered Yaakov's message to Eisav. They returned with bad news. "We went to your brother Eisav, but he doesn't act like a brother. He still hates you. He's coming after you with an army of 400 men!"

Yaakov became very frightened that he and his family might be killed. He was also upset that he might have to kill others to defend his family.

He prepared himself to deal with Eisav in three ways:

- One — By sending Eisav gifts to try and make peace.
- Two — By praying that Hashem should save him.
- Three — By planning military strategies to save himself and his family, if Eisav fought with him.

Yaakov's Strategy

Yaakov took all the people and animals that were with him and split them into two groups. If Eisav attacked one group, they would stand and fight. That would give the other group the chance to run away and save themselves. This way Eisav would not be able to destroy the entire family.

Not knowing how their meeting would turn out, Yaakov told his men to hide swords under their clothes. If Eisav would choose war, they would be ready.

Yaakov's Prayer

Yaakov poured his heart out to Hashem. "G-d of my father Avraham, and of my father Yitzchak, because of all the kindness You have done for me, I hardly have any merits left. I am afraid I am not worthy for You to save me. Still, please save me from my brother Eisav. I am afraid he will kill me and the mothers together with their children. He wants to destroy all of us and You promised that I would have many, many descendants."

Gifts for Peace

Yaakov put together an incredibly expensive gift package of animals. There were herds of sheep, goats, camels, donkeys, and cows, with many animals in each herd.

Yaakov hoped the presents he was sending would cause Eisav to forgive him and stop being so angry.

Some presents come gift-wrapped. Others have bows on them. The nicer a gift is wrapped, and the bigger the box, the more fun it is to get it. Gifts also usually come with a card that has a nice message written on it.

Yaakov wanted his gift to make a great impression on Eisav. He wanted it to look really big and beautifully gift-wrapped. But how? Gifts of animals don't come in boxes.

This is how Yaakov did it. When he sent the gift, he told his servants not to give it to Eisav all at once. Each herd of animals should travel separately, with space between the different herds. That way when Eisav got the first herd, he would think that this was all he was getting. When later he suddenly saw the next herd, he would be happily surprised. More gifts! Another herd of animals all for him! Then once again he would think that this was all there was, and then the next herd would show up, and the next one after that.

Yaakov had figured out a clever way to make the giving of the gift last a long, long time. It was a perfect way to give a present to a greedy man!

Gift Message

What message did Yaakov send with the gift?

Yaakov told his servants that when they would meet Eisav, he would ask them, "Who sent you? Where are you going? Who is

MAASEH AVOS

We can see throughout our history that Hashem uses the same strategy that Yaakov used. Hashem spreads us out in different places so if Jews are having serious trouble in one part of the world, the rest of us will be safe in another part of the world.

When the Romans burned down the Beis HaMikdash and killed or exiled the Jews in Eretz Yisrael, the Jews in Bavel were safe.

When Spain threw out its Jews, the Turkish Empire invited some of the refugees to join their fellow Jews in their country.

When Jews were being murdered in Europe during the Holocaust, the Jews in Eretz Yisrael and America were safe.

FASCINATING FACTS

When Yaakov prayed that Hashem save him from Eisav, he included prayers that Hashem should also save the Jews in the future from Eisav's descendants, who will try to kill them.

Besides the animals, Yaakov also sent many valuable gems.

this gift for?" They should answer him: "Your servant Yaakov sent this gift to my lord Eisav, and he is behind us."

Yaakov sent a different group of servants with each herd of animals. Each group was told to say the same thing to Eisav. That meant that Eisav would hear many times the words that would be so sweet to his ears: being called "lord" and that Yaakov is his servant!

FASCINATING FACTS

Yaakov was afraid that Eisav would see his daughter Dinah and want to marry her. So he hid her in a box, making sure Eisav wouldn't even know she existed.

Eisav Meets His Match

That night Yaakov crossed the River Yabok on his way to Eretz Yisrael. Miraculously, the river split for Yaakov. With his great strength, Yaakov carried his family and all his belongings from one side of the river to the other. While he was crossing the river, angels were beating up Eisav and his men, who were close by.

As Eisav and his men were traveling to attack Yaakov, they suddenly found *themselves* being attacked. By angels!

Angels pushed them and said, "Who are you with?"

They said, "Eisav."

"Beat them, beat them," said the angels.

Trying to protect themselves, Eisav's men screamed, "Leave us alone. Eisav is the son of Yitzchak." It didn't help.

The angels said, "Beat them, beat them!"

Eisav's soldiers cried, "Stop, stop! Eisav is the grandson of Avraham!"

But the angels didn't stop.

Desperate, the soldiers cried out, "Eisav is the brother of Yaakov!"

"In that case, you are one of us," said the angels, and they stopped beating them.

Back Again

Imagine you win a trophy in camp for best athlete. Camp is over and your parents have come to take you home.

You're in the car when you remember your trophy. You didn't pack it. It's still in your bunk! You'll want to go back and get it. Even though the trophy isn't worth much money, it reminds you of your achievement.

Yaakov had moved all his belongings and his family over the river. Later he realized that a few clay jars had been left behind. Yaakov crossed back over the river to get them. For a few jars he went all the way across the river? He was a wealthy man! Why bother going back for them?!

Those clay jars — and everything else he owned — were important to him. They were like a trophy, reminding Yaakov of how hard he had worked so he could buy them with money he earned honestly. Being honest had been a great challenge, since he had lived with Lavan, who cheated him so often. Even so, Yaakov never said, "Since Lavan cheated

FASCINATING FACTS

According to some opinions one jar Yaakov went back for was very valuable. It was the small jar of miraculous oil that, far in the future, would last for eight days instead of just one. It was the small jar of oil the Chashmonaim found in the Chanukah story.

FASCINATING FACTS

Eisav's evil angel has another name: The Angel of Death.

QUESTIONS, ANYONE?

What day in the year did Yaakov fight with the angel?

Seder night. The same night the angels were beating up Eisav's men.

MAASEH AVOS

Yaakov's fight with the angel was also a hint to the Jewish struggle against all their enemies throughout history. Just as Yaakov defeated the angel, in the end the Jews will be victorious when Mashiach comes. The Jews will be recognized by everyone as Hashem's Chosen People. Good will win over evil forever!

me, I can cheat him back!" Yaakov would never be a cheater like Lavan, and that was something that was very important to him.

Many tzaddikim feel this way about what they own. That's because they work so hard to make sure that they would never cheat anyone.

Wrestling with an Angel

It was the dead of night. Yaakov was all alone, looking for the jars he had left behind. Suddenly, a man attacked him! He grabbed Yaakov and wouldn't let him go. They wrestled.

Though it looked like a man, it was actually the angel representing Eisav. He was the most dangerous angel in heaven.

All night Yaakov and the angel wrestled with each other. Each one tried to defeat the other. It was a struggle between good and evil, and it lasted the whole night. The dust kicked up by their struggle reached up, up, all the way to Hashem's throne in heaven!

Finally, at dawn, Yaakov managed to wrestle the angel to the ground. He won the fight! But the angel, who was pinned to the floor, reached up and hit Yaakov's hip, dislocating his leg.

Bless Me!

Despite the pain, Yaakov held on and wouldn't let go. The angel, desperate, begged Yaakov, "It's dawn, let me go!"

"No! Not unless you bless me," answered Yaakov.

The angel asked, "What's your name?"

"Yaakov."

"You won't be called Yaakov, you will be called Yisrael," said the angel, "because you won your battles with an angel and with men."

"What's your name?" Yaakov asked the angel.

"Why ask me my name?"

The angel then gave Yaakov a blessing and Yaakov let him go.

The Angel's Blessings

The angel had to get back to Heaven because he had a very important mission! For the first time since he was created, it was his turn to praise Hashem. If he missed his turn he would never be able to praise Hashem again. But Yaakov wasn't letting him go!

Why is giving Yaakov a new name a blessing?

By giving Yaakov a new name, the angel was saying that people would no longer accuse Yaakov of having tricked his father. The word Yaakov comes from "eikev," which means "tricked." People used to say that Yaakov had tricked his father to give him the blessings. Yaakov's victory over the evil angel, over Eisav, and over Lavan proved that the blessings really belonged to him. And that's why he would also be called "Yisrael." That comes from the Hebrew word "serarah," which means "ruled over." Yaakov "ruled over" the angel — that is, he won their fight.

Actually, Yaakov's name wasn't changed by the angel. The angel was telling Yaakov that his name would be changed later by Hashem, in the future.

The angel refused to tell his name to Yaakov, because angels change their names all the time. Every time they are sent on a new mission they are given a new name.

The angel then blessed Yaakov with the same blessings the Kohanim bless the Jewish people during Bircas Kohanim.

Limping, Yaakov walked away from the battle. The sun rose and its light shone on Yaakov. Suddenly Yaakov was able to walk normally again! How? Hashem gave special healing powers to the sunlight shining on Yaakov.

The Nerve

Jews are not allowed to eat the "gid hanasheh," the animal's sciatic nerve. This nerve runs along the inside of the animal's leg. That is the place where the angel hit Yaakov. This reminds us of Yaakov's battle with the evil angel. It makes us realize how special we are. We come from Yaakov, who fought with an angel — and won!

Hugs and Kisses

Eisav and his men finally caught up with Yaakov and his family. Yaakov stood in front of his family. Step-by-step, he approached Eisav. Every few steps Yaakov would stop and bow low.

Eisav saw his brother coming to him, bowing again and again and again. He loved it! The bowing did its job. Eisav had mercy on his brother.

Eisav ran to Yaakov and gave him a big hug. Then he put his head on Yaakov's neck and kissed him.

What a special moment. Two brothers, after such a long and bitter separation, hugging and crying in each other's arms.

Fascinating Facts

Remember how the sun set early when Yaakov left home to go to Lavan, so that he would go to sleep on Mount Moriah? That day the night started two hours early.

Now the sun rose two hours earlier, so it could heal Yaakov after his fight with the angel. Hashem gave the world back the two hours of daylight it had lost years before.

Maaseh Avos

Yaakov fought with the angel of Eisav all through the night. The angel couldn't kill him, but was able to hurt him. Yet in the end Yaakov won, and Hashem sent the sun to heal Yaakov's injury.

We, too, will have to fight constantly with enemies who try to destroy us. Though they sometimes hurt us, they will never be able to destroy us. In the end, the forces of evil will be destroyed.

When the time comes, Hashem will send us the great light of Mashiach. Like the sun shining on Yaakov, Mashiach's light will heal us from all the pain we suffered in exile!

Love or Hate?

FASCINATING FACTS

There is an opinion that it only looked like Yaakov was bowing to Eisav. He was really bowing to Hashem, praying that he be saved from his brother.

QUESTIONS, ANYONE?

How many times did Yaakov bow?

Seven.

But things are not always as they seem. In the Sefer Torah, on top of the Hebrew word for kiss, vayishakeihu, there are dots!

Some say the dots mean that when Eisav kissed Yaakov, he meant it with his whole heart, and these were tears of joy at seeing his brother again.

Others say that Eisav hugged Yaakov to get him off his guard. Then he put his head on Yaakov's neck — so he could bite him! Hashem miraculously made Yaakov's neck as hard as stone. When Eisav tried to bite Yaakov his teeth broke on Yaakov's neck, and his bite turned into a kiss!

While Eisav and Yaakov were hugging each other, Eisav's four hundred men slipped away, one by one. After seeing what a holy man Yaakov was, they decided it would be smarter to return home. They were afraid to fight him.

Meet the Family

Eisav saw Yaakov's family standing behind his brother, and he asked him who those people were. Each of Yaakov's wives stepped forward, keeping their children behind them, and they all bowed to Eisav.

With one exception: Yosef. He didn't stand behind his mother. He stood in front of her, blocking Eisav's view. Yosef didn't want Eisav's wicked eyes to even look at his righteous mother.

Eisav asked Yaakov about the gifts he had sent. Yaakov told him he sent them so Eisav would like him.

Eisav said, "I have plenty, keep what is yours."

With these words — "keep what is yours" — Eisav admitted that Yaakov had not "stolen" his blessings from their father. They really belonged to Yaakov.

Yaakov refused to take the presents back, and told Eisav to keep them. Eisav didn't argue. He gladly took the gifts. The truth is he never really wanted to give them back in the first place. He offered to return the presents to Yaakov only to show that he was a nice person.

Let's Travel Together

Eisav suggested they travel together. Yaakov explained that he didn't want to slow Eisav down. After all, Yaakov said, he was traveling with young children and large flocks of animals. He couldn't possibly travel as fast as Eisav.

"You go on ahead and I'll follow slowly until I catch up to my master in Seir," Yaakov said.

Actually, Yaakov had no intention of following Eisav. As a matter of fact he wanted to get as far away from him as possible! He didn't want Eisav's evil to influence his family.

Yaakov always told the truth. So what did Yaakov mean when he told Eisav he would catch up with him in Seir?

Yaakov meant in the future! When Mashiach comes, Yaakov's descendants will go to Seir, the homeland of Eisav's descendants. At that time Eisav's nation will be judged and punished for all the bad things they did to the Jews throughout history.

Outsmarting Eisav

Yaakov also wanted Eisav to think that he was traveling to Seir right away, but really Yaakov would go to Eretz Yisrael, not to Seir. Why? Yaakov was afraid that Eisav might have a change of heart and attack him. But if Eisav waited for him, expecting him to pass so that he could attack him, it wouldn't happen! Yaakov would be somewhere else and Eisav's plans would fail.

Eisav left and traveled home to Seir, Yaakov left and traveled to Succos.

Yaakov stayed in Succos for a year and a half.

Questions, Anyone?

Yosef was only 6 years old when he met Eisav. How could such a little boy block Eisav's view of Rachel?

Hashem saw how much Yosef wanted to protect his mother. So He helped him by stretching him to be tall enough to hide his mother from Eisav's sight.

Fascinating Facts

Yaakov said, "I have everything!" He was satisfied with whatever Hashem gave him. He didn't want more.

Eisav said, "I have plenty." No matter how rich he was, he wanted more.

Questions, Anyone?

Why did Eisav live outside of Eretz Yisrael in Seir? Why not live in Eretz Yisrael, where he was born?

Eisav knew that to get Eretz Yisrael, his descendants would have to suffer as slaves in Egypt. For Eisav that was too high a price for Eretz Yisrael, so he wasn't interested. He found a different land to conquer, and he and his descendants lived there.

Next Stop: Shechem

After Succos, Yaakov traveled to Shechem. He arrived with his health and wealth complete and whole. Most important, his Torah was complete. He hadn't forgotten any of his learning.

Over twenty years had passed since he had last studied Torah from his teachers, Shem and Eiver. Yet he remembered all the Torah he had learned from them!

Tragedy!

Yaakov decided to live in Shechem. He bought a piece of land, built himself a house, and moved in.

Yaakov's daughter Dinah went out to see if she could find other girls to be friendly with, when tragedy struck! Shechem, the prince of the city, kidnapped her! He wanted to marry her! Dinah yelled and screamed, but no one came to help her. They were afraid of the evil prince.

Shechem told his father, Chamor, to speak with Yaakov to get permission to marry Dinah.

What a horrible person! First, he kidnaps Dinah from her family. Then he wants his father to ask Yaakov for permission to marry her.

The Brothers Agree ... On One Condition

Yaakov heard what happened, but he didn't do anything right away. He waited for his sons to return home from caring for the sheep.

The brothers were in the fields grazing their animals when they heard the awful news about their sister. Angry and upset, they came running home. They got there just in time to find Chamor and Shechem coming to speak about Dinah.

Chamor said to Yaakov, "My son wants to marry your daughter. Give her to him as a wife. Let our families intermarry. We'll marry your people and you can marry our people. You'll be one of us and I'll let you do business here and buy as much land as you want."

Shechem could see from the look in the eyes of Yaakov and his sons that they weren't happy with the deal Chamor was giving them.

Shechem made a better offer. "I'll give you whatever you want! Ask for as much money and gifts as you want. You'll get it. Let her be my wife."

Yaakov allowed his sons to deal with these evil, heartless people. The brothers had a plan. With great wisdom they knew what to say that would enable them to get their sister back.

They told Shechem and Chamor, "We agree! On condition that all your

FASCINATING FACTS

While he was living in Succos, Yaakov built sheds, called succos, for his animals. These protected the animals from the cold and heat. At that time people had no idea that you shouldn't let animals suffer. They didn't care if their animals lived outside in bad weather. Yaakov was the first one to build shelters for his animals.

The place was called Succos to remind people to build shelters — succos — for their animals, as Yaakov did. Not to let animals suffer!

Shechem had set a trap for Dinah. He sent girls to make music and dance outside her home. Dinah heard the girls and left home to see what was going on. That's when Shechem kidnapped her.

QUESTIONS, ANYONE?

Do we know today where Yaakov lived in Shechem?
Yes, we do! It's the place where Yosef is buried. Kever Yosef, the tomb of Yosef, is one of the graves in Eretz Yisrael that people go to so they can pray to Hashem there.

How important is it to own a piece of Eretz Yisrael?
It is very important! Yaakov bought land in Eretz Yisrael because owning part of Eretz Yisrael is like having a piece of Olam Haba (the World to Come).

people will get a bris milah."

Chamor and Shechem liked the idea.

They returned to the city and convinced everyone to do a bris milah.

However, Chamor and Shechem didn't realize they had been tricked!

A Brilliant Plan

The brothers would never let their sister marry Shechem, even if he had a bris.

So why ask the people to have a bris?

The brothers wanted to rescue their sister. But she was locked up, trapped, in the palace. If they tried to get her out they would have to fight with the palace guards and soldiers. Even if they were able to free her from the palace, they would still have to get her out of the city. The people of Shechem would try to stop them. It would be the brothers against an entire city!

But if all the men in the city were recovering from having a bris, they would be weak and wouldn't be able to fight, so it would be much easier to free Dinah.

A brilliant plan!

Dinah Is Rescued!

Without discussing it with their father, Shimon and Levi picked up their swords and attacked the city. It was the third day after the men of Shechem had gotten a bris milah.

It didn't matter to Shimon and Levi that they were only 13-year-old boys.* Or that there were only two of them to fight an entire city. They were willing to risk their lives to save their sister and punish those who had been a part of this terrible crime. They also believed that in the merit of their father Yaakov, Hashem would save them miraculously.

Shimon and Levi fought their way into the palace and rescued Dinah. They also killed every man in the city, including Chamor and Shechem.

** Even though they weren't twins, Shimon and Levi were born in the same year, so they were the same age at the time they attacked Shechem.*

TORAH IN OUR LIVES

How do we know that a boy becomes obligated in mitzvos when he is 13?

Rashi says it's because here the Torah says that Shimon and Levi were "men," even though they were only 13. This teaches us that a bar mitzvah boy is a man, obligated in all the mitzvos.

A girl becomes bas mitzvah at the age of 12. This is a law given to us by Moshe at Har Sinai ("Halachah L'Moshe MiSinai").

QUESTIONS, ANYONE?

Why did Shimon and Levi attack on the third day after the bris?

Because three days after an operation people are at their weakest.

Shechem's Bitter End

There was great joy when Shimon and Levi came home with Dinah. But the job wasn't over yet. All the brothers now returned to Shechem. They went through their homes and fields, taking everything they could find.

Yaakov Is Upset

Yaakov was upset at Shimon and Levi for having killed the men of Shechem. He told them, "You have put us in danger. We are a small family, what if the Canaanites will attack us for what you did? We will be destroyed!"

Shimon and Levi answered their father, "Should we let people think that our sister is free for anyone to kidnap?"

The Argument

Yaakov felt that Shimon and Levi had been right in killing Shechem and Chamor for what they had done. But they should not have killed all the men in the city. What had those people done? They were innocent bystanders. Because of all the killing, the Canaanite nations would want revenge and attack their family!

Shimon and Levi disagreed. They felt that they had to make an example of the city of Shechem so never again would anyone ever dare to harm a Jewish girl. And they felt that all the men were sinners because they should not have let Shechem and Chamor do such a terrible thing.

Revenge!

Two men from Shechem managed to escape from Shimon and Levi. They ran to the nearby Canaanite city of Tapuach and told the king how two of Yaakov's sons had wiped out their entire city.

Yishvi, king of Tapuach, didn't believe them. Two teenagers wiping out an entire city? He decided to send his own men to check things out. Just in case ….

His men returned and reported to the king. The story was true. Shechem had been destroyed. The king was furious and wanted to take revenge by wiping out Yaakov's entire family!

Yishvi's advisers told him that if two sons of Yaakov could destroy a city, his army wasn't big enough to fight Yaakov's entire family. He had better get other armies to join him.

He sent messages to other Canaanite kings, telling them what happened in Shechem and asking them to join him in a holy war of revenge against Yaakov.

Seven other kings joined Yishvi. Together they were ready to attack Yaakov with tens of thousands of soldiers!

Yaakov Prepares for War

Yaakov armed himself and his men and prayed that Hashem should save them. He sent a message to Yitzchak to send help. Yaakov also asked Yitzchak to pray for them.

Their prayers were answered and they were never attacked.

What Happened?

Before attacking, the kings spoke with their advisers one more time. Their advisers begged them not to attack. The advisers made a long speech to the kings, showing them how dangerous it would be to start up with the Jews.

They reminded the kings that Avraham had defeated the four kings with an army of only two men, and how Avimelech had been punished when he kidnapped Sarah.

By the time their speech was over, Hashem had made the kings very, very afraid of Yaakov.

The kings called off the attack! Yaakov and his family were left in peace.

Next Stop

Remember when Yaakov had the dream of the ladder? When he woke up, he promised that if he would return safely to Eretz Yisrael, he would pray and bring korbanos at Beis El, the place he had his dream.

Now the time had come to fulfill his promise.

Hashem told Yaakov, "Go to Beis El and make a Mizbei'ach there."

Before leaving to Beis El, Yaakov told everyone who was with him to give him anything they took from Shechem that may have once been used for idol worship. He buried everything they gave him under a tree.

When he got to Beis El he built a Mizbei'ach and called it E-l Beis El.

Bad News

When Rivkah had left home to marry Yitzchak, her nursemaid Devorah went with her. She remained a devoted servant of Rivkah for many, many years, living in the home of Yitzchak and Rivkah.

Rivkah wanted to send a message to Yaakov that it was time to come home. Whom could she trust to deliver such an important message? Devorah, of course!

Devorah traveled to Yaakov and joined him and his family on their return journey back to Eretz Yisrael. But she never made it back. She died on the trip back, in Beis El. Yaakov buried her and called the place where she was buried Alon Bachus, the Plain of Crying.

A few days later he received bad news. His mother Rivkah had passed away.

Rivkah's Funeral

Rivkah was buried secretly, at night, in a small funeral. It would have been embarrassing for Rivkah to be buried in a large public funeral. Who from her family would have been there? Yaakov wasn't there, he was still traveling back. Yitzchak was blind and couldn't leave the house to be at the funeral. The only one who could have come would have been Eisav!

Seeing only Eisav there, people at the funeral would remember Rivkah as the mother of one of the most evil men on the planet. It was better that she be buried quietly and secretly at night, with no Eisav around.

So why doesn't the Torah tell us straight out that Rivkah died? Why the secret message?

Because Rivkah's funeral was done secretly, the Torah kept her death secret, not writing about her death and funeral. Instead, the Torah tells us about Devorah's death, which was a secret message to let us know Rivkah had passed away.

Questions, Anyone?

Where was Rivkah buried?

In the Me'aras HaMachpeilah.

Why is Yisrael a better name than Yaakov?

Yaakov can be understood to mean someone who tricks other people. That's what Eisav said. But Yisrael means a prince of G-d.

The Blessing

Yaakov was mourning for his mother when Hashem came to Yaakov to comfort him and bless him.

Hashem told Yaakov that He is giving him another, better name: Yisrael, which would be his main name from now on. Yisrael means prince of G-d.

The Blessings

The blessings were wonderful news. Hashem promised:

- Yaakov would have more children, whose descendants would become large nations. Hashem was hinting to the future births of Binyamin, and Yosef's sons, Ephraim and Menashe, who would each grow into a large shevet.
- From these shevatim that were not born yet, Yaakov would have kings as descendants. This was a hint to the future first king of the Jewish people, Shaul, from Shevet Binyamin. Also, kings of the Aseres HaShevatim would come from Ephraim.
- Eretz Yisrael would be given to the Jewish people and belong to them forever.

Questions, Anyone?

How old was Yaakov when his youngest son was born?

99 years old.

Son of My Pain

Yaakov and his people left Beis El and continued their journey home. On the way, when they were about a half mile from the city of Beis Lechem, they had to stop traveling. Rachel was having a baby!

After waiting eight long years to have a second son, finally Rachel had another child. Yosef had a full brother. Yaakov now had twelve sons.

It should have been a reason to celebrate and be happy, but something terrible happened. Right after she gave birth, Rachel died.

Before she passed away Rachel named her new baby son Ben Oni, which means "Son of my Pain."

Son of the South

Yaakov decided to give the boy a more positive-sounding name. He called him Binyamin.

The name has good meanings:

It can mean son (ben) of my right hand (yamin). The right hand is the stronger one. So Binyamin means "Son of My Strength."

The word "yamin" also means south, so Binyamin can mean "Son of the South." Yaakov had traveled south from Lavan's home to get to Eretz

FASCINATING FACTS

Besides Dinah, Yaakov had many daughters. Each of the shevatim were born with a twin girl. All except Binyamin. Binyamin was born with two sisters. Rachel had triplets!

Even though Rachel is the mother of only two shevatim, she is considered the mother of all Jews. That is why many people who pray at her tomb call her "the Mama Rachel."

Yisrael. So "south" symbolizes Eretz Yisrael. Yaakov named him Son of the South, because he was the only one of his children who had the honor of being born in the Holy Land.

Kever Rachel, Then

Yaakov, surrounded by his family, buried his dear wife Rachel. He built a monument over her kever (grave) to mark the place on the side of the road where he buried her.

Even though it would have been more respectful for Rachel to be buried in the nearby city of Beis Lechem, Yaakov buried her on the side of the road. Why?

Yaakov saw far into the future. He knew that one day the Beis HaMikdash would be burned, and the Jews would be taken to Bavel. The Jewish captives would be led on this very road, and pass the spot where Rachel died.

Yaakov decided to bury her there on the road, so when the Jews would pass by the grave of Mama Rachel, they would pray there and cry bitter tears over the destruction of the Beis HaMikdash.

Yaakov made the right choice! After the destruction of the Beis HaMikdash, Rachel heard her children's cries. She came before Hashem and pleaded for mercy and for the return of the Jews to Eretz Yisrael. Hashem promised her that He would return the Jews to Eretz Yisrael.

Kever Rachel, Today

Today, Kever Rachel is a very popular holy site where Jews come to pray. They come all through the year. It's only about a five-minute drive from Yerushalayim's city limits.

Rachel's yahrtzeit, the anniversary of the day she passed away, is the eleventh of Cheshvan. On that day tens of thousands come to pray there, men, women, and children. Rachel is surrounded by her "children" on that day.

Bad Move

When Rachel was alive Yaakov lived in her tent. But when she passed away he moved in with Bilhah, who had been Rachel's servant before Rachel freed her to marry Yaakov.

Reuven, Leah's son, felt this was an insult to his mother. How could Yaakov choose someone who had once been a servant girl over his mother!

To show honor to his mother, Reuven moved his father's bed out of Bilhah's tent and put it in Leah's tent.

QUESTIONS, ANYONE?

How old was Rachel when she passed away?

She was only 36.

FASCINATING FACTS

The place where Rachel is buried became part of the territory of the tribe of her son Binyamin. The border between the territories of Binyamin and Yehudah is Kever Rachel and Yehudah's city of Beis Lechem.

This was a bad thing for Reuven to do. He was wrong to mix in on his father's personal life. This showed that Reuven was impulsive, acting without thinking or discussing it with others. As a result he wasn't fitting to get the rights of the firstborn.

Many years later, Yaakov took away Reuven's special rights as the firstborn. His double portion in Eretz Yisrael went to the sons of Yosef. The kings of the Jews would come from Yehudah, not Reuven. The Kohanim would be descendants of Levi, not Reuven.

However, at the time Reuven sinned, Yaakov did not criticize him. Reuven himself realized that he had done wrong, and he spent many years doing very serious teshuvah, repenting for his mistake. He didn't repent because someone criticized him or told him to. That is why Hashem Himself singled out Reuven as being very special for being the first person to do "teshuvah mei'ahavah," repenting out of love, which is a very high level.

Home at Last

Finally, Yaakov's journey was over. He was back home. Imagine Yitzchak's joy when he heard that Yaakov had arrived, and when he met his grandchildren for the first time!

Imagine Yaakov's children's joy at meeting their grandfather, the great tzaddik. They'd heard so much about him from their father!

Yitzchak's Funeral

The family was finally reunited. For the next twenty years of his life Yitzchak had the pleasure of living with his son and grandchildren, until he passed away at the age of 180.

Yaakov and his family were at the funeral. So was Eisav. Eisav led the funeral procession, with Yaakov walking behind him.

Unlike Yishmael, who had done teshuvah and allowed Yitzchak to go first at their father's funeral, Eisav never admitted that Yaakov was greater than he. He remained evil to the end of his life.

Like his father and mother, Yitzchak was buried in the Me'aras HaMachpeilah, alongside his wife Rivkah.

TORAH IN OUR LIVES

Ari is angry at his sister Aviva. She's so bossy! He decides to get back at her by hiding her favorite toy. Aviva then spends the next half-hour looking for it, in tears.

Now Ari can do one of two things. He can realize he was wrong, feel bad about it, apologize, and return the toy to Aviva.

Or he can wait and see. And if she finds out that he did it, and threatens to tell his parents, he will apologize and say he is sorry.

Sometimes we do something wrong. We just couldn't resist the urge to do it.

The question is: what should we do now?

Should we be like Reuven and admit that we made a mistake? Or should we wait till someone yells at us for what we did?

Which do you think is better?

FASCINATING FACTS

Reuven didn't lose all his rights.

When the Jews were counted in the desert, Shevet Reuven was counted first. When Eretz Yisrael was divided among the shevatim, Reuven got his share before anyone else.

Yaakov had been away from home for thirty-six years! After leaving home, he learned in the yeshivah of Shem and Eiver for fourteen years. Then he spent twenty years with Lavan, and it took two years for him to get to Chevron.

The End

The parashah ends with a list of Eisav's descendants and their rulers. On the list is the name of the Jewish people's worst enemy: Amalek!

Amalek was the son of Eliphaz, who was a son of Eisav. Amalek's descendants are so evil that we are commanded to destroy them. Meanwhile, we wait for Mashiach, may he come soon, who will end Amalek's evil in the world.

FASCINATING FACTS

Every year, on the Shabbos before Purim, we read Parashas Zachor, the Torah verses that command us to wipe out Amalek.

QUESTIONS, ANYONE?

Who is the most famous descendant of Amalek?

Haman!

פָּרָשַׁת וַיֵּשֶׁב

Parashas Vayeishev

Vayeishev · וַיֵּשֶׁב

Parashah Pointers

- Yaakov and his family are back in Eretz Yisrael.
- Yosef is 17 years old. Yaakov makes a beautiful robe for him. Yosef's brothers are jealous.
- Yosef dreams that he and his brothers are tying wheat into bundles. Suddenly all the bundles stand up. His brothers' bundles bow down to Yosef's bundle.
- Yosef tells his brothers about the dream. They accuse him of wanting to be a king over them. The dream makes the brothers hate Yosef.
- Yosef has another dream. In the dream, the sun, moon, and eleven stars bow down to him. He tells the dream to his brothers and father.
- His brothers are very angry, but Yaakov thinks the dream will come true.
- Yaakov sends Yosef to Shechem, where his brothers are taking care of sheep. When Yosef gets there his brothers throw him into a pit. A group of slave traders go by and the brothers sell Yosef to them as a slave.
- The brothers want Yaakov to believe that a wild animal killed Yosef.
- Traders bring Yosef to Egypt and sell him to Potiphar. Yosef does a wonderful job and is put in charge of Potiphar's mansion.
- Yehudah marries Tamar. She has twins, Zerach and Peretz.
- Potiphar's wife likes Yosef very much, and she wants Yosef to like her. Yosef stays away from her, because she is already married. She is insulted and angry that Yosef ignores her, so she lies and accuses him of attacking her.
- Yosef is thrown into prison.

- The head of the prison is impressed with Yosef. He puts him in charge of the jail and its prisoners.
- Pharaoh's Chief Butler (the man in charge of Pharaoh's drinks) serves him wine that has a fly in it. Pharaoh puts him in jail.
- While Pharaoh is eating he finds a small stone in his bread. Pharaoh puts the Chief Baker in jail also.
- One night these two prisoners each have a dream. They ask Yosef to explain the dreams.
- Yosef tells them that the Chief Butler will be freed from jail in three days. The Chief Baker, on the other hand, will be killed by Pharaoh in three days, and his body will be hanged.
- Three days later, everything Yosef said would happen — happens!
- Yosef asks the Chief Butler to help him, but he doesn't do it.

The Master Plan

As we saw in the last parashah, Yaakov had finally returned home to Eretz Yisrael. But almost four hundred years earlier, Hashem told Avraham that the Jews would be slaves in a different country. That country would be Egypt.

How could Hashem get Yaakov and his family to Egypt? He had a master plan. Yosef would be sold to Egypt as a slave and become ruler of the country. Because of a hunger in the world, there would be no food in Eretz Yisrael. Yaakov and his family would move to Egypt to join Yosef, who had made sure that there was plenty of food in Egypt. Years later, the Egyptians would force the Jews to become slaves.

How did Yosef get sold to Egypt as a slave?

To understand how such a thing could happen, we have to know more about Yosef, how he got along with his brothers, and the dreams he dreamed.

FASCINATING FACTS

Yosef was sold nine years after Yaakov had returned to live with his father in Chevron.

Yosef

Yosef was 17 years old and handsome. He carefully combed his hair so it would look just right.

Yosef was close to the children of Bilhah and Zilpah. Because their mothers had been servants before Yaakov married them, sometimes Leah's children did not treat these brothers nicely. Yosef wanted to show that it didn't matter to him that their mothers were once servants, and he spent his free time with them.

The ways that Yaakov and Yosef were similar to each other

- They looked alike.
- They both had brothers who hated them.
- Their mothers both had only two children.
- They both had angels that Hashem sent to protect them.
- They both got married outside of Eretz Yisrael.
- They both had children outside of Eretz Yisrael.
- They both had important dreams.

The Favorite

Imagine if your parents gave your brother a new bike and not you. What if your brother told your parents every time you did something wrong? How would you feel about your brother? A bit jealous? A little angry? You probably wouldn't like him and wouldn't talk to him, right?

Something like that happened to Yosef and his brothers.

Because he had been born when his father was already much older, Yosef became a favorite of his father. Yaakov gave Yosef a special gift, a beautiful woolen robe of many colors called a kesones passim.

Yaakov learned Torah with Yosef. He taught Yosef all that he had learned in the yeshivah of Shem and Eiver.

There were times when Yosef saw his brothers do things that he felt were wrong, and he went to his father and told him. Though Yosef thought they were wrong, he made a mistake.

Why did Yosef tell on his brothers to his father? Yosef thought that Yaakov would want to know so that he could teach his sons to stop what they were doing.

Because of the way Yosef behaved, and the way Yaakov treated him, the brothers were jealous of Yosef and hated him.

There are dishonest people who make believe they are someone's friend, even though they hate him. They continue to speak to their enemy as if they were his best friend. Not Yosef's brothers. They stopped talking to Yosef, unless they had to. They were too honest to pretend they liked him when they really didn't.

Dreams

One night, Yosef dreamt that he and his brothers were tying together wheat into bundles. Suddenly all the bundles stood up. All his brothers' bundles made a circle around his bundle and bowed down to it.

Yosef told his brothers what he had dreamed. The brothers understood the dream's message. The bowing bundles were the brothers bowing to Yosef. They were very angry that Yosef had dreamed that all his brothers would bow down to him. They told Yosef, "You think you will become a king over us, that you will be our boss?!!"

Hearing Yosef's dream, his brothers hated him even more. Imagine, their kid brother dreaming that they would bow down to him! What chutzpah!

Fascinating Facts

The Hebrew word "alumah" (bundle) appears five times when Yosef tells his dream to his brothers. That's a hint that the brothers would bow down a total of five times to Yosef, when he ruled Egypt under Pharaoh.

Sun, Moon, and Stars

Yosef had a second dream. He dreamed that the sun, moon, and eleven stars bowed down to him. He told this dream also to his brothers and to his father.

The meaning of the dream was clear. There would come a time when Yosef's father Yaakov (the sun), his mother (the moon), and his brothers (eleven stars) would bow down to him.

Yaakov scolded Yosef. "What kind of a dream is this? Are we to come — your mother, your brothers, and I — to bow down to you?"

Yaakov was upset with Yosef for telling his dream to his brothers, causing them to hate him. However, Yaakov believed Yosef's dream. He was sure that at some time in the future, the dream would come true. The question was when? Yaakov patiently waited for when that would happen.

To remember Yosef's dream, Yaakov wrote it down. He included the date, time, and place where Yosef had told them the dream.

Questions, Anyone?

How could the dream be true? The moon, Yosef's mother, couldn't bow down to him. His mother Rachel had already died!!

The moon was not a symbol of Yosef's mother, Rachel, but Bilhah, who raised him after Rachel died. She would bow down to him in Egypt.

A Mission

By now Yaakov was more than 100 years old, so he put his sons in charge of taking care of the sheep. He stayed at home while his sons took the flocks to graze in Shechem.

Yosef also stayed at home, learning with his father. One day, Yaakov sent Yosef on a mission. He asked him to go to Shechem and find out how his brothers were doing. He told Yosef to return and report back to him.

The Trip to Shechem

Yosef left Chevron to go to Shechem. When he got there he couldn't find his brothers. He wandered around looking for them, and met a man who asked him, "What are you looking for?"

"My brothers. Please tell me where they are."

"They left here. I heard them say, 'Let's go to Dosan.'"

Fascinating Facts

The man who met Yosef and told him where his brothers had gone was actually the angel Gavriel.

Danger in Dosan

Yosef traveled to Dosan to find his brothers. When they saw him approaching, Shimon and Levi said, "Look, the dreamer is coming. Let's kill him and throw him into a pit. We'll say that he was eaten by a wild animal."

The brothers discussed Shimon and Levi's plan, and they decided to kill Yosef!

Hashem heard them planning to kill Yosef so his dreams would not come true.

"Let's see whose plans will happen, yours or Mine," Hashem said.

Rescue

Reuven was against killing Yosef. He knew his brothers wouldn't listen to him if he tried to stop them, so he said, "Don't murder him. Just throw him into a deep pit in the desert."

The brothers liked the idea. Instead of killing him with their own hands, they would throw him into a pit. Without food or water, Yosef would soon die.

Reuven had tricked them into not killing Yosef. He planned to come back to rescue Yosef after the brothers left. He would lift Yosef out of the deep pit and bring him back to Yaakov.

Sure that he had saved his brother's life, Reuven went back home, leaving his brothers to take care of the sheep.

Why did he leave his brothers to take care of the sheep?

The brothers always made sure that one of them would be with their father, to take care of him. They took turns and now it was Reuven's turn to take care of Yaakov.

Snakes and Scorpions

When Yosef finally reached the brothers they grabbed him and tore off the kesones passim that he was wearing. Then they threw him into a deep pit. The pit was full of poisonous snakes and scorpions, but they didn't harm Yosef.

The brothers sat down to eat. They noticed a caravan of camels driven by Yishmaelites (descendants of Yishmael) going by. These were merchants on their way to sell spices in Egypt.

When they saw the caravan, Yehudah said, "Why should we kill our brother? Let's sell him to the Yishmaelites instead. After all, he is our brother."

The brothers agreed. They sold their brother Yosef for twenty silver coins.

How Could They Do That?

Are you wondering how the brothers, who were tzaddikim, could do what they did to Yosef?

From the way Yosef was acting, his brothers thought he wanted to rule over them. They believed he was putting the unity of the family in danger, something that would be terrible for the future of the Jewish nation.

In reality, their judgment of Yosef was not accurate. In addition to the special love Yaakov showed Yosef, his dreams of ruling over them made them a bit jealous. This clouded their understanding of Yosef's goals. In reality, Yosef was a tzaddik!

FASCINATING FACTS

Hashem sent three angels to take care of Yosef. One was there to make sure his brothers didn't kill him. Another angel protected him from the snakes and scorpions that were in the pit that his brothers threw him into. The third angel made sure he was brought to Egypt, where he would become ruler of the land.

QUESTIONS, ANYONE?

Why does the Torah tell us that the Yishmaelites were transporting spices? What does it have to do with the sale of Yosef?

Yishmaelites usually sold materials that had a terrible smell. Hashem did not want Yosef to suffer any more than needed, so He arranged that the caravan would be carrying spices with a beautiful fragrance.

FASCINATING FACTS

Twenty silver coins is equal to five shekels. That is one of the reasons we were given the mitzvah to redeem a firstborn boy by giving five shekels to the Kohen.

Each brother got a half-shekel from Yosef's sale. That is one of the reasons the Jews were commanded to give a half-shekel to the Beis HaMikdash every year.

Slave Boy

Yosef was alive, but he had lost his freedom. He was now a slave, owned by others, to be bought and sold. He was the property of his master.

As he was riding on a camel that was taking him away from Eretz Yisrael, further and further from home, Yosef began to cry. Bitter tears streamed down his face. He was being ripped away from his dear father, whom he loved so much.

Yosef's constant crying annoyed the Yishmaelites. They forced Yosef to walk in the blazing desert heat, instead of riding the camels with them. But he wouldn't stop crying! So the Yishmaelites began to beat him.

Then Hashem stopped it all. Anyone who hit Yosef suddenly found his arms paralyzed. After that, they left Yosef alone.

Sold and Resold

On his journey to Egypt, Yosef was humiliated again and again, as he was sold from one group of travelers to another.

The Yishmaelites sold Yosef to Midianite slave traders, who sold him once again to another group from Medan. They brought him to Egypt and sold him to Potiphar for 500 silver coins. Potiphar was an Egyptian nobleman in Pharaoh's royal household.

What Have You Done?

Reuven returned to the pit into which Yosef had been thrown, hoping to lift him out and save him.

"Yosef? Yosef?!" he called down.

No answer.

Frightened of what may have happened to Yosef, Reuven lowered himself into the hole with a rope and searched for his brother. But Yosef was gone!

Very upset, Reuven joined his brothers. "The boy is gone," he cried, "and I ... Where can I go!?"

Reuven felt terrible that he had failed to save Yosef. When Yosef wouldn't return home, Yaakov would cry and mourn for the loss of his son. Who would he blame for what happened? Reuven, because he was the oldest!

"Where can I go to escape our father's sadness?!" Reuven asked his brothers. "What have you done!?"

Blood and Tears

That was a good question. What were they going to tell their father about Yosef?

The brothers decided to take Yosef's kesones passim, rip it into

QUESTIONS, ANYONE?

Can tzaddikim make mistakes?

Yes. Even Moshe Rabbeinu did. We all do. Humans are never perfect. Even if someone makes a mistake, he can still be a tzaddik. That is why Hashem gave us the great gift of teshuvah: for those times when we make mistakes. If we are sorry for what we did and try to correct our mistakes, Hashem forgives us.

FASCINATING FACTS

Remember the kesones passim that Yaakov gave Yosef? In Hebrew, the word "passim" is פסים. Its letters stand for all the groups Yosef was sold to:

פ Peh — Potiphar
ס Samech — socharim (slave traders)
י Yud — Yishmaelim
מ Mem — Medanim

By the time Yosef arrived in Egypt he had been sold four times!

QUESTIONS, ANYONE?

What was Potiphar's job in Pharaoh's palace?

He was in charge of the royal butchers who killed the animals before they were cooked and served at the palace meals.

pieces, and dip it into the blood of a goat.

They sent the robe to their father and asked him, "We found this. Is it your son's robe or not?"

Yaakov instantly recognized the robe.

"My son's robe!" he cried out in sorrow and pain. "He was eaten by a wild animal!"

Yaakov thought his son was dead, and he tore his shirt. That is what Jews still do today when a close relative dies.

Yaakov sat, crying and mourning for his son. His family gathered around him to support and comfort him. But as hard as they tried, they couldn't succeed. He would not stop mourning for his lost son. Yaakov's father, Yitzchak, cried too when he saw his son's suffering.

Blame

The brothers felt really bad about the suffering they had caused their father. They thought that since Yehudah was their leader and he had not stopped them, he was to blame for what happened.

If he would have insisted they leave Yosef alone, they would have listened to their leader, just like they listened to him when he said to sell Yosef.

Since he was to blame, Yehudah would no longer be their leader.

Twins!

Yehudah felt bad, so he decided to leave the family and build a home somewhere else. He married and had three sons. Their names were Eir, Onan, and Shelah.

Unfortunately, his two older sons died. Eventually, Yehudah married again, a woman named Tamar who was the daughter of Noach's son Shem. She and Yehudah had two sons. Twins! They were named Peretz and Zerach.

Back to Yosef

Yosef started to work as a slave for Potiphar. He did an extraordinary job. Hashem made sure that whatever Yosef did for Potiphar was successful.

For example, Potiphar asked Yosef for a cup of cold water. When Yosef brought it to Potiphar, he changed his mind and asked for a cup of hot water. The water in the cup instantly became hot instead of cold. Now that's service!

Hashem blessed Potiphar because Yosef was in his house, and Potiphar got richer and richer.

QUESTIONS, ANYONE?

How long did Yaakov mourn for his son?

Until he found out that Yosef was alive, 22 years later. All the time Yosef was gone Yaakov never forgot his beloved son and cried over his loss every day.

FASCINATING FACTS

King David and King Shlomo were descendants of Yehudah and Peretz. Mashiach will come from them.

TORAH IN OUR LIVES

Yosef was now living with people who believed in idols, but he didn't try to be like them. He did not hide the fact that he was different and believed in Hashem, and not statues.

When Yosef spoke to others he would often mention Hashem, even though it made him different from everyone else.

When you go shopping or travel, you should be like Yosef. Be proud of being Jewish. Don't try to hide it!

Top Slave

Within a year of being brought to Egypt, Yosef had become Potiphar's special servant. He was in charge of all his properties, and was also Potiphar's personal assistant.

Potiphar put Yosef in charge of running his house and gave him the keys to all the rooms in the house. That included the place where Potiphar kept his money and treasures! Potiphar let Yosef run everything. He trusted him one hundred percent!

When Yosef first arrived in Egypt he was sad every day. You can imagine how homesick he was! But after he became an important slave, he stopped being so sad. He began to eat and drink well and comb his hair.

Hashem felt that wasn't right. How could Yosef do that when he knew his father was suffering? Yosef should have been more sensitive and been sadder, knowing his father was crying for him.

Hashem decided it was time to change Yosef's situation. Yosef would stop being an important man. Instead, he would become a prisoner.

This is how it happened.

Potiphar's Wife

Potiphar's wife liked Yosef very much, and she wanted Yosef to like her. Yosef knew that would not be right, since she was a married woman. She was very insulted with the way Yosef ignored her, so she accused Yosef of attacking her. People believed her lies and Yosef was thrown into prison.

Prison

Even in prison, though, Hashem did not abandon Yosef. Hashem made sure that whoever met Yosef liked him. The head of the prison liked and trusted Yosef so much that he soon put him in charge of the entire prison and all the prisoners.

Nine years after Yosef had been put in jail, he greeted two new prisoners. Before going to prison they had been very important officials in Pharaoh's palace. They were Pharaoh's Sar HaMashkim, the Chief Butler in charge of Pharaoh's drinks, and the Sar HaOfim, Pharaoh's Chief Baker. Because they were important officials, the head of the prison gave them special treatment. So he appointed his trusted prisoner, Yosef, to take care of them.

Why were they in prison? What had they done wrong?

Flies and Pebbles

The Chief Butler had served Pharaoh some wine. Pharaoh picked up the cup to take a drink. Ughh! He saw a fly swimming in the cup! This made him angry. What kind of service was this? He ordered his guards, "Throw my Chief Butler in jail!"

Pharaoh reached for a loaf of bread, broke off a piece, and started chewing. Suddenly he felt himself biting down on something hard. It was a pebble! The Chief Baker had served him bread with a pebble in it! Again, Pharaoh was very upset. He yelled to his guards, "Throw the Chief Baker in jail!"

Dreams

Pharaoh's Chief Butler and Chief Baker had been in prison for a year when one night they had disturbing dreams. They were sure the dreams were messages about the future. If they weren't in prison they would have gone to a professional dream interpreter to find out what their dreams meant. But in prison who would be able to explain their dreams? They became anxious and upset.

The next morning, when Yosef saw them, he asked both of them why they looked so worried.

"We had dreams and there is no one to tell us what they mean," they each answered.

"Tell me the dreams and with Hashem's help I will tell you what they mean."

First, the Chief Butler told Yosef his dream.

FASCINATING FACTS

Each of them dreamed two dreams. One dream was about what would happen to him. The other dream showed the meaning of the other prisoner's dream. So the Chief Butler knew the meaning of the Chief Baker's dream, and the Chief Baker knew the meaning of the Chief Butler's dream! This is how they knew that Yosef had interpreted correctly.

Back On the Job

"I saw a grapevine that had three branches. As I watched, bunches of grapes grew on the branches. When the grapes were ripe I saw myself squeezing the grapes into Pharaoh's royal wine cup. Then I placed the cup onto Pharaoh's palm."

Yosef understood the dream.

Yosef told the Chief Butler, "Putting the cup onto Pharaoh's palm means you will be freed from jail and return to your job, being in charge of Pharaoh's drinks. The three branches means that it will happen in three days."

A Request and a Mistake

The Chief Butler was very happy about what Yosef had told him. He would soon be out of prison and back to his old job!

Having given him such good news, Yosef felt he could ask the Chief Butler for a favor. He could help Yosef because he would once again be an important official in Pharaoh's court.

"Please do me this kindness," Yosef asked him. "When you are back in Pharaoh's palace, talk to him about me. Try to convince him to free me from prison. I was kidnapped and I did not do anything wrong."

Yosef was on a very high and holy level. Sold as a slave and in prison for so many years for a crime he did not do, he never once got angry at Hashem. Amazing! He had faith the entire time that Hashem knew what was good for him. Yosef never lost faith. He had complete trust that everything Hashem did was for the best!

For someone as great as Yosef to turn to the Chief Butler for help was a mistake! He should have had complete faith that Hashem would free him at the right time.

To teach Yosef not to rely on anyone else but Him, Hashem left Yosef in jail for an extra two years.

Put to Death

The Chief Baker was next.

"I dreamt that I was carrying three baskets on my head. The top one was full of baked goods. Birds were eating the food in the basket."

Yosef understood that the three baskets meant three days. The other part of the dream meant the Chief Baker would be killed and birds would eat him.

Yosef told the Chief Baker, "In three days Pharaoh will tell his soldiers to kill you by the sword. Then they will hang your body where it will be eaten by birds."

TORAH IN OUR LIVES

One of the reasons for the mitzvah to drink four cups of wine on Seder night is because the Hebrew word "kos," which means cup, is mentioned four times in the Torah when it discusses the Chief Butler's dream and what it meant.

What does his dream have to do with Pesach?

The dream was also a message to Yosef about what would happen to the Jews in the future. The three branches were the three holy people Hashem would send to lead the Jews out of slavery in Egypt: Moshe, Aharon, and Miriam.

QUESTIONS, ANYONE?

Why do you think Pharaoh had the Chief Baker killed, and let the Chief Butler go free?

The Chief Butler wasn't really at fault. It's easy for a waiter to miss seeing a fly jump into a silver cup when he is bringing it out. Or maybe the fly flew in after the Chief Butler had served the wine to Pharaoh, while the cup was standing on the table waiting for Pharaoh to drink.

The Chief Baker was not careful. He should have sifted the flour and checked the dough more before he baked it. He was sloppy about his work. Pharaoh could have broken a tooth on the pebble or choked on it. So Pharaoh felt the Chief Baker was guilty.

Happy Birthday!

Three days passed from when Yosef explained the dreams. It was Pharaoh's birthday and he made a grand party. At the party Pharaoh had the Chief Butler and the Chief Baker taken out of prison. The Chief Baker was killed and hanged. The Chief Butler got his old job back. Everything happened just as Yosef had predicted.

Forget, Forget

The Chief Butler didn't forget Yosef right away. He really wanted to help him. But after some time had passed, he forgot. When you don't want to forget something, you can write it down to remember it. The Chief Butler did something just like that. He tied knots in the loose strings on his clothing to remind him to talk to Pharaoh about Yosef. But Hashem sent angels to untie the knots!

Finally, after two more years in jail, Yosef was finally freed! Find out how that happened in the next parashah!

How many years was Yosef in prison before he was freed?

Twelve years!

פָּרָשַׁת מִקֵּץ

Parashas Mikeitz

Mikeitz · מִקֵּץ

Parashah Pointers

- Pharaoh dreams that seven fat cows are eaten by seven skinny cows. He wakes up and then goes back to sleep.
- He then dreams of seven fat ears of grain that are swallowed up by seven skinny ears of grain.
- No one can explain to Pharaoh what the dreams mean. The Chief Butler tells Pharaoh about Yosef. Two years before, Yosef had correctly explained the dreams of the Sar HaMashkim (the Chief Butler) and Sar HaOfim (the Chief Baker).
- Pharaoh orders Yosef to be brought from jail to explain the dreams.
- Yosef explains that the dreams mean that Egypt will have seven years with plenty of food, but then there will be seven years of hunger.
- Yosef advises Pharaoh to store food during the seven years of plenty. That way there will be food for the years of hunger.
- Pharaoh appoints Yosef as his second in command over all of Egypt! Only Pharaoh has more power than Yosef.
- During the seven years of plenty, Yosef arranges that tons and tons of extra food be stored away.
- Yosef marries Osnas and has two children, Menashe and Ephraim.
- The seven years of hunger begin. No food is growing in Egypt, in Eretz Yisrael, and other nearby countries.
- Yosef sells the food that had been stored away to the Egyptians and to people from the other starving countries. Yaakov sends his sons to buy food in Egypt. Binyamin stays behind with his father.
- Yosef accuses them of being spies. They tell Yosef they came to buy food, and their youngest brother stayed with their father.

- Yosef puts Shimon in prison. He says that if they bring their youngest brother to him, they will get Shimon back.
- The brothers return to Yaakov and tell him what happened. Yaakov refuses to send Binyamin.
- The hunger gets worse. The brothers have to return to Egypt to buy food, but without Binyamin, they can't go!
- Yehudah convinces Yaakov to let Binyamin go with them. Yehudah guarantees that he will bring Binyamin back.
- The brothers return and Yosef frees Shimon, and he invites them to eat with him.
- Yosef tells his son Menashe to hide his silver cup in Binyamin's luggage.
- The brothers leave to return home. Menashe runs after them and accuses them of stealing the cup.
- The brothers deny it and tell Menashe to check their bags. Menashe "finds" the cup in Binyamin's bag.
- The brothers are forced to return to Yosef.
- Yosef tells his brothers that he will punish only Binyamin because the cup was in his bag. The rest of them can return home.

Dreams

Egypt was an enormous empire. Most probably Pharaoh worked very hard: long meetings with government ministers; dinners with many guests and many speeches. By the end of the day he must have been exhausted, falling into bed and looking forward to a good night's sleep.

But Hashem had a different plan. It was time for Yosef to be freed. So Pharaoh began to dream.

Pharaoh dreamt he was standing over the Nile River. Suddenly, something very strange happened. Seven fat cows rose out of the river. They went to graze in a field. Meanwhile, seven other cows rose up out of the river. These were skinny, so starved you could see their bones sticking out. They looked like skeletons!

The seven skinny cows went over to the fat cows, and swallowed them all. But the skinny cows were still skinny and starved.

What a scary dream! Pharaoh woke up in a fright.

It was still in the middle of the night, so Pharaoh just turned over, cuddled in his blankets, and went back to sleep.

And then he had another dream ...

This time he saw seven ears of grain that had large, high-quality kernels growing on them. Then another seven ears grew, but their kernels were small and scrawny, and of very poor quality.

The scrawny ears of grain swallowed the good ones.

Another terrifying dream! Pharaoh woke up shaking and trembling in fright.

The king knew that these dreams had an important message. He had to find out what they meant!

He called a meeting of Egypt's wise men. They were experienced in explaining dreams. He asked them to explain the dreams' message.

Disaster!

They predicted disaster.

His wise men explained that the dream about the cows meant that Pharaoh would have seven daughters, and all seven would die.

The dream about the grain meant that Pharaoh would conquer seven kingdoms, and seven Egyptian districts would rebel against him.

Pharaoh did not accept their answers. He knew they were wrong.

With no explanation of his dreams, Pharaoh was sick with worry. He was so upset that if no one could explain his dreams soon, he would die.

Yosef Is the Answer

One of Pharaoh's officers was very afraid of Pharaoh's death. Who? Someone we met in the last parashah: the Chief Butler, the officer in charge of bringing Pharaoh his drinks.

He was worried a new king might find someone else to replace him. Then he would lose all the honor, respect, and money that went with his important job.

Suddenly he remembered Yosef. That was the answer to his problem! Surely Yosef would be able to explain Pharaoh's dreams. After all, Yosef had explained the dreams he had in prison, and everything had come out just like Yosef had predicted.

Yosef would be able to tell Pharaoh what the dream meant. Pharaoh would live, and he would keep his job!

FASCINATING FACTS

When the Chief Butler left prison, he forgot all about Yosef. But now that the time had come for Yosef to become ruler of Egypt, Hashem made him remember Yosef.

One Night in Jail

The Chief Butler hurried to speak to Pharaoh. He reminded Pharaoh of what had happened a few years before. How the king had thrown him and the Chief Baker into prison.

Then he told Pharaoh what happened one night in jail:

"One night both of us had dreams. We told them to a young Hebrew slave, who was with us there. He explained what our dreams meant. And what he said came true — exactly the way he said it would!"

The Chief Butler wanted Pharaoh to talk to Yosef, but he was also afraid. If Yosef explained the dream correctly to Pharaoh, Pharaoh would reward him by making him an important person. The Chief Butler didn't want that. He was jealous of other people's success. He was a bad man.

How could he talk about Yosef, without encouraging Pharaoh to make Yosef important? The Chief Butler said Yosef was just "a young Hebrew slave." All these words were meant to leave Pharaoh with a bad impression of Yosef. Yosef was "young," meaning that he was immature and foolish. He was a "Hebrew," who spoke Egyptian with an accent, so it was hard to understand him. And he was a "slave." In Egypt, a former slave could not become a ruler.

Yosef Gets Out of Prison!

Pharaoh was very excited about this prisoner who could predict the future from dreams, and get it right. He immediately ordered his guards to bring Yosef to him.

It was Rosh Hashanah when guards took Yosef out of prison. Yosef got a haircut. Instead of a prisoner's uniform, they dressed Yosef in clothes fit to meet a king.

Yosef Meets the Ruler of the Egyptian Empire

Yosef was taken to Pharaoh.

Pharaoh said to him, "I had a dream but no one can tell me what it means. I heard that you can explain the meaning of dreams."

Yosef answered, "The wisdom to explain dreams is not mine. Hashem will tell me what to say."

This was good enough for Pharaoh. He told Yosef his dreams and Yosef began to explain their meaning.

The Dreams Mean ...

Yosef told Pharaoh, "Pharaoh's two dreams are really one dream. Hashem is telling Pharaoh what He will do to Egypt. The seven fat cows and seven good ears of grain stand for seven years when there will plenty of food in Egypt. The seven skinny cows and seven bad ears of grain are seven years of terrible hunger that will come after the years of plenty."

Then Yosef explained why in the dream the skinny cows ate the fat cows and still stayed skinny.

"The hunger will be so bad that all the good times of the years of plenty will be forgotten. The dream was repeated twice to show that Hashem is going to do this right away."

Good Advice

Yosef continued with some good advice for Pharaoh.

"Pharaoh should put a wise man in charge of all of Egypt. He should prepare the country for the years of hunger. He should hire workers who will gather food during the years of plenty and put it away in Pharaoh's warehouses. That way there will be food for the seven bad years. Then people won't starve during the hunger years."

Pharaoh knew that Yosef was right. This was what the dream meant!

Pharaoh's Idea

Pharaoh gathered his advisers and government ministers to discuss the terrible crisis the country would be facing. Egypt might be destroyed by the seven years of hunger. Steps had to be taken during the seven years of plenty. They needed a wise man to save the kingdom! But who?

Pharaoh had an idea. He told his advisers: "If we search all over we

TORAH IN OUR LIVES

Yosef didn't say he was smart enough to explain dreams. He knew that all his talent came from Hashem. When he was praised for what he did, Yosef said, "It's not me, it's Hashem."

Something for us to remember.

When we are praised for getting high marks, playing a musical instrument, for our beautiful voice or making a great basketball shot, remember: It's not us. It's the talent Hashem gave us.

Don't take the credit. Give Hashem the credit.

won't find anyone as wise as Yosef. I want to put him in charge of all Egypt."

Pharaoh's advisers were shocked by this suggestion. They told Pharaoh, "You are going to make a Hebrew slave into a ruler over us?!"

"I can tell that he is a noble man fit for royalty," Pharaoh answered.

"But only someone who knows how to speak all seventy languages can be an Egyptian ruler," the advisers said.

"Okay," Pharaoh said. "We'll test him."

Yosef's Test

While Pharaoh was discussing how to save Egypt, Hashem was making sure that Yosef would become ruler of Egypt. He sent an angel to teach Yosef all the seventy languages spoken in the world at that time.

Yosef was taken back to Pharaoh. Pharaoh was sitting on a very large and beautiful throne covered with silver and gold. The throne was at the top of a high staircase that had seventy steps.

As Yosef walked up each step Pharaoh spoke to him in a different language, and Yosef answered him in that language. For every language they spoke Yosef could move up one step higher on the staircase, one step closer to Pharaoh. To pass Pharaoh's test Yosef would have to be able to get up to the very top step!

From the bottom of the staircase, the advisers watched as Yosef moved up step by step, higher and higher and higher. Finally, he reached the very top step. He had passed the test. Now Pharaoh could make him ruler of Egypt.

FASCINATING FACTS

When Yosef got to the top step he spoke to Pharaoh in one more language. That language was Hebrew. Pharaoh couldn't answer Yosef. Yosef knew one more language than Pharaoh! This frightened Pharaoh.

He didn't want anyone to know that there was a language he couldn't speak. Pharaoh asked Yosef to swear to keep it a secret.

A Ring and a Chain

Pharaoh told Yosef, "There is no one as smart as you. I have placed you in charge of all of Egypt. You are the highest ruler in the land. Only my authority is higher than yours."

To make it official, Pharaoh took the royal ring off his finger and gave it to Yosef. This ring gave Yosef the power to make laws for the entire country.

Pharaoh ordered the finest linen royal robes be brought for Yosef to wear and he put a gold chain around his neck.

QUESTIONS, ANYONE?

How old was Yosef when he left prison and became ruler of Egypt?

Yosef had been in jail for twelve years. At age 30 he suddenly became the ruler of Egypt.

Yosef's Parade

Now Pharaoh had to tell all of Egypt that Yosef was their new ruler. How do you do that when there are no newspapers, phones, or cameras? Pharaoh made a spectacular parade that he sent all

through Egypt so that the Egyptians could meet Yosef, their new ruler.

Imagine being there, and watching the parade from the roof of your house. What a view! Below are crowds of men, women, and children standing on the sides of the road, looking at the new ruler's chariot. Yosef is standing up in the chariot, wearing a fancy set of royal robes. On his neck, a golden necklace gleams in the sun. The chariot is being pulled by the largest, most beautiful horses you've ever seen!

Thousands of musicians are marching behind Yosef playing drums, flutes, and harps. In front of Yosef's chariot are 5000 men, marching and holding out their swords. Some of them are even juggling swords!

Twenty soldiers march right in front of the chariot. In a loud voice, they announce together: "Have you seen Avrech — the king's adviser? He has been appointed the king's second in command — the viceroy. Whoever doesn't bow down to him or obey his orders will be put to death!"

After hearing the announcement, the entire crowd bowed before Yosef and shouted, "Long live the king and long live his viceroy!"

QUESTIONS, ANYONE?

What does Avrech mean?

The simple explanation is the king's adviser. However the Midrash says it may mean "young and wise," or it may mean "kneel to him" because he is the ruler.

Honor and Glory

How does the president feel on the day he is inaugurated? What's going through his mind when he travels in his motorcade, surrounded by motorcycles and cars and seeing the crowds cheering him on?

Probably that he is the greatest and most important person on earth.

Yosef didn't think that way. With all the honor and glory that he was getting during the parade, all he could think about was how much he owed Hashem for his good fortune. He remained modest and thanked Hashem for everything. He said, "Blessed is He Who lifts the needy from the dust. Happy is the man who has faith in You."

TORAH IN OUR LIVES

All those years Yosef was in prison, he turned to Hashem to get him out. When good things were happening to him in the parade he also turned to Hashem, to thank Him.

Some people think of Hashem only when bad things are happening, but not when things are going great.

When things aren't going well we ask Hashem for help. When good things happen (like getting something you really wanted for your birthday) we should also turn to Hashem and, like Yosef, thank Him.

Yosef's New Name

Now that Yosef was the new viceroy, Pharaoh gave him an Egyptian name. He called him Tzafnas-Panei'ach, which means, "Explainer of Mysteries."

Pharaoh also gave Yosef a wife. Her name was Osnas. She was a granddaughter of Yaakov, who Hashem brought to Egypt to be a wife for Yosef.

Yosef and Osnas had two children. The oldest was Menashe and the youngest Ephraim.

The Good Years

During the years of plenty, Yosef hired an army of workers to collect extra food and put it in Pharaoh's storehouses. Egyptian families also put away food for the years of hunger.

The seven years of plenty ended. Suddenly nothing was growing. One minute there was plenty of food, and the next all the food was gone. Even the food they were eating on the table spoiled at the moment the seven years of hunger started!

The Egyptians weren't worried. After all, they thought, they had put food away for themselves. Imagine their surprise when they opened the doors of their warehouses and everything they had put away was spoiled!

Miraculously, the only food that hadn't rotted was the food that Yosef and his workers had stored in Pharaoh's warehouses.

The People Complain

The Egyptians were desperate. They went to Yosef and asked for food. He said, "Whoever wants food will have to get a bris milah."

The Egyptians didn't want to do it, so they went crying and screaming to Pharaoh.

Pharaoh asked them, "He told you there would be a hunger, why didn't you prepare for it?"

"We did! But everything rotted."

"All your crops rotted because of what Yosef said. What he says happens. He has powers! What if he says we should die? We will! You had better do what he tells you."

Egypt Becomes Wealthy

The Egyptians did what Yosef asked. He opened all the warehouses and started selling food to the Egyptians.

There was hunger not only in Egypt, but everywhere else in that part of the world. When people heard food was being sold in Egypt, they came from other countries to buy food from Yosef.

It was big business, and money poured into Egypt. Pharaoh's treasuries were bursting with wealth from Yosef's food sales.

Yosef made Pharaoh very, very wealthy!

Name Please

Yosef knew his brothers would come to buy food because of the hunger in Eretz Yisrael. When they would show up he wanted to know about it. How could he make that happen?

FASCINATING FACTS

Yosef had his workers keep an exact count of how much food was collected. But they collected so much food, they had to stop counting. Why?

Because at that time in Egypt they had no names for numbers that went up so high!

He ordered the guards at the city gates to make everyone fill out a form when entering Egypt. The form asked for their names, and the names of their father and grandfather.

Yosef's son Menashe collected the names and brought them to his father. Imagine Yosef sitting at his desk every evening going through the long lists of names. Searching, searching, and hoping to find his brothers' names. Wondering: "When will they be here? When will they come?"

Hunger in Eretz Yisrael

In Eretz Yisrael, there was also a terrible hunger. Families were sending people to Egypt to buy food.

Yaakov's family was not going hungry. Hashem made sure they still had food to eat. But Yaakov realized that word would get out that his family didn't need food, and people would become jealous.

When surrounded by enemies it's not good to give them an excuse to hate you more. So even though they didn't need food, Yaakov's family needed to do what everyone else was doing. They would have to travel to Egypt.

QUESTIONS, ANYONE?

When Yaakov told the brothers to go to Egypt he didn't say "lechu, go," he said, "redu, go down." Why?

Though he didn't know it, the word "redu" (which Hashem put into his mouth) was saying what would happen in the future.

Yaakov was hinting to them that they and their descendants would live in Egypt for the next 210 years! The numerical value of the Hebrew letters in the word רְדוּ is 210! (Reish = 200, dalet = 4, vav = 6. Do the math: 200 + 4 + 6 = 210.)

The Brothers Set Off

Yaakov called his sons together and explained the situation. He told them to go down to Egypt and buy food.

He instructed them, "When you get to Egypt don't all go in together through one gate. Each one of you should go in through a different gate."

Seems like a strange request, right? Wrong!

Yaakov wanted to protect his sons. They were unusually handsome and strong. If they went as a group they would stand out and be noticed. People might look at them with an evil eye, an "ayin hara." That could be dangerous. If they went in separately they wouldn't be noticed, so no one would give them an evil eye.

The Road Trip

Only ten brothers went. Yaakov was afraid to send Binyamin. In those days the roads were dangerous. If anything happened to Binyamin, Yaakov wouldn't have any children left from his late wife, his beloved Rachel.

The brothers got on their camels for the long trip. They took donkeys with them to carry the food they would bring home from Egypt. As they got closer to Egypt the roads became packed with people coming to buy food.

By now the brothers were sorry for what they had done to Yosef. They decided that they would look for him in Egypt. Once they found him there they would buy Yosef back, no matter how much it would cost them!

Where Are They?

When the brothers got to the city they split up. Each brother went in through a different city gate. At each gate they wrote their names down, as requested by the gate guards.

Once in the city the brothers joined up with one another and started looking for Yosef.

Yosef was so excited when he saw his brothers' names on the lists of people who had entered Egypt that day. His brothers finally had arrived!

Yosef ordered all the warehouses selling food to close. Only one was left open. He called in its manager and gave him his brothers' names. "When these people come to buy food, arrest them and bring them to me!" Yosef commanded.

The first day passed. None of the brothers came to buy food. Another day passed, and another. Still no brothers. Where were they? They had been in Egypt for three days already, and they hadn't come to buy food. Where could they be?

Yosef wouldn't wait anymore. He called for seventy mighty warriors from Pharaoh's palace and gave them a description of his brothers. "Go find them!"

Arrested

The brothers had spent the last three days searching everywhere for Yosef, never imagining that he was in the royal palace. Now they were looking for him in one of the city's open-air markets.

Suddenly there was a commotion in the market. Seventy Egyptian soldiers had come to the market, looking around. The brothers were astonished when they saw the soldiers coming straight at them!

They were surrounded, arrested, and brought to Yosef's palace.

"You Are Spies!!"

The brothers were brought before the viceroy of Egypt. Yosef was in his royal robes, wearing a golden crown and sitting on his throne. In his hands he held a large golden cup. He looked very impressive.

The brothers bowed down before Yosef. That was the custom in Egypt when meeting rulers.

Questions, Anyone?

How could the brothers not recognize Yosef when they met him? He was their own brother. They grew up together!

When the brothers sold Yosef he was only seventeen years old. Now he was grown up, a man of thirty. His face was covered with a beard. That is why the brothers didn't recognize him.

Seeing his brothers bowing before him, Yosef remembered that in his dreams, his brothers bowed to him.

The brothers stood up and he asked them, "Where do you come from?"

"From the land of Canaan (what Eretz Yisrael was called then) to buy food."

They stood and watched as Yosef tapped his golden cup. He spoke to them harshly and said, "I see by my magic cup that you are spies! Only spies come in through separate city gates." He accused them of trying to find the best places to attack Egypt, where its weakest defenses were.

"We aren't spies! We came to buy food. We are a family of twelve brothers. One of our brothers stayed with our father. The other is gone. We are trying to find him. We entered through different gates, hoping to find him faster that way."

"If you had found him and were asked to pay a very high price to get him back, would you have paid?" Yosef asked.

"Yes."

"What would you do if his owner wouldn't sell him to you at any price?"

"We'd fight for him to the death!"

"Aha!" Yosef said. "Just as I said, you are spies coming to kill our people."

Prison

Yosef had the brothers put in prison.

On the third day, they were once again brought before Yosef.

He told them, "I'll let you go and bring food back home, but bring your youngest brother back to me. Then I will know you are telling the truth. One of you will stay here in prison, as a hostage."

Why Are We in Trouble?

The brothers wondered why this was happening to them. Why were they in such trouble? They spoke to each other in Hebrew. They didn't know Yosef understood Hebrew.

"We deserve all that's happening to us because of how we treated Yosef," they said. "He begged and pleaded with us not to throw him into the pit. But we did not feel sorry for him. Now we are suffering for what we did."

Reuven spoke, "Didn't I tell you not to sin against the boy? But you didn't listen, and now we are being punished."

The brothers didn't know the viceroy was really Yosef. He understood every word they said.

When he heard after so many years that his brothers were sorry for selling him, he felt he had to cry. He left the room. The minute the door

Why didn't Yosef tell the brothers who he was right away?

Yosef had to do everything in his power to make his dreams come true, because they weren't just dreams, they were prophecies from Hashem.

He had to arrange for Binyamin to come to Egypt so all eleven brothers would bow to him, like in his first dream. So far, since Binyamin was not in Egypt, only ten brothers had bowed down to him.

closed behind him he cried, tears running down his face. When he was able to stop crying, he washed the tears from his face and went back to his brothers.

Yosef pointed at Shimon, and told seventy soldiers to put handcuffs on him and take him back to prison. When they tried to put their hands on Shimon, he let out a mighty roar. Its power made the soldiers fall over and they ran off in terror.

Yosef turned to his son Menashe and said, "You do it." Menashe closed in on Shimon, hit him hard on his back with his fist, and brought Shimon to jail.

Yosef told the brothers, "He stays in prison until you come back with your youngest brother."

Surprise!

Yosef ordered that the brothers' bags be filled with food and that they be given food to eat for the trip back. The brothers put the bags of food on their donkeys and left Egypt.

Yosef gave another order. He told his assistants to take the money that the brothers paid for the food and hide it in their bags.

At the end of a day of travel through the desert, the brothers stopped at a hotel for the night. Levi opened his bags to feed his donkey and found the money.

Surprised, he told his brothers, "My money has been returned! Here it is in my bag!"

The brothers grew very frightened. This could only mean that they would be in more trouble. Someone had put the money there so they would be accused of being thieves, of taking food without paying. They looked in their other bags — and all the money was there. They would all be in big trouble!

Home at Last

What was supposed to be a simple trip to buy food had turned into a nightmare. They'd been accused of spying, had been put in prison, and their brother was being held hostage!

Yaakov heard his sons returning, and he went out to welcome them. He looked them over anxiously. Where was Shimon?

His sons told him about all the horrible things that had happened to them in Egypt. They gave him the awful news: Shimon was being held as a hostage by Egypt's ruler. He would not be set free until they brought Binyamin to Egypt. And when they'd unloaded their bags of food, they'd found that their money had been returned!

QUESTIONS, ANYONE?

Why did Yosef pick Shimon, and not one of the other brothers?

Yosef wanted to separate Shimon and Levi. Together they were dangerous and they might try to kill him. He remembered what Shimon and Levi had done to the city of Shechem. They'd destroyed it! Shimon was also the one who had pushed Yosef into the pit before the brothers sold him.

FASCINATING FACTS

As soon as the brothers left, Yosef took Shimon out of prison. During his entire stay in Egypt, until his brothers came back with Binyamin, Yosef gave Shimon food and drink and took care of him. Shimon was quite puzzled. *What kind of a viceroy is this?* he wondered. *He puts me in prison and then takes me out.* But Shimon never guessed the viceroy was his brother Yosef!

Yosef Is Gone! Shimon Is Gone!

The brothers wanted to return to Egypt with Binyamin so they could free their brother Shimon. Yaakov was suspicious. Something was wrong. He had sent Yosef to them and he had never returned. He sent Shimon with them to Egypt and he never returned. Now Yaakov was afraid. What if he would send Binyamin and he wouldn't come back either!

"Yosef is gone," he told them. "Shimon is gone! Now you want to take Binyamin?"

His oldest son, Reuven, tried to persuade him. "Put him in my care and I will bring him back. If I don't bring him back, you can punish two of my sons."

Yaakov said, "Aren't your sons my sons? What kind of thing is that to say? Do I want to hurt my grandchildren?"

And then he added firmly, "I will not send my son with you."

Well, that was that. No one would disagree with their father!

Yehudah told his brothers, "Don't worry, when there will be no food left, our father will have to send Binyamin."

No Food

The hunger in Eretz Yisrael got worse and worse. Now even Yaakov's family was low in food. Yaakov called the brothers together and told them to go back to Egypt and buy food.

Yehudah spoke up. "Without Binyamin we can't go. The viceroy told us not to return without Binyamin."

Yehudah said, "Whether Binyamin comes back or not is only a maybe. But if we don't go to buy food we will all surely die. Send Binyamin with me, I will be responsible for him. I guarantee his return. If I don't bring him back, then I will lose my share in the World to Come, my Olam Haba."

Hearing that, Yaakov agreed to let Binyamin go.

Gifts

Yaakov thought it would be a good idea to send gifts to the viceroy. Maybe he would treat his sons better. He instructed the brothers to take gifts for the viceroy. They took expensive items including top-quality honey, the oil of pistachio nuts, and almond oil.

To pay for the food they hoped to bring back, they took twice as much money as they took the first time, just in case prices had gone up. They also took the money that they had found in their bags, to return to the viceroy.

TORAH IN OUR LIVES

Sometimes we work very hard, staying up late studying for a big test, practicing for hours to win a big game or to perform in a production.

You wonder: Are you ready? Have you done enough?

The answer is: That depends.

The brothers worked hard on their preparation, but they knew they weren't ready unless Yaakov prayed for Hashem's help.

No matter how hard we work to succeed, to be ready we also need to ask for Hashem's help. So are you ready to take the test, play the game, or perform in the production?

It depends.

Hard work and prayers — you're ready.

Hard work alone — you're not ready.

QUESTIONS, ANYONE?

In Yaakov's prayer, he used a special Name of Hashem (Sha-dai) that means, "He Who said to the world, 'dai,' enough!" This Name means that Hashem has the power to create the world and then to tell the world, "Enough! Stop getting bigger and bigger."

Why did Yaakov use this Name of Hashem?

Yaakov had suffered so much in his life. He'd suffered from his brother Eisav and his father-in-law Lavan. Rachel had died. Yosef was gone, now Shimon was gone. And now he was sending another son into danger.

In this prayer Yaakov was begging Hashem: "Enough! Please bring my suffering to an end!"

What Else?

The brothers were ready to go.

"What else do you need?" Yaakov asked.

He was very pleased to hear their answer.

"We need your prayers for our success."

Yaakov prayed for them. "Hashem should make the man (he meant the ruler, little knowing it was his own son!) have mercy on you and release your brother (Shimon) and Binyamin."

Is It a Trap?

With Yaakov's blessing for success, the brothers returned to Egypt. They were once again brought before Yosef in the palace.

When Yosef saw them he told Menashe to bring the brothers to his house, and to tell the servants to prepare a fine feast. When the brothers were being brought to Yosef's home they were scared. They believed it was a trap. Once in Yosef's palace they would be ambushed, robbed, and turned into slaves. They were afraid this would be the punishment for not paying for the food they had bought the last time.

At the entrance of the palace, Menashe tried to persuade them to enter. They wouldn't do it.

To protect themselves and to find out if Menashe was trying to trap them, they told him, "On our way home, we stopped over at a hotel. When we opened our bags we found the money we had used to pay for the food. We don't know who put it there, but we brought it back to pay you."

Menashe said, "Be at peace. What you found was a treasure your G-d has given you."

The Dream Comes True!

Once Menashe wished them peace they knew that they were safe, and they entered Yosef's house.

They had a wonderful reunion with their brother Shimon, when Menashe brought him out to join them. The brothers were surprised at the way Shimon looked. They had worried that while Shimon was in jail he wouldn't get much food. But he looked great! While Shimon was in Egypt, Yosef had fed him well.

While waiting for Yosef, the brothers refreshed themselves. They arranged the gifts they'd brought in attractive jars so they would look even more impressive.

Yosef walked into the room and the brothers presented him with the gifts. Then — just as Yosef had seen in his dream so many years before — all of his eleven brothers bowed down to him. The first dream had come true!

Yosef and Binyamin

Yosef greeted the brothers and asked how their father was. They answered that he was still alive and doing well. Then they bowed to Yosef again!

Yosef saw Binyamin. After asking the brothers if this was the youngest brother they had talked about, he blessed him. The blessing was that Hashem should be kind to him.

Seeing Binyamin, his baby brother, Yosef wanted to find out all about him. He asked Binyamin, "Do you have a brother from your mother?"

"Yes, but I don't know where he is."

"Do you have sons?"

"Yes. Ten of them, and they are all named after my lost brother."

Yosef was so emotional over his brother's love for him that he had to cry. He quickly left to another room where he broke down, and the tears came pouring down his face.

Yosef forced himself to stop crying, washed his face, and went out to start the meal.

Binyamin's 10 Children

Binyamin never wanted to forget his lost brother, so he gave his sons names that would remind him of Yosef. Below are what the names he gave them meant:

- **Bela** — He was swallowed up by the nations. That is, he was lost.
- **Becher** — He was my mother's firstborn.
- **Ashbel** — Hashem made him a prisoner.
- **Gera** — He lives in a foreign land.
- **Naaman** — My brother was very pleasant.
- **Echi** — He was my brother.
- **Rosh** — He was my leader.
- **Muppim** — He studied Torah from my father.
- **Chupim** — He wasn't at my chupah, and I wasn't at his.
- **Ard** — He went down to be lost among the nations.

A Test

The time still hadn't come for Yosef to reveal his identity to his brothers.

There was a test the brothers needed to pass before Yosef could reveal who he was. Did the brothers' love for one another include even Rachel's son Binyamin? If Yosef treated Binyamin better than the others, would they be jealous of their youngest brother? If Binyamin got into trouble, would they defend him? Would they risk their lives for him?

Yosef had a plan to find out! He would get Binyamin in trouble and see what the brothers would do about it.

Take a Seat

Like all good guests, the brothers waited for their host to seat them around the table. Yosef looked into his silver cup decorated with jewels and tapped it. He then looked up and said, "Reuven, Shimon, Levi, Yehudah, Yissaschar, and Zevulun. You are the children of one mother. Sit down in the order I called your names. It's your birth order." He tapped the "magic" cup, again and again, seating the brothers around the table in birth order, grouped according to their mothers.

The brothers were astonished. How did he know? It seemed that Yosef's magic cup knew all about them!

When it was Binyamin's turn to be seated Yosef said, "You have no mother, and I don't either. Sit next to me."

Binyamin sat at the head of the table with Yosef and his family. Yosef's wife knew that the people in the room were her brothers-in-law and her children's uncles. Yosef had already told his family the secret of who these special guests were!

FASCINATING FACTS

At the meal, the brothers did something they hadn't done for twenty-two years. They drank wine. Out of sorrow for what they had done to Yosef, they hadn't drunk wine all that time. Yosef, too, had not drunk wine, since he was so sad because he was away from his family.

But since they were eating with the ruler of Egypt, the brothers couldn't refuse to drink his wine. And because Yosef was reunited with his brothers, he had no reason not to drink wine anymore.

Dessert!

The meal was not just a plain meal, it was a royal banquet. At the end of the meal, they served many desserts. A heaping tray of fancy desserts and exotic fruits was placed before Yosef. He passed out the desserts to all the brothers, and then to himself and his family.

The empty platter was removed. But Yosef hadn't finished yet. He honored Binyamin by passing him his own plate of desserts. When Yosef's wife and sons saw what he did, they did it too, showing respect and honor to his brother.

Binyamin was sitting in front of five portions of dessert!

Hide It

Yosef told his son Menashe, "Fill the brothers' bags with food and put their money in their bags, as well."

Yosef then took his magic silver cup and gave it to Menashe. "Hide this in Binyamin's bag," he told him.

The next morning the brothers took their bags and loaded their animals. Happy that everything had gone so well, they rode their animals out into the desert, leaving Egypt and starting their journey home.

They hadn't traveled very far. The city walls were still in sight behind them. Suddenly the silence of the desert was broken by loud noises, the sound of hoof beats made by galloping horses.

Startled by the noise, the brothers turned around. Coming out of a cloud of sand they saw Menashe riding in front of a group of soldiers. They were coming straight at them!

The brothers stopped, allowing Menashe and his soldiers to catch up with them.

Accused

Yosef had told him to chase after the brothers and ask them, "Why have you repaid good with evil? How could you take the viceroy's magic cup, which he uses to see what's hidden and secret?"

"How could you say such a thing?" the brothers replied. "We would never do something like that! We even returned the money we found in our bags from our last trip. How could you accuse us of stealing anything?"

Arrested

The brothers knew they hadn't stolen the cup. To show Menashe how sure they were that none of them had done it, they said, "If you find it, then the one who has it should be put to death. The rest of us will become your slaves!"

Menashe said, "That won't be necessary. I will be merciful. The one who has it will become a slave. The rest of you will go free."

Menashe demanded to search their bags.

Surrounded by soldiers, the brothers took their bags off the animals, placing them on the ground. Menashe opened each of the brothers' bags. He started with Reuven, and then went to Shimon, searching the bags of each of the brothers according to their age, from oldest to youngest.

Menashe finally reached the bags of the youngest brother, Binyamin. Going through Binyamin's bags, Menashe lifted something out for all to see. It was the silver cup!

Menashe wasn't surprised. After all, he had put it there himself. But the brothers were in shock. They knew their brother hadn't stolen the cup. They realized the viceroy was out to get them, and they were in big trouble.

They were arrested.

The brothers loaded their animals and sadly followed Menashe back to Egypt. They were brought straight to Yosef, who was waiting for them.

TORAH IN OUR LIVES

We see from the story of Yosef and his brothers how terrible it is when brothers don't get along. The Torah is sending us a strong message — we can hear it if we really want to.

A Jew is a Jew. It doesn't matter if he is Sephardi or Ashkenazi, from this yeshivah or that yeshivah. Satmar, Bobov, Breslov or any other Chassidic group. We are all brothers and sisters, and we have to treat each other with love and respect.

How do your parents feel when you fight with your siblings? Hashem is the Father of us all. We give Him the greatest pleasure when He sees His children getting along.

He Stays Behind as My Slave

The brothers bowed to Yosef.

"What have you done?" Yosef accused them. "Don't you know this is my valuable magic cup?"

Yehudah said, "We didn't steal it, but we know that this is a punishment from Hashem for a sin we did long ago. We accept the punishment and we will all be your slaves."

"That wouldn't be fair," Yosef answered. "I wouldn't do such a thing! You're all free to go, except for the man in whose bag the cup was found. He stays here as my slave."

Yosef was testing the brothers. Had they really done teshuvah for selling him? Were they prepared to treat their brother with love, even though he was Rachel's son? Would they be willing to risk their lives to save him from becoming a slave?

End of the Parashah

The parashah has ended, but the story is not over. Will Yehudah save Binyamin from slavery? Will Yaakov ever see Binyamin again? What will happen to the brothers? Will Yosef finally tell them who he is?

We'll find out ... in the next parashah!

פָּרָשַׁת וַיִּגַּשׁ

Parashas Vayigash

Vayigash • וַיִּגַּשׁ

Parashah Pointers

- Yehudah tries to convince the viceroy — who, unknown to them, is Yosef — to let Binyamin go free.
- Yosef reveals that he is their brother.
- Pharaoh learns that Yosef's brothers have come and tells Yosef to invite his family to move to Egypt.
- Yosef gives his brothers gifts and clothes.
- Yaakov is told that Yosef is alive.
- Yaakov and his family travel to Egypt.
- Yosef and his father meet for the first time in 22 years.
- Yaakov and his family move to Goshen.
- Yaakov visits Pharaoh and blesses him.
- The Egyptians run out of money to buy food. Yosef makes them pay Pharaoh with their animals, land, and, taxes.
- Yaakov's family becomes very rich. They own a lot of land in Goshen and have very large families.

Yehudah Argues

Yaakov's sons stood in front of Pharaoh's second in command, who, of course, was their brother Yosef, though they didn't know that. Yosef told his brothers, "The rest of you are free to go, but Binyamin stays here with me." Yehudah, who was king of the shevatim, stepped forward. He was going to force Yosef to free Binyamin and let him return to their father, Yaakov.

First, Yehudah warned Yosef that many years ago Pharaoh had kidnapped their great-grandmother Sarah, and he had been punished for it. He said that he and his brothers were powerful warriors. After all, they had fought against the entire city of Shechem and destroyed it.

Yehudah then reviewed everything that happened up to this point. How they had come to Egypt to buy food, and at their meeting, Yosef had told them not to come back to Egypt without their younger brother.

Now, Yehudah pleaded with Yosef, "If we return without our brother, our father will die. I swore to my father that I would bring him back safely. Take me as a slave, but let Binyamin go free."

Yosef asked Yehudah, "Why, of all the brothers, are you doing all the talking?"

"Because I told our father that I guarantee to bring him back."

Yosef said, "Why didn't you speak up for your brother Yosef, when you sold him to the Yishmaelites for twenty pieces of silver?" (The brothers thought Yosef knew this because of his "magic cup.")

Preparing for Battle

Yehudah, realizing Yosef was not being convinced, became angry. Really angry. Seeing Yehudah's anger, the other brothers joined him in a show of strength. They stamped their feet, and the floor beneath them cracked from their powerful blows.

Yosef decided to show them his own extraordinary strength. He kicked a stone pillar. Before the brothers' eyes it crumbled into pebbles.

Seeing what Yosef had done, Yehudah said, "He is stronger than I am!" Still, Yehudah was willing to risk a fight that he would probably lose. He would take a chance that he would be killed, if he could only save his brother Binyamin.

Yehudah tried to pull out the sword that was hanging at his side and begin the battle. He pulled and pulled at it, but the sword wouldn't come out. Yehudah realized that Hashem hadn't allowed the sword to come out. It must have been because Yosef was a G-d-fearing man, and Yehudah would have no power over him.

Naphtali was the fastest runner of the brothers. Yehudah told him to run through the city and tell him how many markets there were. Naphtali

Questions, Anyone?

Yehudah explained to Yosef that his father and Binyamin were "keshurah," connected to each other. What made Yaakov so very close to Binyamin?

The Hebrew word for "connected," keshurah, has the gematria of 611 — the same number as the word "Torah." It was the Torah that they learned together that made them so close.

Fascinating Facts

We think of Binyamin as the "baby brother," but at the time of this story he was 33 years old, married, and had ten children! Each of his children was named to remind Binyamin of his lost brother Yosef.

raced away and quickly returned to Yosef's palace. He reported to Yehudah that he had found twelve major markets.

Yehudah told his brothers, "We will go and destroy them!"

Yosef listened into the brothers' plans. He understood Hebrew, so he realized that Egypt was in grave danger. He asked Pharaoh to send help. Pharaoh sent three hundred soldiers, but they didn't scare Yehudah. When the soldiers approached, Yehudah gave out a loud yell. The force of his yell threw both Yosef and Pharaoh off their thrones. The three hundred soldiers? Their teeth fell out and they ran away in fright.

Yosef Drops His Disguise

At this point Yosef realized that he had to reveal who he really was or Egypt would be destroyed! But first, so that his brothers would not be shamed in front of others, he ordered, "Guards, slaves, leave the room at once!"

Yosef and his brothers were alone in the room.

Yosef said, "Didn't you say that the brother of your youngest brother is dead? You are liars. I will call him to come here!"

Yosef called out in a loud voice, "Yosef, son of Yaakov, come here."

The brothers looked around. Would their lost brother really appear?

No one came.

He then asked his brothers, "What are you looking around for? I AM YOSEF! Is our father still alive?"

The brothers couldn't say a word. They were totally shocked! Yosef? Pharaoh's second-in-command?! They couldn't believe it.

To prove his identity Yosef showed them that he had a bris milah and he spoke to them in Hebrew. That did it. Now the brothers were sure that this man was their brother, Yosef.

Yosef Explains

Yosef told them, "Don't feel bad that you sold me to Egypt. Hashem sent me here, and He made me ruler over Egypt, so I could save you all from starvation. Hurry home. Tell our father that I said Hashem has made me a ruler over Egypt. Come to Egypt and you will live in Goshen. Bring your children, grandchildren, and everything you have. There will still be five more years of hunger. I will feed all of you and no one will starve."

An Emotional Reunion

Finally Yosef broke down. He put his head on Binyamin's neck, gave him a big hug, and cried. Binyamin did the same.

When Yosef was talking to them, his brothers just stood there, in

TORAH IN OUR LIVES

Everything was so confusing and mysterious to the brothers. How did Yosef know everything about them and their lives? Then, with just three words, "I am Yosef," it all became clear. All their questions were answered.

The same way, when Mashiach comes, all he will have to say is, "I am Mashiach," and all the questions we ever had will be answered.

FASCINATING FACTS

When Yosef revealed his identity, the brothers actually died from shame and embarrassment at having sold Yosef. Hashem brought them back to life!

TORAH IN OUR LIVES

In the story of Yosef and his brothers, we see what a great man Yosef was. His brothers sold him and he became a slave and a prisoner, and for many years had no contact with his father and family. Yet after all that, he forgave his brothers!

If Yosef could forgive his brothers for the terrible thing they did to him, can't we forgive others for the not-so-terrible things they do to us (like when your brother or sister takes your stuff without your permission)?

shock, ashamed of what they had done. They were not sure what to say or how to react. Had Yosef forgiven them for what they had done? Did he still love them? Would he act toward them as a brother?

Yosef broke their silence. He lovingly kissed each of his brothers, crying with joy that they were together again.

When they saw that Yosef wasn't angry at them, they came out of their shock. They began talking with Yosef, the way brothers speak with one another.

Pharaoh's Offer

The news spread like wildfire throughout the palace and Egypt. The second most powerful man in Egypt wasn't a slave after all. He came from an important and famous family.

Pharaoh ordered his guards to bring Yosef to him. Pharaoh told him that he should tell his brothers to move their father, their families, and households to Egypt. Pharaoh promised to give them the best land in Egypt: Goshen. He would also give him the best Egypt has to offer.

Pharaoh was so excited about having Yosef's family in Egypt, he even gave them wagons to use to bring their belongings to Egypt!

Parting Gifts

Before the brothers left to go back home, Yosef gave each of them a suit of expensive clothing. Binyamin got even more. Yosef gave him three hundred silver coins and five expensive suits.

Yosef sent a gift for his father as well. Ten donkeys were loaded with aged wine and a special kind of Egyptian bean. These are foods that were a favorite of elderly people, because it makes them feel relaxed. Another ten donkeys were loaded with other foods.

Travel Instructions

Yosef knew his brothers would be hurrying home. He told them not to travel at night and not to travel too fast, because that was dangerous. Also, he told them not to argue about whose idea it was to sell Yosef.

Yosef was afraid that his brothers would discuss questions of Jewish law while traveling. They might get into a Torah argument and lose track of where they were going, or they might make a wrong turn and get lost. Their trip would take much longer! He begged them not to get involved in deep Torah discussions while they were traveling, and just keep the Torah discussions easy and simple for safety reasons.

Fascinating Facts

Yosef cried from joy over being able to hug his younger brother after so many years. But there was also another reason. The Beis HaMikdash was built on land that belonged to Binyamin's shevet. Yosef saw that in the future both of the Batei Mikdash would be destroyed.

Binyamin cried because he saw that the Mishkan of Shiloh, which was in the land belonging to Yosef's shevet, would be destroyed.

When Yehudah saw the wagons that Pharaoh sent, he burnt them! Why did he destroy them? The wagons had images of idols on them. Yosef then replaced the wagons with new ones that had no idol images on them.

Questions, Anyone?

Why did Binyamin get five sets of clothing?

This was a hint to something that would happen in the future. Mordechai, the hero of the Purim story, was a descendant of Binyamin. And he, too, would one day wear five sets of clothing.

After Haman was hanged, Achashveirosh gave Mordechai permission to wear five types of royal clothing: one blue garment, one white, one purple, a crown, and a linen robe.

Beautiful Music, Great News

The brothers returned to Eretz Yisrael. They were very excited about telling Yaakov that Yosef was still alive. The question was how to break the news to him.

At the time Yaakov was 130 years old. The brothers were afraid to surprise him and say, "Guess who we found alive? Yosef!" The shock of hearing that, after so many years of believing Yosef was dead, could kill a man of Yaakov's age!

What to do?

The brothers decided they had to prepare Yaakov for the news. They sent Yaakov's granddaughter Serach, Asher's daughter, to do the job. How? Serach came to Yaakov's tent, carrying a harp. She played her instrument and sang a song with the words, "Yosef is still alive." This was a gentle way of preparing Yaakov.

Slowly Yaakov began to understand what Serach was singing about. The brothers then came in and told him the great news: Yosef is alive and is ruler of Egypt.

Is It True?

Even though Yaakov had heard Serach's song, and the brothers had told him that Yosef was alive, Yaakov wasn't sure he could believe them. They had told him that Yosef had been killed by animals. Now they were saying Yosef was alive. Which story was true?

WHO'S WHO IN THE TORAH

Serach

Since Serach was the first one to give Yaakov the good news about Yosef, he gave her a blessing. He blessed her that she would live forever! And indeed, Serach never died. She lived for a very, very long time, and she went straight to heaven without dying.

Before Yosef died, he asked the Jews to promise to take his coffin with them when they left Egypt. When the time came to leave Egypt, no one knew where Yosef had been buried. Moshe Rabbeinu went to Serach, who had been there when Yosef died. She remembered Yosef's funeral and told Moshe where he would find Yosef's remains.

Serach was still on this earth in the time of King David. That was 650 years after she told Yaakov that Yosef was still alive!

TORAH IN OUR LIVES

During the entire time – 22 years — that Yosef was away from his father, Yaakov was sad. Because he was sad, he could not have the high level of Hashem's Presence that he used to have. Once Yaakov found out that Yosef was alive, he became happy again. Then Hashem's Presence returned.

The happier we are, the closer we feel to Hashem, and the closer Hashem is to us. And that's a good reason to be happy with what **we have**, instead of being sad and complaining about things we **don't have**.

Next time you see an advertisement for something you don't have, don't be sad because you don't have it. Think about all you do have — and be happy!

And even if Yosef was alive, Yaakov wondered, was he still a tzaddik? Had he become like an Egyptian in the way he talked and acted? Did he still believe in Hashem?

The Message

At first, the brothers didn't get the reaction they expected. Yaakov didn't seem happy to hear his son was alive, because he wasn't sure Yosef was still a tzaddik. Then they told him that Yosef had sent a special message.

When Yaakov heard the message, he knew the news was true! Imagine Yaakov's joy at that moment.

He said, "Yosef is alive! I will go and see him before I die."

What was the message that made Yaakov suddenly believe that his son was alive and still a good Jew?

Yosef knew that he had to send his father proof that he still believed in Hashem. How could he do that? By letting Yaakov know that he still remembered the last thing in the Torah they learned together. That was something only the real Yosef could know.

The last thing they had learned together were the laws of Eglah Arufah* So Yosef told his brothers to send agalos, wagons, and to tell Yaakov that he had learned those laws with him right before he disappeared, and he still remembered them.

Yaakov realized that if Yosef had become like the Egyptians, he would not have sent a message about Torah learning.

The Time Has Come

Hashem had promised Avraham that sometime in the future his descendants would go into exile. There they would become slaves in a foreign country.

Yaakov realized that the time for exile had come. He and his family were leaving Eretz Yisrael and going to live in Egypt.

It's All Yours

Yaakov and his eleven sons and their families packed all they owned. They left their homes and set out on their journey to Egypt.

Yaakov took only the wealth that he had made during the time he lived in Eretz Yisrael. He didn't want the wealth he had earned while he lived with Lavan. Those earnings didn't have the holiness of the Holy Land.

* *The law of eglah arufah is about what to do if a murder victim is discovered between two cities and the killer can't be found. The Torah describes what has to be done by the Jewish court of the city closest to where the murder victim was found. Part of the procedure is the killing of a young calf.*

Yaakov piled up everything he'd earned outside of Eretz Yisrael and showed the pile to Eisav. "It's all yours," he told his twin brother, "if only you let me have your burial plot in Me'aras HaMachpeilah."

When Yitzchak died there were two burial plots left in Me'aras HaMachpeilah. One plot was for Yaakov and one for Eisav. Yaakov did not want Eisav buried in such a holy place, and he also wanted a plot for his wife, Leah. (His wife Rachel had already died and was buried near Beis Lechem.) So Yaakov decided to buy Eisav's plot. He would use the fortune he had made when he lived with Lavan.

Eisav took one look at the pile of glittering gold and silver, and he agreed to the deal. Right away!

Trees

On the way to Egypt, Yaakov and his family stopped in Beersheva. They went there to pick up something very important to take with them to Egypt: cedar trees.

Avraham himself had planted the trees. He planted them so they could be used hundreds of years later to build the Mishkan. By the time Yaakov arrived in Goshen the trees were very tall and wide. They had been growing for almost two hundred years!

Yaakov had them cut down and loaded on the wagons. These trees would go to Egypt with them. There they stayed in storage for 211 years.** During all that time the Jews protected them. Even in the darkest times, when the slavery was at its worst, the Jews protected those trees. They never lost hope that Hashem would one day take them out of Egypt. They knew that on that day they would take the trees with them — to build the Mishkan.

Worried

In Beersheva, Yaakov prayed to Hashem. He was worried about what would happen to his family while they were exiled in Egypt. In answer to his prayers, Hashem appeared to him and told him: "Don't be afraid of going to Egypt. You will become a great nation there. I will go down with you to Egypt. (This means, "I will be with the Jews in Egypt, watching over them.") I will bring you back to Eretz Yisrael to be buried."

Once again the family got back on their camels, wagons, and donkeys to finish their journey to Egypt.

Yaakov was concerned. When they got to Egypt, where would they live? They needed a home. A place where they could build their own Jewish community, a place that would protect them from the influence

Why did Yaakov pray specifically in Beersheva?

Hashem had appeared to his father Yitzchak in Beersheva, and his father had prayed there. Yaakov knew that if that's where his father prayed and Hashem appeared, it must be a special place to pray.

*** The Jews were in Egypt for 210 years, and there was one more year until they built the Mishkan.*

of idol-worshiping Egyptians. They would need a place to study Torah, a yeshivah where their children could learn.

Who could he send ahead to set all this up before the whole family arrived?

Yaakov decided to send Yehudah. After all, he was the one whose descendants would be kings of the Jews.

Mazel Tov!

Finally, after days and days of travel, the land of Egypt came into sight. Their journey was almost over!

To the Egyptian border guards looking out over the desert sands, Yaakov and his family must have been quite a sight. A long, slow-moving caravan of donkeys and camels. Flocks of sheep and goats. Wagons piled high with bundles. Men, women, and children of all ages.

The caravan began to pass through the Egyptian city gates. One of the wagons suddenly stopped, right in the gates. A few moments later there was the sound of a newborn baby crying. It was Levi's wagon. His wife had just given birth to a beautiful baby girl, just as they entered Egypt's border. The news spread up and down the caravan. Yaakov smiled, a big smile, when he heard the news about his new granddaughter. Cries of mazel tov could be heard in the air.

Moshe's mother, Yocheved, had just been born!

Yaakov and his family, a total of 70 people, had finally arrived in Egypt. They went straight to Goshen where Yehudah had prepared places for them to live and, of course, a yeshivah in which to learn.

Yosef and the Horses

After Pharaoh, Yosef was the richest and most powerful man in Egypt. Imagine how many servants he had! But when Yosef found out that his father had arrived, he went to the stables and tied the horses to his best chariot. He wanted to go out and meet Yaakov. And he did it all himself, out of love of his father, and because he knew he would do it faster than any servant.

Yosef Welcomes His Father

Yosef put on his most beautiful robes. He got on his chariot and drove through the city to greet his father and family. The second most powerful man in Egypt doesn't travel alone! His bodyguards and important officers went with him. When they passed Pharaoh's palace, more officials saw Yosef go by, and they joined him. After all, if the viceroy was going somewhere, they wanted to go with him!

Questions, Anyone?

The Torah lists the names of the people that came to Egypt with Yaakov, all his children and grandchildren. Including Yosef and his sons, who were already in Egypt, there are 69 names.

But the Torah says 70 people went down to Egypt! Who is the seventieth one?

There are numerous opinions:

Hashem, Who went with them to Egypt to watch over them.

Yocheved, who was born just as they arrived.

Yaakov who led them down into Egypt.

Torah in our Lives

Sometimes it's not easy to do the jobs and errands our parents ask us to do. We might persuade one of our brothers or sisters to do it instead. Not a good idea. Be a tzaddik like Yosef and do it yourself!

As this parade of important people went by, the Egyptians went along as well, to see what all the excitement was about.

Imagine the scene. Yosef, dressed royally, on his chariot. Spread out behind him were more chariots, pulled by galloping horses, carrying generals and important members of the government. Following them was a huge crowd of Egyptians.

When they reached Yaakov, Yosef's chariot came to a stop. The whole parade stopped too. What a great welcome Yaakov was given when he arrived in Egypt! What honor they showed him!

Shema Yisrael!

Yosef ran to Yaakov, whom he hadn't seen for so long. Hugging him, Yosef couldn't stop crying. Tears of happiness streamed down his face.

While Yosef was embracing his father, Yaakov covered his eyes with his hand and said the words of Shema Yisrael, which includes the words of "ve'ahavta," the mitzvah to love Hashem.

Yaakov poured out all his feelings, all the love he had for Hashem, Who had given him back his beloved Yosef. He put all those feelings into the words of Shema. He used his feelings of great happiness to serve Hashem, by doing the mitzvah to love Hashem with great love and joy.

The Family Meets Pharaoh

Yosef chose his five weakest brothers to meet Pharaoh. Why the weakest? Yosef didn't want to introduce Pharaoh to the strongest brothers. He was afraid that Pharaoh would want to make them soldiers in his army.

Pharaoh asked them, "What do you do for a living?" They answered him, "We are shepherds."

Pharaoh told Yosef to settle his father and brothers in Goshen. Yosef then brought his father Yaakov to meet Pharaoh. Pharaoh saw a man who looked very old standing before him.

"How old are you?" Pharaoh asked.

Yaakov answered, "I am 130, and I have had a hard life."

Even though 130 is quite old, Yaakov looked even older than he was, because of all the troubles he had with Lavan and Eisav.

The Blessing

Then Yaakov blessed Pharaoh that whenever he would go to the Nile River, it would overflow.

Why is that a special blessing?

QUESTIONS, ANYONE?

Who were the weakest brothers that Yosef took to meet Pharaoh?

Reuven, Shimon, Levi, Yissaschar, and Binyamin.

FASCINATING FACTS

The Egyptians didn't like shepherds. They felt shepherds didn't have the proper respect for sheep. Who treats sheep with respect? The Egyptians did. Because sheep were their gods!

This blessing is very important because it hardly rains in Egypt. The Egyptian fields were watered when the Nile River would rise onto the land and water their fields.

Yaakov's blessing ensured that Egypt would have a lot of food. If crops aren't growing because the Nile didn't overflow — no problem! Pharaoh would visit the Nile, and then the water would rise and then water their fields.

As a result of Yaakov's blessing, the hunger in Egypt stopped. Instead of seven years of hunger that Pharaoh saw in his dream, there were only two.

Galus Begins

We have now read about how Yaakov and his family were forced to leave their beloved Eretz Yisrael.

It turns out that Yosef was sold by the brothers as part of Hashem's grand plan. The time had come when the Jews had to live in exile, just as Hashem had told Avraham. But Hashem did not want Yaakov to be dragged down to Egypt in chains! So Hashem arranged for Yaakov to go to Egypt in comfort and honor as a guest of Pharaoh.

Yaakov and his family built their community in Goshen. Yosef was a good son and brother, and he made things easier for them. As long as he was alive, Yosef provided all the food his father and the family needed.

But as time went by, Yaakov's family stopped feeling that they were in Egypt only as visitors, for a short time. They began to get too comfortable. They settled down as if they belonged in Egypt. They built homes and bought land.

A terrible mistake! They should have lived their lives as if they had one foot out the door, ready to go home to Eretz Yisrael as soon as they could — back to their real home.

Maaseh Avos Siman La'banim

Galus (Exile)

For much of our long history, the Jews have been in galus in countries all over the world.

In many countries, the exiles were like the one in Egypt. Here are some examples:

- Pharaoh invited Yaakov and his family to Egypt and treated them very well. In the end, however, Egypt turned the Jews into slaves and tried to destroy them. Many nations at first invited the Jews but later they made their lives miserable — maaseh avos siman la'banim — what happened to our forefathers, happened to their descendants.

  In the year 1343, King Casimir invited the Jews to come to Poland. They were treated pretty well for about three hundred years. After that, the Jews in Poland suffered terribly. In World War II many of the Polish people helped the Germans kill millions of their Jewish citizens.

In 1492, the sultan of the Ottoman Empire, Bayezid the Second, invited the Jews who had been thrown out of Spain and Portugal to come to his empire. They were treated well for about 200 years. Then many laws were made against the Jews.

In the 1800's Germany was one of the first countries in Europe to give the Jews civil rights. Jews from Poland and Russia, where Jews had no rights, were welcomed by Germany. The Jews did well and some of them even became leaders of government. And then, in 1932, the Nazis came to power. Germany became worse than Egypt. Jews became slaves and Germany murdered six million.

- Before Yaakov arrived in Egypt he sent Yehudah ahead to prepare a yeshivah where the family could learn Torah. Before Hashem sends Jews into exile He often sends tzaddikim first, to set up yeshivos and shuls for the Jews who will arrive later. Just like what happened in Egypt — maaseh avos siman la'banim.

Before the destruction of the First Beis HaMikdash, King Nevuchadnetzar of Bavel conquered Yerushalayim. He took some of the greatest talmidei chachamim to Bavel. Why did Hashem send them there before the destruction? So that yeshivos would be ready when the Jews were taken to Bavel after the destruction of the First Beis HaMikdash. Those talmidei chachamim who were taken to Bavel before the destruction were waiting to greet the exiles and help them.

Before World War II, the Torah centers of the world were in Europe. After the war, many Jews who survived the Holocaust went to a new exile: America. But many years before World War II, Hashem arranged for great men from the European Torah centers to move to America. They began to build Torah in America, so that when European Jews came after the war, there were already shuls and yeshivos waiting for them.

- When Yaakov and his family arrived in Egypt, Yosef arranged for them to live in Goshen, their own area. Here they could live together, away from Egyptian influence. When Jews are in exile they often live together in their own communities, just like they did in Egypt — maaseh avos siman la'banim.

Why do the Jews like to live together? Because in numbers there is strength. Living together helps us to stay true to the Torah. We can help each other resist ideas that are against the Torah.

No More Money

Before Yaakov came to Egypt there were two years of hunger. What was going on in Egypt during that time? Now, at the end of the parashah, the Torah tells us.

The hunger hit Egypt hard. There was no food, except the food Yosef had collected and stored during the years of plenty.

Now Yosef began selling food. It wasn't long before Yosef had all the money in Egypt. He put that money into Pharaoh's treasuries.

No one had any more money to buy food. The Egyptians were desperate. Without money they would starve! They came and begged Yosef for food. "Give us bread! Why should we die of hunger because we have no money?"

Yosef said, "I'll sell you food in exchange for your animals."

By the end of the first year of hunger, Pharaoh owned all the money in Egypt — and all the animals as well!

Year Two of Hunger

By the second year the Egyptians had no money and no animals left. What now? They sold their land to Pharaoh, and they also sold themselves, becoming Pharaoh's servants.

Now that all of Egypt and its wealth belonged to Pharaoh, Yosef removed the Egyptian population from their homes and made them move to new places. People who had lived in the same towns for generations were forced to move somewhere else.

Yosef did this to make sure the Egyptians understood that the land they lived on wasn't theirs anymore. They had sold it all to Pharaoh. Yosef did this so that the Egyptians should not call his brothers exiles, for they, too, were exiles.

FASCINATING FACTS

The Gemara tells us the reason we eat romaine lettuce as maror on Pesach. When romaine lettuce starts growing it tastes sweet, but later the leaves turn bitter. Just like the Egyptian exile. It started with sweetness, and an invitation from Pharaoh, but it ended with bitter slavery.

Grateful

After Yaakov came to Egypt, the hunger ended. The land once again grew crops. Yosef gave everyone seeds to plant, and he made a law that 20 percent of whatever grew had to be given to Pharaoh's treasuries.

The people of Egypt were very grateful to Yosef for saving them from dying of hunger.

פָּרָשַׁת וַיְחִי

Parashas Vayechi

Vayechi • וַיְחִי

Parashah Pointers

- Yaakov is very old. He asks Yosef to make sure he will be buried in Me'aras HaMachpeilah. Yosef swears that he will do what his father has asked him.

- Yosef is told that his father, Yaakov, is very sick. Together with his sons, Menashe and Ephraim, Yosef goes to visit him.

- Yaakov makes Menashe and Ephraim equal in status to his own children. They will be treated like the other shevatim. When Eretz Yisrael is divided up among the shevatim, the shevatim of Menashe and Ephraim will each get a portion.

- Yaakov blesses Menashe and Ephraim by putting his hands on their heads. Yaakov crosses his arms so that his right hand rests on the head of Ephraim, the younger brother. His left hand rests on Menashe, the older brother.

- Yosef tries to uncross his father's hands. Yaakov stops him. He explains that he was blessing Ephraim with his right hand because Ephraim's descendants will be greater than Menashe's.

- Yaakov promises that the angel who saved him from his problems will bless Yosef's children. They will have many, many descendants, as many as the fish in the sea.
- Yaakov gives Yosef the city of Shechem.
- Yaakov calls together his 12 sons to bless them before he dies.
- After blessing his sons, Yaakov passes away at the age of 147. He had lived peacefully in Egypt for 17 years.
- Yosef asks Pharaoh for permission to bury Yaakov in Eretz Yisrael. Pharaoh approves, and Yosef arranges for his father's funeral. The whole family goes. Yaakov is laid to rest in Me'aras HaMachpeilah.
- When they return to Egypt, his brothers ask Yosef to forgive them for having sold him. He tells them that as things turned out, "It was a good thing I was sold." As leader of Egypt, Yosef was able to prevent many people from dying of hunger. He wholeheartedly forgives his brothers.
- Before Yosef dies, he calls his brothers together and tells them that Hashem will take their descendants out of Egypt and bring them to Eretz Yisrael.
- Yosef asks his brothers to swear that when the Jews leave Egypt they will take his bones out with them and bury them in Eretz Yisrael.
- Yosef dies at the age of 110. He is laid to rest in a casket that was placed in the Nile River.

Mystery of the Missing Spaces

The parashah begins with a mystery. Most other parshiyos in the Torah scroll are separated from the previous parashah by a space. Sometimes, the parashah begins on a new line. But Parashas Vayechi begins right after Parashas Vayigash, with no space between them. That doesn't happen anywhere else in the Torah.

What happened to the extra space between parshiyos?

There's no space because Hashem wanted Parashas Vayechi to be called a "closed parashah," to tell us that on the last day of his life, Yaakov wanted to tell his sons when Mashiach would come. But Hashem "closed off" Yaakov's ability to see the future, so he couldn't tell them.

Another answer is that this is a hint that when Yaakov passed away the eyes and hearts of the Jews were "closed," because with Yaakov's death, exile in Egypt started getting worse and worse.*

Funeral Arrangements

Yaakov was now very, very old. He realized it was time for him to make preparations for his funeral. There was only one place he wanted to be buried: in Me'aras HaMachpeilah, where his parents, grandparents, and his wife Leah were buried.

Yaakov knew that Pharaoh would want him to be buried in Egypt. The Egyptians knew he was a powerful and holy man, because when he came to Egypt the terrible hunger came to an end. Pharaoh would want to build a temple over his grave and turn him into an idol.

Egyptians made idols out of everything! Crocodiles, cobras, cats, sheep, and even people. Yaakov's grave would become a place where people would come to bow down, and Yaakov did not want that to happen!

He knew that his children would need Pharaoh's permission to bury him in Eretz Yisrael. Yosef was the only one with the power to do that.

Yaakov sent a message from Goshen to Yosef to come see him.

FASCINATING FACTS

There were other reasons why Yaakov didn't want to be buried in Egypt.

- Yaakov saw that in the future Hashem would punish the Egyptians with the plague of lice. He didn't want lice crawling all over his body.
- When Mashiach comes, the dead will come back to life in Eretz Yisrael first. Jews buried in other countries will have to roll through miles of underground tunnels till they arrive in Eretz Yisrael. Then they will stand up out of the ground, alive once again. Yaakov wanted to be with the first group of people to be brought back to life, and he didn't want to suffer the pain of having to roll.

Swear!

Yosef arrived and Yaakov told him, "I want you to do for me a chessed shel emes (a true kindness). Swear that you will not bury me in Egypt. Bury me in the grave of my ancestors."

** After Yaakov's death, the slavery was mild. The Jews were only sometimes used for government building projects. But the Jews were worried that their slavery would become permanent, which eventually was what happened.*

"I'll do what you told me," said Yosef.

Yosef's agreement wasn't enough. Yaakov told Yosef to swear he would do it, and Yosef swore. Didn't Yaakov trust Yosef? Why did he ask him to swear? If Yosef hadn't sworn to take Yaakov out of Egypt, Pharaoh wouldn't have let Yaakov's body leave.

Come Quickly!

Menashe worked together with his father, Yosef, while Ephraim spent his time learning Torah with his grandfather, Yaakov, in Goshen.

Ephraim realized that his grandfather had become very sick. Ephraim hurried to tell Yosef to come quickly.

Yosef arrived with Menashe and Ephraim. Out of respect for Yosef's royal status, Yaakov sat up in bed. That was not easy for him. He was very weak. But he did it because royalty has to be respected.

Yaakov said, "Ephraim and Menashe are mine, just like Reuven and Shimon."

This was an astounding gift from Yaakov to Yosef! His two sons would have the same holy status as his brothers. They would have their own flags, their own prince, and get an equal share in Eretz Yisrael with the other shevatim.

Rachel Is Crying

Yaakov was putting Yosef through the trouble of bringing him all the way to Eretz Yisrael to be buried. Yet when Yosef's mother died near the city of Beis Lechem, Yaakov buried her on the side of the road! He didn't bring her to be buried honorably in a city!

Yaakov explained to Yosef why he did that. "I buried Rachel there on the road because Hashem told me to. In the future when the Jews will go into exile, they will travel on that same road where I buried Rachel. When they pass her grave, Rachel will come before Hashem and cry that He should have mercy on her suffering children. Because of her tears, Hashem will promise to bring the Jews back from exile."

If Rachel had not been buried by the roadside, the Jews would not have passed her grave!

Evil Descendants

Yaakov was about to bless Ephraim and Menashe when the Presence of Hashem left him. Suddenly the tzaddik saw the future of his grandchildren, and he was upset. Both Menashe and Ephraim

FASCINATING FACTS

When a person is kind to someone else, he can return the favor. For example, if you give a friend who forgot his lunch half of your sandwich, he might give you some of his lunch when you forget your sandwich on the kitchen table! Doing a kindness for someone after he has passed away, though, is called chessed shel emes, true kindness, because the dead have no way of ever repaying the good deed you have done for them. That proves that your kindness to them was truly only for the good — so it's a true kindness.

TORAH IN OUR LIVES

After Yosef swore not to bury Yaakov in Egypt, Yaakov bowed down in the direction of the head of his bed. What's special about the head of a sick person's bed? Hashem's Presence rests there, watching over the sick person.

Hashem is with every sick person. That's good to remember if a person is sick in bed and feeling miserable. It makes things easier if one knows Hashem is right there with him.

FASCINATING FACTS

When Yaakov blessed Yosef's sons he was already blind from old age.

would have very wicked descendants: Ephraim would have Yeravam and Achav, and Menashe would have Yehu, all kings of the Aseres HaShevatim. They would influence the Jews to bow down to idols instead of worshiping Hashem.

Yaakov asked Yosef, "Who are these evil people who will be your descendants? How can I bless your sons if they will have wicked descendants?"

Yosef prayed that Hashem would allow Yaakov to bless his sons. In answer to Yosef's prayers, Hashem's Presence returned to Yaakov, and he blessed his grandchildren.

Right, Left, Left, Right

Yaakov hugged and kissed his grandsons. Turning to Yosef he said, "When you were missing I didn't think I would ever see you again. Now Hashem has even let me see your children!"

Yosef got his sons ready for their blessing. He placed Menashe, the older one, on Yaakov's right, and Ephraim to his left. That way the older son would get the strongest blessing, the one coming through Yaakov's right hand. Then Yosef backed away and bowed down to his father as a sign of respect.

Yaakov stretched out his hands to Menashe and Ephraim, but instead of stretching them out straight in front of him, he crossed his hands! Now his right hand was on Ephraim's head, and his left hand was on Menashe's head!

Like Fish

FASCINATING FACTS

During Kerias Shema that we say before going to sleep, we recite the words "Hamalach hagoeil osi mikal ra ... — the angel who saved me from everything bad ...." These words come from the blessing Yaakov gave his grandsons.

Yaakov blessed his grandsons that the angel that had saved him from his troubles should bless them. And that they would have many children and descendants — as many as the fish in the sea.

Seeing that Yaakov had crossed his hands, Yosef tried to uncross them. He said, "This is the older son. Put your right hand on his head."

Yaakov answered, "I know I know, he (Menashe, the older one) will also become a great shevet. But his younger brother will become greater; his descendants will be famous even among the nations."

The Sun Stops

When would Ephraim's descendant become so well known? Yaakov saw that Yehoshua, who brought the Jews into Eretz Yisrael after Moshe's death, would come from Shevet Ephraim. During one of his battles to conquer Eretz Yisrael, Yehoshua prayed that the sun should not set, so that the Jewish army could keep fighting in daylight. He became

world famous when suddenly, all over the world, the sun stood still and time stopped, all because of him!

There would be a Jewish leader from Menashe as well. His name would be Gideon. He miraculously wiped out a Midianite army of 135,000 soldiers with an army of only 300 men!

Like Ephraim and Menashe

Yaakov then gave his grandsons a special blessing. Jews would always bless their sons that "Hashem should make you like Ephraim and Menashe."

Till today, on those special times when parents bless their sons, whether it's on Friday night before Kiddush or on Erev Yom Kippur, they bless them to be like Ephraim and Menashe.

What's so special about Menashe and Ephraim that we want our children to be like them?

They grew up in Egypt, which was the world's most powerful country. Egyptian culture was evil. The Egyptians didn't believe in Hashem and they were not modest. Yet Menashe and Ephraim were not influenced by those living around them. When everyone was out having fun celebrating Egyptian holidays, they didn't. They grew up to be tzaddikim, believing in Hashem, acting and dressing modestly. They became so holy that they were on the level of their uncles, who had been raised by Yaakov!

We bless our children to be like them. To grow up to be Torah Jews, and to have the strength not to be influenced by evil values.

After finishing blessing his grandsons, Yaakov told Yosef that Hashem would be with the Jews in Egypt and would give them the Torah.

A Gift

Because Yosef agreed to bury Yaakov in Eretz Yisrael, Yaakov gave him a present. An entire city! Yosef was promised that when the Jews came to Eretz Yisrael, they would take his bones out of Egypt and bury him in the city of Shechem.

Mashiach

Yaakov called together all his sons. He wanted to let them know when Mashiach will finally come.

When all twelve sons arrived, Yaakov tried to tell them when Mashiach would come. Suddenly Yaakov felt Hashem's Presence leave him, and he could not remember when it would happen. Hashem made him forget because He didn't want the Jews to know how long it would take before the exile would end.

Shema Yisrael!

Yaakov wondered why Hashem's Presence left him, just when his children arrived. He had a terrifying thought. Maybe it happened because one of his sons was not a tzaddik?

"Does anyone doubt that Hashem Who is in Heaven is the true G-d?" he asked them.

The brothers answered with the same six words we say today, morning, evening, and before we go to sleep.

"Shema Yisrael Hashem Elokeinu Hashem Echad — Listen, (our father) Yisrael (Yaakov's other name), Hashem is our G-d, Hashem is the One and Only."

Later, when the Torah was given, Hashem made it a mitzvah for us to say these words.

Hearing his sons say these words, Yaakov answered:

"Baruch Shem k'vod malchuso l'olam va'ed — Blessed is the Name of His glorious kingdom forever."

Yaakov then blessed his sons. In these blessings, he let them know what would happen to their shevet in the future. (To read more, see the special section at the end of the parashah called "Yaakov's Blessings," p. 252.)

Questions, Anyone?

How were Ephraim and Menashe different from the other pairs of brothers in the Book of Bereishis?

They were the first pair of brothers in the Torah that loved each other like brothers should and didn't fight. Kayin killed his brother Hevel. Yishmael tried to kill Yitzchak, Eisav hated Yaakov and wanted to kill him.

Menashe was very special. Yaakov gave Ephraim the bigger blessing, but Menashe wasn't jealous. He continued to love his younger brother.

Yaakov told Yosef, "I'm giving you Shechem, which I took from the Emori with my sword and bow." But wasn't the city of Shechem conquered by Shimon and Levi, and not by Yaakov?

Seven years after Shimon and Levi destroyed Shechem, Yaakov and his family decided to settle there. The Canaanite nations were furious about this. They combined all their large armies and attacked Yaakov and his family. Yaakov, holding a sword and bow in hand, went out to lead the battle. Though he was outnumbered, he won the war. The city of Shechem became his property.

Yaakov knew he didn't win the war with his weapons. A Jew's power in battle comes from his prayers. His prayers are his sword, and asking Hashem for help are his bows and arrows. Today also, our tefillos are better than tanks and planes.

When he finished blessing his sons, Yaakov told them to bring his body back to Eretz Yisrael and to bury him in Me'aras HaMachpeilah.

Crying and Mourning

Then Yaakov passed away. All his sons were now mourners, and they ripped their shirts in grief. They cried bitter tears at the loss of their father.

The news spread throughout Egypt. The great man, Yaakov, who had stopped the terrible hunger, had passed away. The man who had brought the blessing of the Nile, so that it overflowed and caused the crops to grow, was gone. All of Egypt cried and went into mourning when they heard the terrible news.

The mourning for Yaakov didn't last just a week or a month. It lasted for 70 days! That's how bad everyone felt that he had died.

Yaakov was 147 years old when he died. He had lived a peaceful life in Egypt during his final seventeen years.

Can I Go?

The days of mourning passed, and it was time for Yaakov's funeral. Yosef asked Pharaoh for permission to take Yaakov's body to Eretz Yisrael for burial. Pharaoh refused.

"I swore to my father I would bury him in Canaan," said Yosef. (Canaan was what Eretz Yisrael was called then.)

"Get your promise canceled," answered Pharaoh.

"If I do that, I'll also cancel my promise to you."

What promise was that? When Yosef was released from prison Pharaoh tested him on how many languages he knew. Yosef passed the test, since he knew all 70 languages, just like Pharaoh. But he also knew a language Pharaoh didn't: Hebrew.

Pharaoh was embarrassed that Yosef knew more languages than he did. After all, he was the awesome Pharaoh, ruler of the Egyptian Empire! No one could be better than he was! He made Yosef swear to tell no one. The fact that Pharaoh didn't know Hebrew would be their little secret.

Yosef had kept his word and didn't tell anyone. But now Yosef warned him: "Pharaoh, don't make me cancel my promise to my father. If you make me do that, I will also cancel my promise to you, and everyone will find out that I know more languages than you."

When Pharaoh heard that, he suddenly changed his mind, and he gave Yosef permission to bury Yaakov in Eretz Yisrael.

FASCINATING FACTS

When Yaakov died, his family had grown from the 70 people who had come to Egypt into a nation of 600,000!

TORAH IN OUR LIVES

Most of Yaakov's life was difficult. He was forced to run away from home because his brother wanted to kill him. He worked for Lavan, who constantly tried to cheat him. His daughter Dinah was kidnapped. He thought his son Yosef had been killed by a wild animal. Through it all Yaakov never lost faith in Hashem and he constantly prayed to Him.

What can we learn from this?

1. When things are tough, have faith in Hashem and pray to Him.
2. Just because someone is having a hard life does not mean he is wicked. Yaakov, one of the greatest tzaddikim who ever lived, had a hard life.

FASCINATING FACTS

The Gemara tells us that Yaakov did not really die. What does that mean? In a sense, Yaakov didn't die because as long as the Jews exist and continue to behave like Yaakov Avinu wanted, he lives through us!

The Funeral

Yaakov's funeral was one of the most amazing events the world had ever seen. Yaakov was honored not only by Egypt, but by the nations of Canaan, Eisav, and also the descendants of Yishmael. The greatest honor of all? Even the Presence of Hashem was there!

Yaakov's body lay on a golden bed surrounded by all kinds of jewels. The body was covered with a sheet made of the finest linen. Next to Yaakov's head was a magnificent golden crown. Though it was a clear day, a cloud was floating over the bed. It was the Presence of the Shechinah, which also came to be at the funeral!

Ten of Yaakov's sons, and also Menashe and Ephraim, carried the bed, three on each side. Levi walked behind the bed, and Yosef rode in a carriage out in front. He was not wearing his crown. That was the crown on Yaakov's bed.

Pharaoh's servants, magicians, and wise men led the funeral procession. Pharaoh also sent a team of chariots and horsemen to protect the crowds. Servants threw nice-smelling spices and flowers all around to give the air a pleasant smell.

Danger!

After many days of travel, the procession finally crossed the border to Eretz Yisrael. On the way to Chevron, where Yaakov was to be buried in Me'aras HaMachpeilah, the funeral stopped at Goren Ha'atad, where terrible danger awaited them. The armies of the Keturah, Yishmael, and Eisav nations had come to make war on Yaakov's family.

The armies saw Yosef's crown lying on Yaakov's bed, gleaming in the sunlight. They recognized the crown as the one worn by the Egyptian viceroy who had sold them food when they were all starving during the years of hunger. He had saved their lives! Seeing the crown, they put away their weapons. They were afraid to go to war against the viceroy. After all, if there was another hunger, they would need him again! They were not going to bite the hand that fed them and might feed them in the future.

Out of respect for Yosef, the kings of all these nations took their crowns off their heads and placed them around Yaakov's body! Yaakov's body was surrounded with 36 royal, golden crowns!

A speech was made in Goren Ha'atad describing Yaakov's greatness. The people at the funeral remained there for seven days of mourning.

Questions, Anyone?

Why didn't Levi and Yosef help their brothers carry their father's body?

Because in the future Shevet Levi would carry the Holy Ark. Yaakov felt it wouldn't be right for Levi to carry his body. And Yosef was a king. It wasn't proper for him to join his brothers carrying the body.

Fascinating Facts

Naphtali, Asher, and Dan stood on the north side of the bed where Yaakov's body rested. Reuven, Shimon, and Gad were on the south side. Yehudah, Yissaschar, and Zevulun were in front, and Binyamin, Menashe, and Ephraim stood behind the bed.

Many years later, when the Jews had left Egypt and were in the desert, their camps were around the Mishkan, and the shevatim followed the exact same order.

Challenge!

The funeral finally reached Me'aras HaMachpeilah, where Yaakov was to be buried. Unfortunately, the burial could not take place. Why? Eisav was blocking the entrance of the cave.

"You can't bury Yaakov here," he announced in a loud voice. "After our parents died there were two graves left. Yaakov buried his wife Leah in one of them. The other belongs to me!"

The brothers answered, "You sold your grave to our father!"

"Prove it," said Eisav.

Eisav had sold his grave to Yaakov, and there was a signed contract. The problem was, the contract was back in Egypt. Someone would have to go and bring it back to show Eisav.

The brothers chose Naphtali, the fastest runner of all of them. He raced back to Egypt. While he was gone, everyone just waited around. Yaakov's body was not being buried. It was a terrible situation.

Suddenly, Chushim, the son of Dan, saved the day!

Problem Solved!

Chushim was deaf. He saw Eisav, but he couldn't hear him, so he had no idea what was going on. "Why are we just waiting around?" he asked. The others pointed to Eisav and let Chushim know that he was holding up the funeral.

Chushim got very angry that this wicked man was causing Yaakov such dishonor. "Should my grandfather lie in disgrace until Naphtali returns!?" he shouted. Then Chushim picked up his sword and hit Eisav so hard that he knocked Eisav's head off, and it fell into the cave!*

Chushim had solved the problem!

Yaakov was then buried in Me'aras HaMachpeilah by his son Yosef. The brothers chose Yosef because it was an honor to their father to be buried by the ruler of Egypt, second only to Pharaoh.

Yosef Remembers

After the funeral, Yosef and his brothers headed back to Egypt. On the way, Yosef stopped at a pit. It was the pit where his brothers had thrown him so many years before.

Staring into the deep hole, Yosef remembered the snakes and scorpions that had been inside. If Hashem hadn't protected him from their poisonous bites, he would have died that day.

** According to the Gemara, Chushim hit Eisav with a club so hard that Eisav's eyes were knocked out of his head and he died.*

FASCINATING FACTS

The Canaanite nations were evil. They would have been destroyed shortly after Yaakov's death. But Hashem pushed off their destruction as a reward for their mourning Yaakov. He let them survive for many more years.

The Egyptians were also rewarded for mourning Yaakov. After the sea split, the dead Egyptians were spit out of the water, and they were buried in graves instead of lying at the bottom of the sea.

Yaakov was one of six people who were so holy that the angel of death had no power over them. They did not die through the angel of death; Hashem took them up to Shamayim. They died without pain.

The other five were Avraham, Yitzchak, Moshe, Aharon, and Miriam.

Eisav's head is buried in Me'aras HaMachpeilah.

QUESTIONS, ANYONE?

What was Yosef's reward for burying Yaakov?

When the time came to leave Egypt, who dealt with bringing Yosef's coffin out of Egypt? The greatest Jew alive, leader of the Jewish people – Moshe Rabbeinu!

What was Moshe's reward for bringing Yosef's coffin?

Moshe was buried by Hashem himself!

He would never have had a family; he'd never have become Egypt's ruler. He would never have seen his father again.

Overcome with thankfulness to Hashem, Yosef said a berachah. "Blessed are You, Hashem ... Who performed a miracle for me in this place." That is the blessing a person says when he passes a place where a miracle happened to him.

The brothers watched Yosef standing alone, looking into the pit. They were worried. Was he thinking about what they had done to him? Did he hate them for it? Was he planning revenge? They didn't know that Yosef had stopped only to make that berachah.

Dinner Invitations

When they returned to Egypt something else happened that made them think that Yosef hated them. Yosef stopped inviting them over for dinner. When Yaakov was alive, sometimes the family got together at Yosef's house to have dinner together. But since the funeral there were no more invitations. The brothers were afraid that Yosef might take revenge for selling him, now that their father had died.

Once again the brothers had misunderstood. Yosef didn't hate them. He stopped inviting them because he didn't want to embarrass them.

Yosef Has a Problem

You know what it's like when the whole family gets together for a bar mitzvah or wedding? Your parents spend a lot of time thinking about how the guests should be seated, making sure that no one's feelings are hurt because of where they were put. Yosef had the same problem.

When Yaakov was alive he told his sons where to sit. Even though Reuven was the oldest, and Yehudah was the leader of the shevatim, Yaakov put Yosef at the head of the table next to himself, because Yosef was ruler of Egypt. That was fine, because it was their father who told everyone where to sit.

But after Yaakov passed away, Yosef felt it would hurt his brothers if he invited them for dinner. Because he was the Egyptian ruler, he couldn't put Reuven and Yehudah at the head of the table. He worried they might feel bad about that.

Not wanting to embarrass them, he stopped inviting them. Unfortunately, the brothers took it the wrong way. They thought it was because he hated them for what they had done to him.

Peace Mission

The brothers decided they had to act. They sent Bilhah's sons, Dan and Naphtali, with a message.

They told Yosef that before Yaakov passed away he had commanded them to tell Yosef, "Please forgive the sin of your brothers." And then they pleaded with Yosef to forgive them all.

QUESTIONS, ANYONE?

Why did they choose Dan and Naphtali to send the message of peace?

When Rachel died, Bilhah raised Yosef and Binyamin as if they were her own children. Bilhah's children, Dan and Naphtali, were Yosef's close friends.

TORAH IN OUR LIVES

Why did the brothers make up the story if their father had never said it? They did it for a good reason: to keep peace in the family. It is permitted to say something that is not true if it will bring peace to a family.

Let's say your brother and sister are fighting with each other and haven't spoken to each other for days. Or you have two friends who were the best of buddies, but now are upset with each other. You want to make peace. **What can you do?**

You can make up a story about how one of your siblings or friends told you that they want to make up with the other one, and that they feel bad that there was a fight. Tell each of them the same story. When they hear that the other side wants to make up, they will probably be happy to hear it and become friends again.

But before doing this, be sure to check with a parent or teacher if they think that it will help and what would be the best way to do it.

Yosef Cries

Yosef knew that the brothers had made up this story. It never happened! If his father Yaakov wanted him to forgive his brothers, he would have told him so himself! Yosef realized that his brothers thought he didn't love them. That made him cry!

The rest of his brothers walked in and bowed to Yosef. "We are ready to be your slaves," they said.

Yosef's Answer

Yosef wanted to calm his brothers and convince them that they had nothing to worry about. He loved them and never had any plan to take revenge. Yosef spoke wisely (see special section below) and convinced them that he really meant what he said. He promised to continue to send food for them and their families.

The brothers realized their mistake and the family was united in love and peace.

How Yosef convinced his brothers they had nothing to worry about

Yosef explained to the brothers:

- Ten candles couldn't blow out the light of one candle, so how can one candle blow out ten candles? What he meant was: All ten of you tried to hurt me but Hashem didn't let it happen. He even made it turn out well. I became ruler of Egypt because of what you did.
- How could I possibly harm all of you all by myself? Hashem wouldn't permit it!
- Our family is indestructible. Hashem told our great-grandfather, Avraham Avinu, that the Jews will be like the stars. No one can destroy a star, so how can I destroy any of you?
- Before you came to Egypt, people whispered that I was born a slave and didn't deserve to be viceroy. When you arrived they stopped whispering, because you were my brothers. That proved that I came from one of the most famous families on earth. If I kill you, people will say you weren't really my brothers, and that I made it all up. They will say: "We always said he was born a slave, and this proves it. If they were really his brothers, would he kill them?"

The End

When Yosef felt that he was going to pass away he called together his family, the Bnei Yisrael — the Children of Yisrael. He let them know that one day Hashem would send someone to free them from Egypt and bring them to Eretz Yisrael, the land Hashem had promised to give to the Jewish people.

Yosef then told them the code words that the one who would take them out would say: "Pakod yifkod" (He will remember). When the Jews will hear those words they will know that Hashem sent him and the time to leave Egypt had come.

He made the Bnei Yisrael swear that they would take his bones with them when they left Egypt, and that they would bury him in Eretz Yisrael.

Yosef lived a long life. He had the joy of seeing his sons become grandfathers and great-grandfathers. When Yosef died at 110 he was a great-great-grandfather!

FASCINATING FACTS

Yosef was buried in the city of Shechem, today an Arab city. It's the city where his brothers had sold him. We know exactly where his grave is and many Jews go and pray there.

Yosef was the first of the brothers to die. He ruled Egypt for 80 years. Levi was the last of the brothers to die. He was 137 years old.

Final Journeys

Yosef's body was put into a very heavy metal coffin. The Egyptians threw it into the Nile River, where it sank to the bottom.

This was a mean plan to stop the Jews from ever leaving Egypt. The Jews had sworn to take Yosef when they left. If his coffin was at the bottom of the Nile River, they could never get to it. The Jews would be stuck in Egypt forever!

But the plan failed. The time came to leave Egypt. But how could the Jews leave? Yosef's coffin was still at the bottom of the river!

Moshe Rabbeinu went to the Nile and, miraculously, Yosef's heavy metal coffin floated to the surface. Moshe lifted it out of the water.

Not only did they take Yosef's coffin, they also took the bodies of all his brothers, who had been buried in Egypt. They were taken back to Eretz Yisrael, where they were laid to rest. When Mashiach comes, they will be brought back to life. We will be able to see the shevatim, and the Avos and Imahos whom we have met in Sefer Bereishis, in person. Bimheirah, b'yameinu — it should be soon, in our days.

TORAH IN OUR LIVES

Yosef passed away Shabbos afternoon, at Minchah time. So did Moshe Rabbeinu and King David. To remind us of the death of these tzaddikim we say a special prayer, Tzidkascha, before Aleinu at Shabbos Minchah. It has three verses, one for each of the tzaddikim who passed away at that time.

Yaakov's Blessings

Each son of Yaakov became the head of a shevet in Israel. Yosef was the head of two shevatim, Menashe and Ephraim.

Before Yaakov died he blessed his sons, letting them know what their shevet would be like and what would happen to them in the future. Some of the shevet's strengths were compared to animals. These animals became the symbol of the shevet.

Here are the main points of each shevet's blessing:

Reuven

Yaakov told Reuven that as the eldest of the brothers, his shevet should have been the kings and Kohanim of the Jews. Also, they would have gotten twice as much land in Eretz Yisrael as any of the other shevatim, because the oldest brother inherits a double share of what his father owned.

But because of his sin of removing Bilhah's bed from his father's tent and replacing it with Leah's bed, Reuven lost these privileges.

Reuven is compared to fast-flowing water. He sinned because he acted too quickly. He did not think things through before taking action. Someone like that is not fit to be a leader.

Still, Yaakov gave him many blessings:

- His shevet would be strong and powerful.
- In the future, when Moshe blesses the Jews, he would be forgiven.

Fascinating Facts

The gifts of the firstborn that were taken away from Reuven were given to some of his brothers.

Jewish kings came from Yehudah.

The Kohanim were from Levi.

Yosef was given twice as much land in Eretz Yisrael as any of the other shevatim.

Shimon and Levi

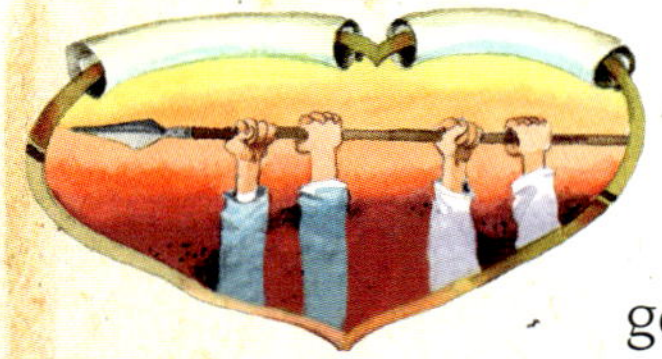

Yaakov then spoke to Shimon and Levi together. He reminded them of the time when Dinah was kidnapped. Shimon and Levi acted like Eisav. They used violence to get what they wanted, and they wiped out all the males of Shechem to free their sister.

Also, Shimon and Levi came up with the plan to kill Yosef, and they convinced their brothers to agree.

- Yaakov cursed their anger. This was a blessing, because, as a result of this, the shevatim of Shimon and Levi were able to control their anger.
- Shimon and Levi would be spread out, spending their time traveling. Shevet Levi would travel to farmers all

over the country to get their maaser. Shimon's shevet would travel throughout the country collecting funds for the poor, teaching Jewish children, and selling mezuzos, tefillin, and Sifrei Torah. This was a blessing because when Shimon and Levi got together they caused great harm. By separating them from each other they wouldn't make trouble.

Yehudah

Yaakov told Yehudah that at first, he suspected him of trying to have Yosef killed. But then he found out that Yehudah had actually saved Yosef, by telling his brothers to sell Yosef instead of killing him.

Yaakov blessed Yehudah:

- The symbol of Yehudah's shevet is a lion. Just like a lion is the king of beasts, the descendants of Yehudah will be the kings and leaders of the Jewish nation.
- King David and Mashiach will come from Shevet Yehudah.
- At first King David will be like a lion cub, leading the Jewish armies under King Shaul. But then he will become like a full-grown lion — a king who is strong, ferocious, and terrifying. When King David will go out to war, the enemy will turn their backs on him, running away in fear. He will be victorious over his enemies.
- After King David dies, Shevet Yehudah will continue to provide Jewish kings and leaders. Even after the Beis HaMikdash was destroyed, the Jewish leaders in Bavel and Eretz Yisrael came from Yehudah.
- Yehudah's land will produce a lot of wine and his animals will give a lot of milk. There will be so much wine and milk that the eyes of the people of Yehudah will be red from drinking wine and their teeth will be white from milk.
- King Shlomo, who came from Yehudah, will build the Beis HaMikdash, and during his time the Jews will live in peace.

Zevulun

- Zevulun will live by the seashore.

Fascinating Facts

Yaakov saw that in the Wilderness, a leader of Shimon's shevet, Zimri, would challenge Moshe and would want to marry a non-Jewish Midianite woman. He also saw that Korach, from Shevet Levi, would lead a rebellion against Moshe's leadership.

Yaakov asked Hashem not to mention his name when the Torah writes about these two terrible men. So when the Torah tells us who they came from, it doesn't mention Yaakov as their ancestor.

Where in the Torah is Mashiach mentioned?

Yaakov told Yehudah that his shevet would be leaders of the Jews from the time of King David until "Shilo" comes. Shilo is another name for Mashiach. It stands for two words — "shay lo" — which means "gift to him." When Mashiach finally comes, all the nations of the world will accept his leadership, and they will bring him gifts.

TORAH IN OUR LIVES

The shevatim of Yissaschar and Zevulun had a very special partnership. Yissaschar would learn Torah. Zevulun would support them.

Yissaschar got a share of Zevulun's business profits, and Zevulun shared in Yissaschar's reward for learning Torah, which they would both receive in the next world.

Today there are many kollels in Eretz Yisrael that have a "Yissaschar Zevulun" partnership with generous supporters. The kollel students can continue to study Torah because of the money they receive from their partners. The businessmen who support the kollels have a share in the great zechus of Torah learning.

QUESTIONS, ANYONE?

Why was Zevulun blessed before his older brother Yissachar ?

Yissaschar is able to study Torah all the time because of Zevulun's donations to him, so Yaakov blessed Zevulun first.

- The shevet will make a living traveling the high seas, doing business with other countries.
- Zevulun will support the scholars of Yissaschar, so that they can devote their time to learning Torah.

Yissaschar

Shevet Yissaschar will be blessed with many Torah scholars and experts in halachah, Jewish law. They will carry a large load of Torah knowledge in their heads. They have to know Gemara, Shulchan Aruch, and countless other works of Jewish law. That is what Yaakov meant when he told Yissaschar that his shevet would be like a donkey. Donkeys are the animals used to carry large, heavy loads — and this shevet has to carry a large and heavy load of Torah knowledge.

- The whole shevet will be devoted to Torah learning.
- Many of them will be in the Sanhedrin (the Supreme Court of the Jews). They will make decisions about Jewish law, and answer many complex and serious questions.

Dan

- When the Jews were being oppressed by the Plishtim, Hashem sent a tzaddik who would lead them and fight for them. His name was Shimshon, and he came from Shevet Dan. Hashem gave Shimshon miraculous, extraordinary strength.
- Shimshon would deal with the Plishtim like a snake, which is the symbol of his shevet. How?
- Snakes don't hunt their prey in packs, like wolves and other animals. Instead, they travel alone. Shimshon fought the Plishtim without help from anyone! He fought without regular weapons or an army. Yet he won! Once, Shimshon killed a thousand Plishtim all by himself. What was his weapon? The jawbone of a donkey.
- Snakes can kill humans who are out of their reach without biting them. If a snake wants to kill a man riding on a horse, he bites the horse. This causes the horse to suddenly jump up on its back legs, which throws the rider off its back. The

rider hits the ground and the impact kills him.

- In a similar way, Shimshon won his final victory against the Plishtim. It happened after he had lost his strength, and the Plishtim captured him. They brought him to their temple to make fun of him. Three thousand Plishtim stood on the roof of the temple to watch. Shimshon stood between two high, heavy pillars, which supported the roof. He prayed to Hashem to return his strength.
- In his blessing to Dan, Yaakov saw this vision of the future, and he prayed that Hashem should listen to Shimshon's prayer.
- Miraculously, Shimshon's great strength returned and he pushed against the pillars until they broke. The roof came crashing down, killing all the Plishtim. Unfortunately, when the building collapsed, Shimshon was killed as well.
- Like the snake who killed the rider without biting him, Shimshon killed his enemies without laying a hand on them.
- Shimshon was a nazir. His whole life he never drank wine or cut his hair. This made him very holy and deserving of the gift of great strength.
- One day Shimshon's wife cut his hair when he was sleeping. When he woke up his strength was gone.
- Shimshon would judge the Jewish people as King David did many years later. He would be a good ruler, a righteous judge, and he would defeat his enemies.

Gad

- In the future, Gad will live in the part of Eretz Yisrael that lies on the east side of the Jordan River.
- Even though Gad already had their territory even before the Jews entered Eretz Yisrael, the men of Gad will go fight for the other shevatim. They will cross the Jordan and fight with them until Eretz Yisrael is conquered.
- No one from Gad will die during this conquest of Eretz Yisrael. When the wars are over, they will all return back home to the east side of the Jordan, safe and sound.
- They will be outstanding warriors.

Torah in our Lives

Torah is infinite. We begin studying Torah when we are young and we never stop, no matter how much we know. There are people over a hundred years old and they are still learning Torah. There is always more Torah to learn! Torah study lasts a lifetime.

Fascinating Facts

Over two hundred men who served as the head of the Sanhedrin came from Shevet Yissaschar.

Yaakov Avinu thought that Shimshon would be Mashiach. When he saw that Shimshon was destined to die he was very sad, and he prayed that Hashem bring Mashiach as soon as possible.

Asher

- The olives groves in Asher's land will produce great amounts of oil.
- The women of Asher's shevet will marry Kohanim, and some of their descendants will be Kohanim Gedolim.
- Kings will marry women from Asher.
- The oil used to anoint kings will be made by Asher.
- Asher's food will be so tasty that it will be served at the meals of kings.

Naphtali

- Did you ever see a deer run? They are very fast! Naphtali himself was the fastest runner of all his brothers, and his shevet's symbol was a deer.
- In the future, King Yavin of Chatzor will send his army under the command of General Sisera to attack the Jews. Naphtali's soldiers will quickly go out and fight Sisera. They played an important role in the battle, and helped the Jews win.
- The fruits growing in Naphtali's land will be the fastest fruits to ripen in Eretz Yisrael.
- As we read in this parashah, when Eisav will try to stop Yaakov's funeral, the brothers will send Naphtali, the fastest runner, to run back to Egypt and return with the contract that proved that Eisav sold his grave to Yaakov.
- Part of Naphtali's land will be on the shores of Lake Kinneret.

Yosef

Yaakov praised Yosef:

Because of what he suffered at the hands of his brothers and when he was a slave, Yosef could have become bitter. Instead, with Hashem's help, he overcame all his troubles and became ruler of Egypt.

Yosef didn't sin with Potiphar's wife.

He was the highest of all the brothers — their crown.

He fed the family during the hunger.

Years before, when Yaakov met Eisav on his return to Eretz Yisrael from Lavan's house, Yaakov introduced his family to Eisav. As they walked by Eisav, all the children stood behind their mothers. Not Yosef. He stood up tall in front of his mother, protecting her from being seen by the wicked Eisav.

Yaakov blessed Yosef's shevatim (Menashe and Ephraim):

- They would have a large population.

- Ayin hara would have no effect on them.*
- Their lands would be fertile even in dry seasons, because underwater springs will water their crops.
- Hashem had blessed Yaakov with unlimited blessings. Yaakov let Yosef know that his shevatim would have those same blessings without limit.

Binyamin

- The shevet's symbol is a wolf.
- A wolf grabs the food it kills, snatching it away to eat somewhere else. Jewish kings are supposed to come from Shevet Yehudah, but first, Shevet Binyamin will grab that right for itself. King Shaul from Binyamin will be the first king of the Jews.
- A large part of the Beis HaMikdash will be built on land lying in the borders of Binyamin, including the Mizbei'ach on which the meat of the korbanos was burned.
- Binyamin's shevet will be strong, just like wolves are strong animals.
- In the future, Mordechai and Esther, descendants of Binyamin, will defeat Haman. King Achashveirosh will take Haman's money and palace, and give them to Queen Esther. She will put Mordechai in charge of it all.

• • •

Yaakov gave a specific blessing to each of his sons. He then blessed them that, in addition to their own blessing, they also would have all of their brothers' blessings. All of the Jews would be strong as lions, quick as deer, dangerous as snakes etc.

* *When a person causes someone else to be jealous of him, it can cause that person to be punished. If someone shows off his riches as good fortune, causing others to be jealous, the "show-off" sometimes is also punished. That's called ayin hara.*

Fascinating Facts

Yaakov compared Yosef to an ox. An ox is strong. He is the king of the farm animals. Yehoshua, a descendant of Yosef, will rule the Jews after Moshe. He will lead the Jews in their wars to conquer Eretz Yisrael.

Questions, Anyone?

If Yaakov blessed all the brothers with the same blessings, why did he first give each one a specific blessing?

Each shevet was superior in the blessing he was given over his other brothers. For example, though all the brothers were strong like lions, Yehudah would be the strongest of all.

Chazak Chazak V'nischazeik

Mazel tov! We have come to the end of Sefer Bereishis: the first of the Five Books of Chumash.

The sefer begins with Hashem's creation of the world: the sun, the moon, the stars, the planets, the oceans, mountains and valleys, all living creatures and, of course, the first man and woman. This gives us the message that Hashem exists and He created everything. The stories of the first sin, the first murder, and the generation of the Mabul remind us not to sin, because Hashem sees everything and evil is punished.

Sefer Bereishis also tells us how Hashem chose one man and woman, our ancestors, out of all the people in the world. Avraham Avinu and Sarah Imeinu founded a nation that would have the privilege and honor to receive the Torah and Eretz Yisrael from Hashem. That nation is us.

The fascinating stories of our Fathers and Mothers show us how to serve Hashem and have a good life. To be kind like Avraham, who fed strangers. To love Hashem like Yitzchak, who would do anything for Hashem, and was ready to even give up his life. To be devoted to Torah like Yaakov, who studied Torah and kept the mitzvos even when he was living with Lavan.

The brothers' sale of Yosef shows us that even when things seem to be very bad, Hashem has a reason, though it may take us a long time to understand how it was really for our good. It wasn't until Yosef became ruler of Egypt and was able to send food to his family that he knew why Hashem had let him be sold as a slave to Egypt.

And, of course, Sefer Bereishis teaches us that we are all grandchildren of Avraham and Sarah. That makes all of us one family, and every Jew is like our brother or sister.

Now we are ready to begin Sefer Shemos and see how Hashem took us out of terrible times in Egypt and brought us to Mount Sinai to give us the Torah.

Glossary

Aron: A casket for someone who died. Also, a box to keep something safe.

Avos: Fathers. Usually it means Avraham, Yitzchak, and Yaakov, the forefathers of the Jews

Ayin Hara: Evil eye (when someone is jealous of another person's good fortune)

Bechor: The firstborn son

Beis HaMikdash (plural Batei Mikdash): The Holy Temple in Yerushalayim. Two Batei HaMikdash have been destroyed. Hashem .... has promised to build a Third Beis HaMikdash for us.

Berachah (plural: berachos): Blessing

Bikur Cholim: Visiting the sick

Chassan: A groom

Chessed: An act of kindness

Chupah: Wedding canopy. A bride and groom stand beneath it during their wedding.

Daven: Pray

Derech Eretz: Being polite

Eretz Yisrael: the Land of Israel

Gan Eden: Garden of Eden

Hachnasas orchim: Hospitality to guests

Halachah: Jewish law

Hashem: G-d

Havdalah: Prayer said at the end of Shabbos

Imahos: Mothers, usually Sarah, Rivkah, Rachel and Leah, the mothers of the Jewish people

Kadosh Kedoshim: Holy of Holies, located in the Beis HaMikdash. The only person who could enter was the High Priest, and only on Yom Kippur.

Kallah: Bride

Kehunah: The Kohanim, descendants of Aharon HaKohen, performed the services in the Beis HaMikdash.

Kohen Gadol: High Priest, head of the Kohanim, who performed many of the services in the Beis HaMikdash

Kohen (plural: Kohanim): Descendants of Aharon HaKohen, who performed the services in the Beis HaMikdash

Korban: An offering to Hashem

Lashon hara: Speaking badly about someone, which is not allowed by Jewish law

Maariv: Evening prayer

Mabul: the great Flood

Mashiach: The Messiah, whom Hashem has promised to send to us to end our exile. We pray and wait for his arrival every day.

Mitzvah: Commandment

Mizbei'ach: Altar where korbanos were brought to Hashem

Neshamah: The soul, something that every person has. The soul cannot be seen, but it is what makes us want to connect with Hashem and with holiness.

Olam Haba: The World to Come, where people are rewarded (or punished) for their actions

Parashah: A portion of the Torah

Rasha: Wicked person

Sefer: Book

Shadchan: Someone who helps people find their husband / wife

Shamayim: Heaven

Shechitah: Slaughter of an animal following Jewish law

Sheva Berachos: Blessings given to a bride and groom during their wedding and the week after they get married

Shevet (plural: Shevatim: Tribe

Shidduch (plural: Shidduchim): Meeting a man/woman to see if you want to marry him/her

Shul: Synagogue

Teivah: Ark, the boat that Noach built to save his family from the Mabul

Teshuvah: Repentance, feeling bad about something you did wrong, and promising to do better

Tzaddeikes: A pious and good woman

Tzaddik: A pious and good man

Yerushalayim: Jerusalem

Yetzer hara: Something inside that tempts a person to do wrong

Zechus: Merit

Sources

MRB = Midrash Rabbah Bereishis

Parashas Bereishis

page 3 "Bring a Mabul" ... *Rashi* 6:7
page 6 "He created the world" ... *MRB* 1:1; *Maharzu*
"Hashem said, 'Bereishis'" ... *MRB* 17:1
"Came into existence" ... *Rashi* 1:24
"With everything else" ... *Rashi* 1:24
Questions Anyone? ... *MRB* 3:5
"Why Beis?" ... *MRB* 1:10
"The Light Was Good" ... *Chagigah* 12a
"World to the other" ... *MRB* 12:6
"Torah in Our Lives" ... *Berachos* 2a, 26a
page 7 "World's waters in half" ... *MRB* 4:4
Questions Anyone? (2) ... *Chagigah* 12a
"Created on this day" ... *MRB* 1:3, 3:8
"Was also created" ... *Pesachim* 54a
"That's not good" ... *MRB* 4:6, *Rabbeinu Bachya* 1:4
Fascinating Facts ... *MRB* 5:5
"Fourth Day" ... *Chullin* 60b
"The same place" ... *Toras Chaim, Bereishis* 1:16
"Light up the night sky" ... *Rashi* 1:16
page 8 "When Mashiach comes" ... *Rashi* 1:21
Fascinating Facts ... *Rashi* 1:26; *MRB* 10:5
"Making a sculpture" ... *Rashi* 1:27
"To make Adam" ... *Yerushalmi Shabbos* 2:6
"Mixed it with the earth" ... *Targum Yonasan* 2:7
"Form of a human being" ... *Sanhedrin* 38b
page 9 "To speak and think" ... *Targum Onkelos* and *Rashi* 2:7
"In His Image" ... *Malbim* 1:27, 2:7
"Like he was twenty" ... *MRB* 14:7
"Lashon Hakodesh" ... *Rashi* 11:1
Fascinating Facts ... *Rashi* 1:31
"Created Last" ... *Pirkei Avos* 5:6
"Used for miracles" ... *Avos* 5:6; *Magen Avos L'Rashbatz* and *Derech Chaim* there
page 10 "The Seventh Day" ... *Ohr HaChaim* 2:2; *Nesivos Shalom* (II pp. 61-2)
"Creating the world" ... *Chizkuni* 2:3
Fascinating Facts (1) ... *MRB* 11:8, *Eitz Yosef*
"Friday and Shabbos" ... *Rashi* 2:3
"Only for holiness" ... *Rabbeinu Bachya*
"Eaten on Shabbos" ... *MRB* 11:4
"Shop for Shabbos" ... *Ohr HaChaim* 2:3
Fascinating Facts (2) ... *Rashi* 1:1
"Rain" ... *Rashi* 2:5
page 11 Questions Anyone? (1) ... *Rashi* 2:5
"Created just for him" ... *Rashi* 2:15
"Grew on trees" ... *MRB* 15:7
"Served him wine" ... *Sanhedrin* 59b
Questions Anyone? (2) ... *Rosh Hashanah* 11a
"Serving Hashem" ... *Rabbeinu Bachya* 2:15
"Name It" ... *MRB* 17:4
Fascinating Facts (2) ... *"Recanati" Bereishis*
page 12 "Very beautiful" ... *MRB* 40:5
Fascinating Facts (1) ... *Rashi* 1:27
"Chayah" ... *Rashi* 3:20, *R' Hirsch* 3:20
"The Wedding" ... *MRB* 18:1
"Next to Adam" ... *MRB* 8:13
"Danced for them" ... *Osios D'R' Akiva At-Bash*
"Children and descendants" ... *MRB* 8:13
Questions Anyone? ... *Sefer HaChinuch* 1
"Became parents" ... *Sanhedrin* 38b
"A boy and two girls" ... *MRB* 22:3
"Center of the Garden" ... *Targum Onkelos* and *Rashi* 2:9
"Tree of Life" ... *MRB* 15:6
page 13 Questions Anyone? ... *MRB* 15:7
"The Six Commandments" ... *MRB* 16:6
"It was evil" ... *MRB* 19:1
page 14 "Able to create worlds" ... *Rashi* 3:5
"Against Hashem" ... *MRB* 19:4, *Eitz Yosef*
"Believed his lies" ... *Rashi* 3:6
"Animals to eat" ... *Rashi* 3:6
"Disobeyed Hashem" ... *Sanhedrin* 38b
Fascinating Facts ... *Sanhedrin* 38b
"Cover themselves with them" ... *Sanhedrin* 70b
"Punish them" ... *MRB* 19:8, *Eitz Yosef*
page 15 "Done wrong" ... *MRB* 19:11, *Maharzu*
Questions Anyone? ... *MRB* 17:4, *Eitz Yosef*
page 16 "Animals and birds" ... *MRB* 63:13
Fascinating Facts (1) ... *Rashi* 1:1
Questions Anyone? ... *Bamidbar Rabbah* 14:12, *Eitz Yosef*
"Shabbos" ... *MRB* 11:2
"Bright as day" ... *MRB* 11:2
Fascinating Facts (2) ... *MRB* 11:2
"Shabbos was over" ... *MRB* 11:2
"Where he was created" ... *Targum Yonasan* 3:23
"The First Murder" ... *Rashi* 4:3
page 17 "The Best" ... *Rashi* 4:4
"Jealous of his brother" ... *Midrash Tanchuma* 9
"Fight" ... *Shemos Rabbah* 21:17
"He could kill him" ... *Rashi* 4:8
page 18 "Let him get up" ... *Midrash Tanchuma* 9
"Killed him" ... *MRB* 22:8
"He was sorry" ... *Rashi* 3:9, *Sifsei Chachamim*
"Do teshuvah" ... *Rashi* 4:9
Questions Anyone? ... *Rashi* 4:10
"Live in one place" ... *Rashi* 4:12
"Done wrong" ... *Ramban* 4:13
"Because of what he did" ... *MRB* 22:12
"Being killed" ... *Rashi* 4:15
Fascinating Facts ... *MRB* 22:12
"Hevel Is Buried" ... *Yalkut Shimoni* 38
page 19 Questions Anyone? ... *MRB* 22:4
"Living in tents" ... *Rashi* 4:20
"Weapons for warriors" ... *Rashi* 4:22
"A good woman" ... *Mishlei Rabbasi* 30
"Married Noach" ... *Rashi* 4:22
Fascinating Facts (2) ... *Rashi* 4:20
"It hit Kayin" ... *Rashi* 4:23
"'Given' is 'shos'" ... *Targum Onkelos* 4:25
page 20 "Hashem existed" ... *Rambam, Avodah Zarah* 1:1-2
"Mabul!" ... *Rashi* 6:4
"Chanoch" ... *Targum Yonasan* 5:24
"In the Me'aras HaMachpeilah" *Seder Olam* 1; *Sotah* 13a
Questions Anyone? (2) ... *Bamidbar Rabbah* 4:8
"Bringing the Mabul" ... *Avos D'R' Nosson* 32:1

Fascinating Facts .... *Asarah Ma'amaros, Ma'amar Aim Kol Chai* 3:22
"Noach Is Born" .... *Rashi* 5:29
page 22 "To rest, 'nach'" .... *MRB* 25:2
"A farmer even easier" .... *Rashi* 5:29
"Shem and Cham" .... *Sifsei Chachamim* 5:32
"What Took So Long" .... *Rashi* 5:32
Torah in Our Lives .... *Sefer Chareidim, Mitzvos HaTeluyos Ba'Aretz* 4
"Bring a Mabul" .... *Rashi* 6:7

Parashas Noach

page 25 "Murdering each other" .... *MRB* 31:6
Questions Anyone? (1) .... *Rashi* 5:32
"Cham was the second" ... *Rashi* 10:21, *Sifsei Chachamim*
"One More Chance" .... *Rashi* 6:14
"120 years to build it" .... *Rashi* 6:14
Questions Anyone? (2) .... *Rashi* 6:9
"Everyone Is Talking About It" .... *Rashi* 6:14
Fascinating Facts .... *Rashi* 6:13
page 26 Fascinating Facts (1) .... *MRB* 31:7, 31:14, *Yefeh To'ar; Rashi* 9:20; *MRB* 36:3
"Crazy old man" .... *MRB* 30:7
Questions Anyone? (2) .... *Rashi* 6:18
"A window at the top" .... *Rashi* 6:16
"One of the corners" .... *MRB* 31:11, *Eitz Yosef*
Fascinating Facts (2) .... *Rashi* 6:16
"Waters of the Mabul" .... *Rashi* 6:14
"His family stayed" .... *Rashi* 6:16
"Hundreds of rooms" .... *MRB* 31:9
page 28 "The Death of a Tzaddik" .... *Rashi* 7:4
Torah in our Lives .... *Pesachim* 3a; *MRB* 32:4
"Family from the Mabul" .... *Rashi* 7:2, 8:20
"Am I a Hunter?" .... *MRB* 32:8
Questions Anyone? (2) .... *Rashi* 7:22
page 29 Questions Anyone? .... *Rashi* 7:2
Fascinating Facts (1) .... *Zohar Chadash* 22b
"All life on earth" .... *Rashi* 7:7
"Door behind him" .... *Rashi* 7:16
Fascinating Facts (2) .... *Rashi* 7:7; *Me'am Loez* 7:7
"Seventeenth day of Cheshvan" .... *Rashi* 7:12, 8:3
Fascinating Facts (3) .... *Rashi* 7:13
"Would have been saved" .... *Rashi* 7:12
"The Teivah Is in Danger" .... *Rashi* 7:16
"Rain began to fall" .... *MRB* 28:9
"Shot out of the ground" .... *Rashi* 8:2
"Mabul's hot water" .... *Ramban* 7:18-19
"Burned to nothing" .... *MRB* 28:7
"Then the animals" .... *Berachos* 61a
"And the fish" .... *MRB* 28:3
page 30 Questions Anyone? .... *Rashi* 4:22; *Mishlei Rabbasi* 30
"Feeding the Animals" .... *Tanchuma* 9
"Awesome Chessed" .... *MRB* 33:3
"Not to bring the Mabul" .... *Zohar* 106a
"Leave the Teivah" .... *Be'er Moshe* 8:1
"First of Sivan" .... *Rashi* 8:4
"First of Av" .... *Rashi* 8:5
"Back into the Teivah" .... *MRB* 33:5
page 32 Fascinating Facts (1) .... *Sanhedrin* 108a
Fascinating Facts (2) .... *Berachos* 61a
Fascinating Facts (3) .... *Tanchuma* 9
Fascinating Facts (4) .... *Pirkei D'R' Eliezer* 23
Questions Anyone? .... *Sanhedrin* 108b
"Noach sent a dove" .... *Rashi* 8:8
"Rosh Hashanah" .... *Rashi* 8:13
"Leave the Teivah" .... *Rashi* 8:13
"Permission to do so" .... *MRB* 34:4
"Noach entered the Teivah" .... *Rashi* 7:12, 8:14
page 33 Questions Anyone? .... *MRB* 33:6, *Eitz Yosef*
Fascinating Facts (1) .... *Sefer HaYashar, Noach*
"For saving him" .... *Pirkei D'R' Eliezer* 23
"Stand in Yerushalayim" .... *MRB* 34:9
"Passed down to Noach" .... *Bamidbar Rabbah* 4:8
Fascinating Facts (2) .... *Rashi* 8:2
"Saved them from the Mabul" .... *Ohr HaChaim* 9:3
"Eiver min hachai" .... *Rashi* 9:4
"To kill themselves" .... *Rashi* 9:5
page 34 "Destroyed it again" .... *Rashi* 9:9, *Sifsei Chachamim*
Fascinating Facts .... *Rashi* 9:12
"Brought with him to the Teivah" .... *Rashi* 9:20
"They grew grapes" .... *MRB* 36:4
page 35 Fascinating Facts (1) .... *MRB* 36:4, *Matnos Kehunah*
"He told his father" .... *Rashi* 9:22
"Made fun of their father" .... *Midrash Aggadah* 9:23
"With some clothing" .... *Rashi* 9:23
Fascinating Facts (2) .... *Rashi* 9:23
"Dark and ugly" .... *Abarbanel, Noach* 10:1; *Maharsha Taanis* 20b
"Would get Eretz Yisrael" .... *Rashi* 9:26
"Which they built" .... *MRB* 36:8, *Eitz Yosef*
"His descendants" .... *Rashi* and *Targum Yonasan* 9:27
"Art and music" .... *Commentary on Chumash* by *R' S.R. Hirsch* 9:27
"Yefes took Europe" .... *Abarbanel* 10:2
"The world's seventy nations" .... *Rabbeinu Bachya* 10:1
"Noach Passes Away" .... *Abarbanel* 9:18
page 36 Questions Anyone? (1) .... *MRB* 36:7
"The First King" .... *Sefer HaYashar*
"They attracted animals" .... *Pirkei D'R' Eliezer* 24; *MRB* 63:13
"Against Hashem" .... *Rashi* 10:9
"First man to become a king" .... *Pirkei D'R' Eliezer* 10; *Targum Sheini* 1
"Evil Again" .... *Sefer HaYashar*
"To be a god" .... *Midrash HaGadol, Bereishis* 11:28
"Tried to stop it" .... *Mishnas R' Eliezer* 8
Fascinating Facts .... *Rashi* 10:9
"Another Mabul" .... *MRB* 38:1
"Hashem in heaven" .... *Rashi* 11:9
"Another Mabul" .... *Rabbeinu Bachya* 11:4
"Top of the tower" .... *Sefer HaYashar*
page 38 "Build the tower" .... *Sefer HaYashar*
"Plastered over with clay" .... *Rashi* 11:3
Fascinating Facts (1) .... *Pirkei D'R' Eliezer* 24
"Iimashita ka" .... *Rashi* 11:7
"Torah in Our Lives" .... *Rashi* 11:9
page 39 "Others into monkeys" .... *Sefer HaYashar*
Questions Anyone? (1) .... *Sanhedrin* 109a
"Made it better" .... *Bamidbar Rabbah* 14:2
"Sold idol statues" .... *MRB* 38:13
"Priest of the idols" .... *Midrash HaGadol, Bereishis* 11:28
"Seventy years old" .... *Rashi* 11:32
"A child genius" .... *Rambam, Hilchos Avodah Zarah* 1:3
"Youngest brother, Haran" .... *MRB* 38:14

"Bothered him day and night" .... Rambam, Hilchos Avodah Zarah 1:3
page 40 "Spoke to him"..................................... Zohar I 86a
"Ran the world" .... Rambam, Hilchos Avodah Zarah 1:3
"Change their minds" .... Rambam, Hilchos Avodah Zarah 1:3
"Went back home"..................................... Sefer HaYashar
"Idol Smash-Up" .... MRB 38:13
"Fighting Idols" .... MRB 38:13
page 41 "Avram Argues with Nimrod" .... MRB 38:8
"Fiery Furnace" .... MRB 38:13
Fascinating Facts .... Avos D'R' Nosson 33:2
"Became a fiery furnace"..................... Yalkut Shimoni 77
Questions Anyone? .... Rashi 11:28
"I will do it Myself" .... Pesachim 118a
"Into the Fire!..................................... MRB 38:13
page 42 Questions Anyone? .... "Sfas Emes" Lech Lecha 5637
"Expecting a Miracle" .... Rashi, Vayikra 22:32
"Change her name to Sarah" .... Rashi 11:29
Fascinating Facts (1) .... Maharal
"Goodbye, Terach"..................................... Rashi 11:32

Parashas Lech Lecha

page 45 "It's in the genes"..................................... Rambam 12:6
page 46 "Whom he taught to believe"..................... Rashi 12:5
"How long the trip will take"..................... MRB 39:9
Questions Anyone? .... Chizkuni 12:5; MRB, Parashas Vayeishev 38
page 47 "A Great Smell"..................................... MRB 39:2
Fascinating Facts..................................... Bava Basra 158b
"A lot of money" .... Rashi 12:2
"Will come true" .... Rashi 12:3
"Because of you" .... MRB 39:12
"Be like you" .... Rashi 12:3
page 48 Maaseh Avos .... Rashi 12:6
"A Mizbei'ach in Ai" .... Rashi 12:8
"His wife's tent" .... Rashi 12:8
"Take care of her needs first"..................... Yevamos 62b
Fascinating Facts..................................... Bava Metzia 59a
Questions Anyone? .... MRB 39:14
"Only in Eretz Yisrael"..................................... Rashi 12:10
"From Charan"..................................... MRB 41:3; Maharzu
"Hashem's test" .... Rashi 12:10
page 49 "Hidden in a box" .... Rashi 12:14
"Border Police" .... MRB 40:5
"Shone with her beauty" .... MRB 40:5
"Hidden in the box" .... MRB 40:5; Yefeh To'ar
page 51 "A Seder-night Prayer" .... Pirkei D'R' Eliezer 26
"Pharaoh Whipped" .... MRB 41:2
"Honor Guard" .... Rashi 12:19-20
"A short way as well" .... Sotah 46b
"Kidnapping his wife"............ Yalkut Me'am Loez 12:20; Baal HaTurim 12:20
"King of another country" .... MRB 45:1
Maaseh Avos .... MRB 40:6; Pirkei D'R' Eliezer 26
page 52 Fascinating Facts..................... Rashi 13:3; MRB 41:3
"Made him rich too" .... Rashi 13:5
"Use it now" .... Rashi 13:7
"Uncle Avram" .... Rashi 13:8
page 53 "Protection or help" .... Rashi 13:9
"Avram or his G-d" .... Rashi 13:11
"I already am" .... Sanhedrin 109a
"An evil place" .... Rashi 13:10
"Terrible sins" .... MRB 41:7
"Anger Hashem" .... Rashi 13:13
"In all directions" .... Or HaChaim 13:15
"Walking through it" .... MRB 41:10
"Dust" .... MRB 41:9
page 55 "Not be able to exist" .... Rashi 13:16
"Soldier's name was Og"..................... Shocher Tov 136:12
Questions Anyone? .... Rashi 26:5; Beis HaLevi, Shemos 13:8
"Would marry Sarai" .... MRB 42:8
page 56 "Hole in the Teivah"..................... Pirkei D'R' Eliezer 23
Fascinating Facts (1) .... Rashi 14:1
Fascinating Facts (2) .... MRB 43:6
"Nicknamed Og" .... Shocher Tov 136:12
"Over 500 years" .... MR Bamidbar 19:32
"Lot had been captured" .... MRB 42:8
"Peacefully in his bed"..................... ibid. MRB; MRD 1:25
"Og fell over, dead" .... Berachos 54b
"To War" .... MRB 43:2; Maharzu
"Dirt and Straw" .... Sanhedrin 109a; MRB 43:3
Fascinating Facts (3) .... MRB 43:2; Maharzu
"King of Kings" .... MRB 43:5
"Called Shalem .... Shocher Tov 76;3
page 57 "Fighting in battle" .... Rashi 14:18
"Miraculous victory" .... Rashi 14:20
"Mistake!" .... Nedarim 32b
"Only from Hashem" .... Rashi 14:23
"While he was away" .... Rashi 14:24
Fascinating Facts .... Rabbeinu Bachya 14:23
page 58 "Into Gan Eden" .... Rashi 15;1
"Take revenge" .... MRB 44:4
page 59 "Against enemy attack" .... Rashi 15:1
Questions Anyone? .... Heard from R' E. Biderman, Lech Lecha 2018; Berachos 26b
"He told him" .... Rashi 15:5
"Able to hurt us" .... Megillah 16a
"Definitely have a child" .... Rashi 15:5
"Not deserve Eretz Yisrael" .... Rashi 15:6
"Keep Eretz Yisrael" .... Rashi 15:8-9
"Through their prayers" .... Yoma 86a
page 60 "Between the pieces" .... Rashi 15:10
Fascinating Facts................ Rashi 15;12; Ramban 15:12; Rashi 15:14; Rashi 15:10
"Through the pieces" .... Rashi 15:10
page 61 "Eretz Yisrael to live" .... Rashi 15:13-14
"Eisav becomes wicked" .... Rashi 15:15
"Sarai's Plan" .... Rashi 16:2; Gur Aryeh
"No Respect .... Rashi 16:4
"In front of Avram" .... MRB 45:5; Rashi 15:4
"Don't know what they are"..................... Berachos 5a-b
"Hagar shows disrespect" .... ibid. MRB; Rashi 16:5
"A Lesson" .... MRB 45:6
page 62 "Angels with a Message" .... Rashi 16:9
"Hashem heard your prayers"..................... Onkelos 16:11
"Everyone will hate"..................... Rashi 16:12; MRB 45:9
"She had seen angels"..................................... Rashi 16:13
page 63 Questions Anyone? .... Teshuvos HaRambam 448
"Princess of all the nations"..................................... MRB 47:1
Fascinating Facts..................... MRB 47:1; Rashi 17:5
page 64 "Of course, the Jews"..................................... Rashi 17:6

"Eretz Yisrael will be their country" ... *Rambam, Melachim* 10:8
"When you heard the news" ... *Rashi* 17:19
Fascinating Facts ... *Rashi* 17:19

Parashas Vayeira

page 70 "The Visit" ... *Rashi* 18:1
"Invite in as guests" ... *Rashi* 18:1
Questions Anyone? ... *MRB* 48:9, *Eitz Yosef*
"Three Guests in Disguise" ... *Rashi* 18:1
"Destroy the evil city of S'dom" ... *Bava Metzia* 86b
"Disguised themselves as Arabs" ... *Bava Metzia* 86b
page 72 "Three Tongues" ... *Rashi* 18:7
Fascinating Facts (1) ... *Rashi* 18:2
Questions Anyone? ... *Rashi* 18:4
"Adam and Chavah are buried here" ... *Midrash Aggadah* 18:7; *Zohar Chadash Ruth* 79b; *Zohar* 1:127a
Fascinating Facts (2) ... *Zohar Chadash Ruth* 79b; *Zohar* 1:127a
"Tongues in mustard" ... *Bava Metzia* 86b
Fascinating Facts (3) ... *MRB* 48:12
"Place you are visiting" ... *Rashi* 18:8
"Huge Rewards" ... *MRB* 48:10
page 73 Fascinating Facts (1) ... *Bava Metzia* 87a
"Should have said amein" ... *Ramban* 18:15
"Began their journey" ... *Rashi* 18:16
Fascinating Facts (2) ... *Sema C.M.* 427:11
"Would be born" ... *Rashi* 18:33
"Work to do there" ... *Bava Metzia* 86b
"The Five Evil Cities" .. *Rashi* 18:17, *citing Bereishis* 10:19
"With anyone" ... *Sanhedrin* 109b
"Was called S'dom" ... *Rashi* 18:26
Questions Anyone? ... *Lekach Tov* 18:24
"Help the poor" ... *Sanhedrin* 104b, *based on Yechezkel* 16:49
"Screamed in pain" ... *Sanhedrin* 109b; *Rashi, Iyov* 28:4
"Other terrible sins" ... *Sanhedrin* 109b, *Sefer HaYashar*
"Make Hashem angry" ... *MRB* 41:7
"Fit him just right" ... *Rashi* 13:13
page 74 "Must be destroyed" ... *Sanhedrin* 109b; *Sefer HaYashar*
Fascinating Facts ... *Zohar* 1:106b
Questions Anyone? (1) ... *MRB* 49:11, *Maharzu*
"Stop being so mean" ... *R' M. Feinstein, Stone Chumash* 22-33
"Tenth in each city" ... *Rashi* 18:28
"City will be saved" ... *Rashi* 18:29
Questions Anyone? (2) ... *Rashi* 18:32, *Gur Aryeh, Sifsei Chachamim*
"A Secret" ... *Rashi* 19:2
"Couldn't give it up" ... *Rashi* 19:1
page 75 Questions Anyone? ... *Rashi* 19:1
Fascinating Facts ... *MRB* 50:1
"Feeding the Angels" ... *MRB* 50:4, 51:5
"Since it was Pesach" ... *Rashi* 19:3
"Lot's wife, Edis" ... *Pirkei D'R' Eliezer* 25
"Married a S'domite" ... *Targum Yonasan* 19:26
"City was evil" ... *Rashi* 19:4
page 76 "Two married daughters" ... *Rashi* 19:14
"Money? Gold? ... *Rashi* 19:16
Questions Anyone? ... *MRB* 51:6; *Eitz Yosef*
page 78 "Lot's Descendants" ... *MRB* 50:10
"Lived on a mountain" ... *Rashi* 19:17
"Lot was wicked" ... *Rashi* 19:19
"It wasn't as evil" ... *Rashi* 19:20
"Fire falling from heaven" ... *Rashi* 19:24
"Back in the earth" ... *MRB* 51:4
"The trees and grass" ... *MRB* 51:4
page 79 Questions Anyone? (1) ... *Rashi* 19:24
"Near to S'dom" ... *Rashi* 19:30, *Mizrachi*
Questions Anyone? (2) ... *Rashi* 19:26
"For many people" ... *Rashi* 20:1
"She's my sister" ... *Rashi* 20:11
"She was his sister" ... *MRB* 52:6
page 80 Questions Anyone? ... *Rashi* 20:11; *ArtScroll Saperstein Rashi note* 2
page 81 Fascinating Facts (1) ... *Rashi* 21:6
"Letters of Yitzchak's Name" ... *Pirkei D'R' Eliezer* 32
Fascinating Facts (2) ... *MRB* 53:6, *Eitz Yosef*
"Made a big party" ... *Rashi* 21:8
"Was there as well" ... *Rashi* 21:8; *MRB* 53:10
"Idols and grasshoppers" ... *MRB* 53:11
"Attempted Murder" ... *MRB* 53:11
page 82 "To do teshuvah" ... *Rashi* 21:11
"Questions Anyone? (1) ... *Rashi* 21:12
"A Test" ... *Avos* 5:3, *Bartenura*
"Sick and Dying" ... *MRB* 53:13, *Eitz Yosef*
Questions Anyone? (2) ... *Rashi* 21:14
"Yishmael was seventeen" ... *Yalkut Shimoni* 95
Questions Anyone? (3) ... *Rashi* 21:14
"Old Egyptian gods" ... *Rashi* 21:14
"Water in the bottle was gone" ... *Rashi* 21:15
page 83 "Not a Jewish Mother" ... *Rashi* 21:16
"Saved" ... *MRB* 53:14
"The Arab nations" ... *Mishnah Sachir, Devarim* 29:9; *Sfas Emes, Vayeira* 5654
Torah in Our Lives (1) ... *Rosh Hashanah* 16b
"Stay and live there" ... *Pirkei D'R' Eliezer* 30
"Champion" ... *MRB* 53:15, *Eitz Yosef*
page 84 "Avraham was still alive" ... *Bava Basra* 16b
"Very old man" ... *Rashi* 21:22
"Seven Sheep" ... *Yalkut Me'am Loez* 21:22-32
page 85 "Belonged to Avraham" ... *MRB* 54:5
Maaseh Avos ... *MRB* 54:5
Questions Anyone? ... *Midrash Sechel Tov* 21:31
"Different kinds of fruit trees" ... *Targum Yonasan, Rashbam* 21:33
"Code Word" ... *Otzar HaMidrashim, Alpha-Beta, p.* 37
Fascinating Facts ... *MRB* 54:6, *Eitz Yosef*
"Satan Makes Problems" ... *Rashi* 22:1
page 86 "I Chose" ... *Sanhedrin* 89b; *MRB* 55:4
"The Tenth Test" ... *Rashi* 22:2
"Hashem spoke to Avraham" ... *Pirkei D'R' Eliezer* 31
Fascinating Facts ... *Rashi* 22:2
Questions Anyone? ... *Rashi* 22:2
"A great nation? No" ... *Yerushalmi Taanis* 2:4
page 87 "On Their Way" ... *Rashi* 22:3
Maaseh Avos ... *MRB* 55:8
"Avraham's Donkey" ... *Pirkei D'R' Eliezer* 31
"Eliezer with him" ... *Rashi* 22:3
"The Journey" ... *MRB* 56:2
"Cloud in the distance" ... *Rashi* 22:4
"Over the mountain" ... *Pirkei D'R' Eliezer* 31
Questions Anyone? ... *MRB* 55:4

"Didn't see anything special" .... *MRB* 56:2
"I'm Going" .... *MRB* 56:4; *Yalkut Shimoni* 98,100,101
page 89 Fascinating Facts .... *Rashi* 22:5
"To do Hashem's will" .... *Rashi* 22:6
"Brought with them on it" .... *Tanchuma Vayeira* 23
"Mizbei'ach they had built" .... *Yalkut Shimoni* 101
page 90 Fascinating Facts (1) .... *Targum Yonasan* 22:9; *Pirkei D'R' Eliezer* 31
Questions Anyone? .... *Rashi* 22:9
"Angel's Tears" .... *Yalkut Shimoni* 101; *MRB* 56:8
"Saw what was going on" .... *Targum Yonasan* 22:10
Fascinating Facts (2) .... *Rashi* 27:1
"Hard to do" .... *Abarbanel* 22:11
page 91 "Who Are You" .... *Yalkut Shimoni* 101
Questions Anyone? (1) .... *Rashi* 22:11
Questions Anyone? (2) .... *Rashi* 22:12
"Satan's tricks" .... *Rabbi Moshe HaDarshan*
Questions Anyone? (3) .... *Rashi* 22:12; *MRB* 56:7, *Yefeh To'ar*
"How Can It Be" .... *MRB* 56:8
"Branches of a tree" .... *Rashi* 22:13
page 92 "The Ram" .... *Yalkut Shimoni* 101
"Right before Shabbos" .... *Avos* 5:6
"He Will See" .... *Rashi* 22:14
Questions Anyone? .... *MRB* 56:10, *Eitz Yosef*
page 93 "Presence of Hashem" .... *Rashi* 22:14
"Torah in Our Lives" .... *Rosh Hashanah* 16a
Questions Anyone? .... *Tzitz Eliezer*, 17:74, *citing Pesikta D'Rav Kahana*
"Stars and Sand" .... *Kli Yakar* 22:17
"A Baby Is Born" .... *Rashi* 22:20

Parashas Chayei Sarah

page 97 "Are buried there as well" .... *Sotah* 13a
"Esav's head is buried there" .... *Pirkei D'R' Eliezer* 38
"On the way to heaven" .... *Zohar Chadash*, *Parashas Noach* 35b
"From the Akeidas Yitzchak" .... *MRB* 58:5
"Doesn't wear makeup" .... *MRB* 58:1
Questions Anyone? .... *Targum Yonasan* 22:20; *MRB* 58:5; *Rashi* 23:2
page 98 Fascinating Facts .... *Rashi* 23:2
"Came to her funeral" .... *MRB* 58:7
"Mamrei came as well" .... *Me'am Loez* 23:17-19
"Eishes Chayil" .... *Midrash Tanchuma* 4
"Hadn't died young" .... *Baal HaTurim* 23:2
page 99 "Straight to Gan Eden" .... *Kli Yakar* 23:2
Questions Anyone? (1) .... *Baal HaTurim* 23:2; *Kli Yakar there*
Questions Anyone? (2) .... *MRB* 58:3; *Midrash Aggadah* 23:1
"Adam and Chavah were buried" .... *Sotah* 13a; *Zohar Bereishis* 127a
Fascinating Facts .... *Rashi* 23:9
Questions Anyone? (3) .... *MRB* 58:8
"Buy the field as well" .... *Ha'amek Davar* 23:11
page 100 Fascinating Facts (1) .... *Rashi* 23:10; *MRB* 58:7
"One million regular shekels" .... *MRB* 58:7
Fascinating Facts (2) .... *Bava Metzia* 87a
"Burial" .... *Zohar Bereishis* 128a
Questions Anyone? .... *Esther Rabbah* 7:11
"Face Change" .... *Bava Metzia* 87a; *MRB* 65:9
page 102 "'Ben' and 'bakol' is 52" .... *Rashi* 24:1
"Some say 'Bakol' teaches us" .... *Bava Basra* 16b.
"His servant Eliezer" .... *Pirkei D'R' Eliezer* 16
"Taught them to others" .... *Yoma* 28b
"With him to the battle" .... *Rashi* 14:14
Fascinating Facts .... *Rashi* 24:39
Questions Anyone? .... *MRB* 59:10, *Maharzu*
page 103 "Aner, Eshkol or Mamrei" .... *Rashi* 24:8, *Mizrachi*
"Wealth to Yitzchak" .... *Rashi* 24:10
Questions Anyone? .... *Rashi* 24:10
"Trip by camel" .... *Pirkei D'R' Eliezer* 16
"Out of the well into her pitcher" .... *Rashi* 24:17
Fascinating Facts (1) .... *Yalkut Shimoni* 109
page 104 "Weighing a half silver shekel" .... *MRB* 60:6
"Torah in Our Lives" .... *MRB* 60:6
page 106 "Ran out to kill him" .... *Yalkut Shimoni* 109
"Camels in the Air" .... *Yalkut Shimoni* 109
"Feeds his animals" *Gittin* 62a; *"Magen Avraham"* 167:18
Fascinating Facts .... *Rashi* 24:50
page 107 "Lot or Yishmael" .... *Rashi* 24:49
"Poison" .... *Yalkut Shimoni* 109
"Switched the dishes" .... *Midrash Aggadah* 24:53
"There is another opinion" .... *MRB* 60:12
page 108 "To go or not" .... *Rashi* 24:58
"Like it or not" .... *Be'er Mayim Chaim* 24:58
Fascinating Facts .... *Berachos* 26b *Berachos* 26b
page 109 "Yitzchak ... daven Minchah" .... *Pirkei D'R' Eliezer* 16
"Beis HaMikdash ... stand" .... *Rashi*, *Chullin* 91b
"Like looking at an angel" .... *Shocher Tov* 90:18
"Who the man was" .... *MRB* 60:15
"With her veil" .... *"Akeidas Yitzchak"* 22
"Clouds, Candles, and Dough" .... *Rashi* 24:67
"Answered so quickly" .... *Rashi* 24:66
Questions Anyone? .... *MRB* 60:16, *Maharzu*
Fascinating Facts (1) .... *MRB* 68:4
"Gave him his freedom" .... *Pirkei D'R' Eliezer* 16
"Without dying first" .... *Derech Eretz Zuta* 1
Fascinating Facts (2) .... *Yalkut Shimoni* 109
page 110 "Eisav becomes evil" .... *Rashi* 25:30
"Remarriage" .... *MRB* 61:4 *Zohar Bereishis*, 133b
"Yitzchak Gets It all" .... *MRB* 61:6
Fascinating Facts (1) .... *Chiddushei Radal* 21, *MRB* 61
"To be at the funeral" .... *MRB* 62:5
"A great tzaddik" .... *MRB* 62:3
"Sarah's grave .... *MRB* 62:3
Fascinating Facts (2) .... *MRB* 62:3
Questions Anyone? .... *MRB* 59:1
page 111 "He blessed him" .... *Rashi* 25:11

Parashas Toldos

page 115 "A Rose" .... *MRB* 63:4
Fascinating Facts .... *Rashi* 25:19
"From this tzaddeikes" .... *MRB* 63:5
"Pray there for children" .... *Targum Yonasan* 25:21
"Prayers that were answered" .... *Rashi* 25:21
"The same thing happened" .... *Rashi* 25:22
"Have a child" .... *Rashi* 25:22
page 116 "Was a prophet" .... *MRB* 20:6, *Eitz Yosef*
"One would be good" .... *Rashi* 25:23
"Evil son and his descendants" .... *Rashi* 25:23
"Prince of the Jews" .... *Rashi* 25:23
"Serve Rebbi his meals" .... *Avodah Zarah* 10b

Questions Anyone? (1) .... *Stone Chumash commentary* 25:22
Torah in Our Lives .... *MRB* 63:6, *Eitz Yosef*
"Fighting back" .... *MRB* 63:6
Questions Anyone? (2) .... *Niddah* 30b; *Chiddushei HaGriz (Brisker Rav), Toldos* 2
"It was too late" .... *Rashi* 25:25
page 117 "Not cute at all" .... *Targum Yonasan* 25:25
Questions Anyone? .... *Rashi* 25:25
Fascinating Facts .... *Rashi* 25:25
"Born with a bris" .... *Avos D'R' Nosson* 2:5
"The baby's name" .... *Rashi* 25:26
page 118 "Eisav's body, his heel" .... *Rashi* 25:26
Torah in Our Lives .... *Sifri, Bamidbar* 69
"Loving Hashem" .... *MRB* 63:10
"Birds to kill" .... *Rashi* 25:27
"Becoming wicked" .... *Ohr HaChaim* 25:28
"Give him wine" .... *MRB* 63:10
"Truly was a tzaddik" .... *Zohar* 146b
Fascinating Facts .... *Pesikta* 23; *MRB* 65:16
"Fooled people" .... *Rashi* 25:27
"From straw" .... *Rashi* 25:27
Questions Anyone? .... *Ben Poras Yosef Parshas Vayeitzei*
"Into a fire" .... *Midrash Aggadah* 27:15
"Very hungry" .... *Rashi* 25:29
page 119 "Yaakov Is Cooking .... *Rashi* 25:30
Fascinating Facts .... *Rashi* 25:30
"Eisav Sins Again!" .... *MRB* 63:11
"What he had ordered" .... *MRB* 63:12
page 120 "To be like the Kohanim" .... *Rashi* 25:31
"Eisav and Friends" .... *MRB* 63:14
Fascinating Facts .... *MRB* 63:12
"Land of Eretz Yisrael" .... *MRB* 64:3
page 122 Questions Anyone? .... *MRB* 64:3
"They got careless" .... *Rashi* 26:8
"Marry Rivkah himself" .... *Rashi* 26:10
"Not good land for farming" .... *Rashi* 26:12
"Grew to the poor" .... *Rashi* 26:12
page 123 "An army of servants" .... *Ramban* 26:14
"Richer than the king" .... *Ramban* 26:16
"Will drink this water" .... *Rashi* 26:15
"'Belongs to us!' they said" .... *Ramban* 26:17
Maaseh Avos .... *Ramban* 26:20
"Who wanted to kill him" .... *Ramban* 26:24
page 124 "Couldn't stop scratching" .... *MRB* 64:9
page 125 "A tzaddik just like my father" .... *Rashi* 26:34
"He became blind" .. *Drashos R' Y. Ibn Sho'ib, Vayishlach*
"Yitzchak's blindness" .... *Rashi* 27:1
"Made him blind" .... *Rashi* 27:1
"It is Hashem's will" .... *MRB* 67:9; *Ohr HaChaim* 27:5; *Ramban* 27:4
page 126 "On Erev Pesach" .... *Chizkuni* 27:4
"Take your sword and bow" .... *Rashi* 27:3
"Sharpen your knife" .... *Rashi* 27:3
"Belongs to someone else" .... *Gur Aryeh* 27:3
"To eat a good meal" .... *Rabbeinu Bachya* 27
Fascinating Facts (1) .... *Rashi* 28:9
Fascinating Facts (2) .... *Rashi* 27:9
"Me and not you" .... *MRB* 65:15, *Eitz Yosef*
page 128 Questions Anyone? .... *Targum Yonasan* 27:9
"Surrounded by animals" .... *MRB* 63:13
"Took the clothing" .... *MRB* 65:16
Fascinating Facts .... *Pirkei D'R' Eliezer* 24
"Stolen by his wives" .... *Rashi* 27:15
page 129 "Yitzchak's firstborn" .... *Rashi* 27:19
"Make sure it's Eisav .... *Rashi* 27:21-22
page 130 "Cursed him" .... *MRB* 44:3, *Eitz Yosef*
"Pushed him forward .... *MRB* 65:19
"'My son Eisav,' he said" .... *Ohr HaChaim* 27:24; *but see Alshich* 27:24; *Midrash Sechel Tov* 27:24
Fascinating Facts .... *MRB* 67:2
"Smell of Gan Eden" .... *Rashi* 27:27
Questions Anyone? .... *Targum Yonasan* 27:25
"Should always give you" .... *MRB* 66:3
"Listen to Hashem" .... *Rashi* 27:28
page 131 "Prayed for victory" .... *MRB* 66:3, *Yefeh To'ar*
"Those who learn it" .... *MRB* 66:4, *Maharzu*
"The Jews will rule" .... *MRB* 66:4
"Realizing he was there" .... *MRB* 66:5
"Yitzchak's tent had two" .... *MRB* 66:5
"Extraordinarily powerful" .... *Pirkei D'R' Eliezer* 32
page 132 Fascinating Facts .... *Pirkei D'R' Eliezer* 32
"Before Eisav got back" .... *MRB* 67:2
"Being served dog meat" .... *Targum Yonasan* 27:31
"Open under him" .... *Rashi* 27:33
"'Opening for Eisav,' He said" .... *MRB* 67:2, *Yefeh To'ar*
"Deserve the blessings" .... *Rashi* 27:33
page 133 "Belongs to his master" .... *Rashi* 27:37
"His father's mercy" .... *Malbim* 27:39
"Freed from being his slave" .... *Rashi* 27:40
"Nature would give him" .... *Kli Yakar* 27:39
"To destroy them" .... *MRB* 67:7
"The victors in war" .... *Ramban* 27:40
page 134 "He would kill Yaakov" .... *Rashi* 27:41
"Wanted to kill Yaakov" .... *Rashi* 27:42
"When Yitzchak will die" .... *Ohr HaChaim* 27:43
"Might kill each other" .... *Even Ezra* 27:45
Fascinating Facts (1) .... *Rashi* 27:45; *Sotah* 13a
"Family to marry" .... *Ohr HaChaim* 27:46
Fascinating Facts (2) .... *Yerushalmi Bikkurim* 3:3
page 135 "Prophecy about the future" .... *Rashi*, *Gittin* 57b
"Destroyed our Beis HaMikdash" .... *Gittin* 57b
"Kill their enemies" .... *MRB* 65:20, *Eitz Yosef*
"Eisav's nations .... *MRB* 65:20

Parashas Vayeitzei

page 138 "Built in the future" .... *Rashi* 28:11
page 139 "Enter Eretz Yisrael" .... *MRB* 74:17
page 140 "The journey begins" .... *Rashi* 29:11
Fascinating Facts (1) .... *Rashi* 28:10
Fascinating Facts (2) .... *MRB* 68:11, *Eitz Yosef*
"So Yaakov could walk across" .... *Rashi* 32:11
Fascinating Facts (3) .... *Yalkut Shimoni Shemos* 168, 173
"Yaakov Turns Back" .... *Sanhedrin* 95a-b; *Chullin* 91b
"From Beersheva to Charan" .... *Pirkei D'R' Eliezer* 16
"The same day" .... *MRB* 68:8
"From Mount Moriah" .... *Sanhedrin* 38b; *Yalkut Shimoni Vayikra* 455
page 141 Questions Anyone? .... *Berachos* 26b
"Wall against wild animals" .... *Rashi* 28:16
Fascinating Facts .... *Akeidas Yitzchak*, *Vayeitzei* 25
"Talking Rocks" .... *Rashi* 28:16
"One united Jewish nation" .... *MRB* 68:11
page 143 Maaseh Avos .... *MRB* 70:6; *Taanis* 11a

"Come down with the Torah" .... *MRB* 68:12
"To Hashem in Heaven" .... *MRB* 68:12, *Eitz Yosef*
"Mashiach will come" .... *Vayikra Rabbah* 29:2
"Could fit under a person" .... *Rashi* 28:13
"Will be a large country" .... *Seforno* 28:14
page 144 "Back to Eretz Yisrael" .*Rashi* 28:15; *Ohr HaChaim* 28:13
"Live in Eretz Yisrael" .... *Rabbeinu Bachya* 28:13
"The gate of heaven" .... *Shelah*
"Will one day be built" .... *Seforno* 28:17
"Hashem had given him" .... *MRB* 69:8
Fascinating Facts .... *Midrash Tehillim* 91:7
"Korbanos to Hashem" .... *Rashbam* 28:22
"Hashem's blessings" .... *Rambam* 28:20
"Bring korbanos" .... *Ibn Ezra* 28:21; *Chizkuni* 28:18
"Feeling very happy" .... *Rashi* 29:1
page 146 "Easily, without effort" .... *Rashi* 29:10
Fascinating Facts (1) .... *Zohar II* 12b
"Will You Marry Me" .... *Megillah* 13b
"Taken everything from him" .... *Rashi* 29:11
Fascinating Facts (2) .... *Rashi* 29:11
Questions Anyone? .... *Riva Al HaTorah* 29:25
page 147 "No Money!? .... *Rashi* 29:13
Questions Anyone? (1) .... *Rashi* 29:12
"A Guest in Lavan's House" .... *Rashi* 29:14
"Please, Not Eisav" .... *MRB* 70:16
Questions Anyone? (2) .... *Rashi* 29:18
page 148 Questions Anyone? .... *MRB* 68:5
"Would be so ashamed" .... *Rashi* 29:25
Fascinating Facts .... *Midrash Rabbah Eichah*, *end of Introduction* 24
"Yaakov Marries Rachel" .... *Rashi* 29:27
page 149 Questions Anyone? (1) .... *Yerushalmi Moed Kattan* 1:7
"He loved Rachel more" .... *Ramban* 29:31
"Leah couldn't have children" .... *Midrash Sechel Tov* 29:31
"Hagar to Avraham" .... *Rashi* 30:3
"Give her a child too" .... *Rashi* 16:3, *Gur Aryeh*
"She raised him" .... *Rashi* 30:3
page 150 "A miracle and give her a child" .... *Rashi* 30:22
"Finally had a child" .... *Rashi* 30:22
Fascinating Facts .... *MRB* 73:1
"Knew the future .... *Rashi* 29:34
"Safe to go home" .... *Rashi* 30:25
"Now he did" .... *Rashi* 30:27
"Very wealthy man" .... *Zohar I* 161a
Questions Anyone? .... *MRB* 73:8
page 151 "In the care of his sons" .... *Rashi* 30:35
"Rings around their ankles" .... *Rashi* 30:32
"Sick and weak ones" .... *Rashi* 30:36
"Yaakov came up with a plan" .... *Rabbeinu Bachya* 30:38
Questions Anyone? .... *Rashi* 31:7
page 152 "Lots of servants" .... *Rashi* 30:43
"Hashem told you to do" .... *Rashi* 31:15
"Group of his relatives" .... *Rashi* 31:23
"To kill Yaakov" .... *Midrash Tanchuma Parashas Eikev* 3
Fascinating Facts .... *Targum Yonasan* 31:22
page 153 "Belief in idols" .... *Rashi* 31:19
"From being stolen" .... *Rav Hirsch* 31:19
"The mountain before dark" .... *Ramban* 31:23
"He was going to kill him" .... *Pirkei D'R' Eliezer* 35
"To work for him" .... *Rashi* 31:24; *Sifsei Chachamim*
Questions Anyone? .... *MRB* 74:7; *Zera Avraham*
page 154 "Payment one hundred times" .... *Rashi* 31:7
Fascinating Facts .... *MRB* 74:4, *Eitz Yosef*
"They come from me" .... *Rav Hirsch* 31:43
page 155 "When Yaakov left" .... *MRB* 74:16, *Eitz Yosef*
page 156 "Reuven" .... *Rashi* 29:32
"While she carried the baby" .... *Chizkuni* 29:34
"To accompany" .... *Rashi* 29:34
"Yehudah" .... *Seforno* 29:35
page 157 "Zevulun" .... *Rashi* 30:20
"Dinah" .... *Rashi* 30:21
"Dan" .... *MRB* 71:7
"Her son also" .... *MRB* 71:7, *Eitz Yosef*
"Naphtali" .... *Rashi* 30:8
page 158 "Gad" .... *MRB* 71:9, *Eitz Yosef*
"Asher" .... *MRB* 71:10, *Eitz Yosef*
"Yosef" .... *Rashi* 30:23
"She prayed for another son" .... *Rashi* 30:24

Parashas Vayishlach

page 162 "Yaakov Sends a Message" .... *Rashi* 32:4-6
"Bad news" .... *Rashi* 32:8-9
Maaseh Avos .... *Ramban, introduction to the parashah*
"They would be ready" .... *Midrash Tanchuma* 6
page 163 Maaseh Avos .... *Ramban* 32:9
Fascinating Facts (1) .... *MRB* 76:6
"Gifts for Peace" .... *Rashi* 32:17
Fascinating Facts (2) .... *Rashi* 32:14
page 164 "Eisav Meets His Match" .... *Rashi* 33:8
"Side of the river to the other" .... *MRB* 76:9, *Eshed HaNechalim*
Fascinating Facts (1) .... *Rashi* 32:23
"Back Again" .... *Chullin* 91a
Fascinating Facts (2) .... *Shelah*, *Vayeishev* 4-9
page 166 "Wrestling with an Angel" .... *Kli Yakar* 32:25
Fascinating Facts .... *Kli Yakar* 32:25
"Throne in heaven" ... *MR Shir HaShirim* 3:2-3; *Eitz Yosef*
Questions Anyone? *Haggadah, Piyut Vayhi Bachatzi Halaylah*
"Angel to the ground .... *MRB* 77:3, *Eitz Yosef*
Maaseh Avos .... *Lekach Tov*
"The Angel's Blessings" .... *Rashi* 32:29
"Turn to praise Hashem" .... *Chullin* 91b
"Able to praise Hashem again *MRB* 78:2, *Yefeh To'ar*
page 167 "Given a new name" .... *Rashi* 32:30
"During Bircas Kohanim" .... *Rabbeinu Bachya* 32:30
"Special healing powers" .... *Rashi* 32:32
Fascinating Facts .... *MRB* 68:10
"Where the angel hit Yaakov" .... *Sefer HaChinuch* 3
"And won" .... *Chizkuni* 32:33
Maaseh Avos .... *Sefer HaChinuch* 3
"Mercy on his brother" .... *Rashi* 33:4
page 168 Fascinating Facts .... *MRB* 78:8, *Eitz Yosef*
"Love or Hate?" .... *MRB* 78:9
"Seeing his brother again" .... *Ibn Ezra* 33:4
"Afraid to fight him" .... *MRB* 78:15, *Eitz Yosef*
page 169 "Look at his righteous mother" .... *Rashi* 33:7
Questions Anyone? (1) .... *MRB* 78:10, *Eitz Yosef: Bereishis* 30:25, 31:41; *Rashi* 28:9
"Really belonged to Yaakov" .... *Rashi* 33:9
"A nice person" .... *MRB* 78:12
"Let's Travel Together" .... *Rashi* 33:14
"Influence his family" .... *Ramban* 33:15
"Outsmarting Eisav" .... *Rashi* 33:14

Questions Anyone? (2) .... *Rashi* 36:7
page 170 Fascinating Facts (1) .... *Ohr HaChaim* 33:17
"Next Stop: Shechem" .... *Rashi* 33:18
Fascinating Facts (2) .... *Pirkei D'R' Eliezer* 38
"A house, and moved in" .... *Sefer HaYashar*
Questions Anyone? .... *MRB* 79:7
Questions Anyone? .... *Ibn Ezra* 33:19
"Afraid of the evil prince .... *Ohr HaChaim* 34:2
"With great wisdom" .... *Rashi* 34:13
page 171 "Discussing it with their father" .... *Rashi* 34:25
"Thirteen-year-old boys" .... *MRB* 80:10, *Yefeh To'ar*
"This terrible crime" .... *Rashi* 34:25
"Save them miraculously" .... *MRB* 80:10
Torah in Our Lives .... *Rashi*, *Nazir* 29b
"Halachah L'Moshe MiSinai" .... *Maharil*, *responsa* 51
Questions Anyone? .... *Rabbeinu Bachya* 34:25
page 173 "Everything they could find" .... *Sefer HaYashar*
"The Argument" .... *Rav Hirsch* 34:25
"Revenge!" .... *Sefer HaYashar*
page 174 "Bad News" .... *Rashi* 35:8
page 175 "Rivkah's Funeral" .... *Rashi* 35:8
"Comfort him and bless him" .... *Rashi* 35:9
"Name from now on" .... *Berachos* 12-13a
"Prince of G-d" .... *Rashi* 35:10
Questions Anyone? (2) .... *Rashi* 35:10
Questions Anyone? (3) .... *Seder Olam*
page 176 "A half mile" .... *Ramban* 35:16
Fascinating Facts (1) .... *Rashi* 35:17
"After waiting eight" .... *Seder Olam*
Fascinating Facts (2) .... *MRB* 82:10, *Eitz Yosef*, *Yefeh To'ar*
"Positive sounding name" .... *Ramban* 35:18
"Good meanings" .... *Rashi* and *Ramban* 35:18
page 177 "Kever Rachel, Then" .... *MRB* 82:10
Questions Anyone? .... *Seder Olam*
Fascinating Facts .... *Ramban* 35:16
page 178 "Put it in Leah's tent" .... *Rashi* 35:22
"A very high level" .... *MRB* 84:19, *Eitz Yosef*
Fascinating Facts (2) .... *Megillah* 17a; *Rashi* 35:29
"At the age of 180" .... *Rashi* 35:29
"Their father's funeral" .... *Rashi* 25:9
"End of his life" .... *Megillah* 11a
page 179 Questions Anyone? .... *Midrash Rabbah Esther* 7:13

Parashas Vayeishev

page 184 "The Master Plan" .... *Rashi* 37:14
"Yosef" .... *Bereishis* 39:6; *Rashi* 37:2
"Similar to each other" .... *MRB* 84:6
"They looked alike" .... *MRB* 84:8
page 185 "Robe of many colors" .... *MRB* 84:8, *Yefeh To'ar (quoted in Stone Chumash)*
"Shem and Eiver" .... *Rashi* 37:3
"His best friend" .... *Rashi* 37:4
Fascinating Facts .... *MRB* 84:10
page 187 Questions Anyone? .... *Rashi* 37:10
"Causing them to hate him" .... *Rashi* 37:10
"When that would happen" .... *Rashi* 37:11
"Told them the dream" .... *MRB* 84:12
Fascinating Facts .... *Rashi* 37:15
"Eaten by a wild animal" .... *Rashi* 49:5
"Yours or Mine" .... *Rashi* 37:20
page 188 Fascinating Facts (1) .... *MRB* 84:14, *Eitz Yosef*
"Rescue" .... *Rashi* 37:22
"Take care of Yaakov" .... *Rashi* 37:29
"Didn't harm Yosef" .... *Rashi* 37:24
Questions Anyone? .... *Rashi* 37:25
Fascinating Facts (2) .... *Yerushalmi Shekalim* 2:3; *MRB* 84:18
"How Could They Do That" .... *Stone Chumash Commentary* 37:11
page 190 "Slave Boy" .... *Sefer HaYashar*
"Sold and Resold" .... *MRB* 84:22
"500 silver coins" .... *Sefer HaYashar*
Fascinating Facts .... *MRB* 84:8, *Eitz Yosef*
Questions Anyone? (2) .... *Rashi* 37:36
"Searched for his brother" .... *Sefer HaYashar*
"He was the oldest" .... *Rashi* 37:22
"Our father's sadness" .... *Rashi* 37:30
page 191 "Rip it" .... *Ramban* 37:32
"Yaakov sat, crying" .... *Sefer HaYashar*
"His son's suffering" .... *Rashi* 37:35
Questions Anyone? .... *Rashi* 37:34
"Blame" .... *Rashi* 38:1
"Noach's son Shem" .... *MRB* 85:10
Fascinating Facts .... *Ruth* 4:18-22
"Now that's service" .... *Midrash Sechel Tov* 39:2
page 192 Torah in Our Lives .... *Rashi* 39:3
"Within a year" .... *MRB* 86:6, *Eitz Yosef*
"Let Yosef run everything" .... *Rashi* 39:6
"Combing his hair carefully" .... *Rashi* 39:6
"Change Yosef's situation" .... *Rashi* 39:6
page 193 "Flies and Pebbles" .... *Rashi* 40:1
"In prison for a year" .... *Rashi* 40:4
Fascinating Facts .... *Rashi* 40:5
"What they mean" .... *MRB* 88:4, *Eitz Yosef*
page 194 Torah in Our Lives .... *MRB* 88:5
"A Request and a Mistake" .... *Rashi* 40:23
"Eaten by birds" .... *Targum Yonasan* 40:19
Questions Anyone? .... *Rashi* 40:1, *Mizrachi*, *Gur Aryeh*
page 195 "Forget, Forget" .... *MRB* 88:7, *Yefeh To'ar*
Questions Anyone? .... *Yalkut Shimoni* 146

Parashas Mikeitz

page 201 "Trembling in fright" .... *Rashi* 41:8
"Rebel against him" .... *MRB* 89:6
"They were wrong" .... *Rashi* 41:8
"He would die" .... *MRB* 89:7
"His important job" .... *MRB* 89:7
"Remember Yosef" .... *Rashi* 40:23
page 202 "He was a bad man" .... *Rashi* 41:12
"Could not become a ruler" .... *Rashi* 41:12
"Took Yosef out of prison" .... *Rosh Hashanah* 11a
page 203 "Still stayed skinny" .... *Rashi* 41:30-1
"Do this right away" .... *Rashi* 41:32
"Advice for Pharaoh" .... *Sefer HaYashar*
"Pharaoh's idea" .... *Sotah* 36b; *Sefer HaYashar*
page 204 "Yosef's Test" .... *Sefer HaYashar*
Fascinating Facts .... *Sotah* 36b
"Yosef's Parade" .... *Sefer HaYashar*
Questions Anyone? .... *Rashi* 41:43
page 206 "Faith in You" .... *Sefer HaYashar*
"Explainer of mysteries" .... *Rashi* 41:45
page 207 "The Good Years" .... *Rashi* 41:55; *Sefer HaYashar*
"Years of hunger started" .... *MRB* 90:6

Fascinating Facts .... *Seforno* 41:49
"The People Complain" .... *Rashi* 41:55
"Screaming to Pharaoh" .... *MRB* 91:5
"Name Please" .... *MRB* 91:4
page 208 "Lists of names" .... *Sefer HaYashar*
"Hunger in Eretz Yisrael" .... *Rashi* 42:1
"The Brothers Set Off" .... *Rashi* 42:5
Questions Anyone? .... *Rashi* 42:2
"Roads were dangerous" .... *Rashi* 42:4
"They took donkeys" .... *Sefer HaYashar*
page 209 "What it cost them" .... *Rashi* 41:3
"Where Are They" .... *MRB* 91:6; *Sefer HaYashar*
"Arrested" .... *MRB* 91:6; *Sefer HaYashar*
"You Are Spies!" .... *MRB* 91:6
Questions Anyone? .... *Rashi* 42:8
"Wearing a golden crown" .... *Sefer HaYashar*
page 211 "Faster that way" .... *Rashi* 42:13
"Kill our people" .... *Rashi* 42:14
Questions Anyone? .... *Rambam* 42:9
"Every word they said" .... *Rashi* 42:23
"He had to cry" .... *Rashi* 42:24
page 212 "Stop crying, he washed" .... *Sefer HaYashar*
"Back to his brothers" .... *Rashi* 42:24
"Soldiers fall over" .... *MRB* 91:6
"Ran off in terror" .... *Sefer HaYashar*
"Shimon to jail" .... *MRB* 91:6
"Your youngest brother" .... *Sefer HaYashar*
Questions Anyone? .... *Rashi* 42:24
Fascinating Facts .... *Rashi* 42:24
"Found the money" .... *Rashi* 42:27
"Taking food without paying" .... *Rashi* 42:28
"To welcome them" .... *Sefer HaYashar*
page 213 "Two of my sons" .... *Ohr HaChaim* 42:37
"Aren't your sons my sons" .... *MRB* 91:6
"To send Binyamin" .... *MRB* 91:6
"All surely die" .... *Rashi* 43:8
"Almond oil" .... *MRB* 91:11
"They also took" .... *Rashi* 43:12; *MRB* 91:11
page 214 "What Else" .... *MRB* 91:11
Questions Anyone? .... *Rashi* 43:14
"Is It a Trap?" .... *Rashi* 43:18
"He told Menashe" .... *Midrash Sechel Tov*
"They wouldn't do it" .... *Rashi* 43:24
"They entered Yosef's house" .... *Rashi* 43:24
"Yosef had fed him well" .... *MRB* 92:4
"Even look more impressive" .... *Rashi* 43:25
page 215 "Yosef and Binyamin" .... *Rashi* 43:30
"Binyamin's 10 children" .... *Sotah* 36b
"Foreign land" .... *Sotah* 36b; *see Rashi there*
"A Test" .... *Artscroll Stone Chumash* 43:16-34
page 216 "Take a Seat" .... *Rashi* 43:33
"Decorated with jewels" .... *Sefer HaYashar*
"Special guests were" .... *MRB* 92:5, *Eitz Yosef*
"Dessert" .... *MRB* 92:5, *Eitz Yosef*
Fascinating Facts .... *Rashi* 43:34
page 218 "A sin we did long ago" .... *Rashi* 44:16

Parashas Vayigash

page 220 "In 22 years" .... *Rashi* 35:29
"Becomes very rich" .... *Midrash Sechel Tov* 47:27
page 221 "King of the shevatim" .... *MRB* 84:17
"Punished for it" .... *Rashi* 44:18
"Magic cup" .... *Yefeh To'ar*
Questions Anyone? .... *Baal HaTurim* 44:30
"No power over him" .... *MRB* 93:7
page 222 "Ran away in fright" .... *Yalkut Shimoni* 150
"Egypt would be destroyed" .... *Midrash Tanchuma Vayigash* 3
"Their brother Yosef" .... *Rashi* 45;12
Torah in Our Lives (1) .... *Tiferes Shlomo, Moadim, Shevi'I Shel Pesach*
Fascinating Facts .... *Midrash Tanchuma Vayigash* 3
page 224 Fascinating Facts (1) .... *Rashi* 45:14
"What they had done" .... *Rashi* 45:3
"Speak with one another" .... *Rashi* 45:15
"Famous family" .... *Ramban* 45:16
"Best land in Egypt: Goshen" .... *Rashi* 45:18
Fascinating Facts (2) .... *MRB* 94:3
"Egyptian bean" .... *Rashi* 45:23; *MRB* 94:2, *Eitz Yosef*
"Elderly people" .... *Megillah* 16b
"Feel relaxed" .... *Rashi* 45:23, *Gur Aryeh*
"Travel Instructions" .... *Rashi* 45:24
Questions Anyone? .... *Megillah* 16a-*b*; *Megillas Esther* 8:15
page 225 "Beautiful Music, Great News" .... *Sefer HaYashar* 14; *Midrash HaGadol* 45:26; *Yalkut Me'am Loez* 45:25
"To heaven without dying" .... *Sefer HaYashar* 14
"Find Yosef's remains" .... *Mechilta Beshalach* 13:19
"Yosef was still alive" .... *MRB* 94:9
page 226 "The message" .... *Rashi* 45:27
Torah in Our Lives .... *Rashi* 45:27; *MRB* 94:3
"It's All Yours" .... *Rashi* 46:6
page 227 "Trees .... *MRB* 94:4
"To be buried" .... *Rashi* 46:4
Questions Anyone? .... *Emes L'Yaakov*
page 230 "Kings of the Jews" .... *MRB* 95:3
"Mazel Tov" .... *Rashi* 46:15
Questions Anyone? .... *MRB* 94:9
"Yosef and the Horses" .... *Rashi* 46:29; *MRB* 55:8
"Yosef Welcomes His Father" .... *Midrash Tanchuma* 7
page 231 "Shema Yisrael" .... *Rashi* 46:29
"Great love and joy" .... *Malbim* 46:29; *Gur Aryeh* 46:29
"Brothers to meet Pharaoh" .... *Rashi* 47:2
Questions Anyone? .... *Rashi* 47:2
Fascinating Facts .... *Rashi* 46:34, *Sifsei Chachamim*
"Lavan and Eisav" .... *Rashbam* 46:9
"The Blessing" .... *Rashi* 47:10
page 232 "There were only two" .... *Tosefta Sotah* 10:9; *Midrash Lehkach Tov* 47:18
"Galus Begins" .... *Shabbos* 89b
"And bought land" .... *Midrash Sechel Tov* 47:27
"A terrible mistake" .... *Kli Yakar* 47:27
page 234 Fascinating Facts .... *Yerushalmi Pesachim* 2:5
"Sold it all to Pharaoh" .... *Rashi* 47:21

Parashas Vayechi

page 238 "Mystery of the Missing Spaces" .... *Rashi* 47:28
"Worse and worse" .... *Mizrachi* 47:28
"Idols out of everything" .... *MRB* 96:5
"That to happen" .... *Rashi* 47:29
"With the power to do that" .... *Rashi* 47:29
Fascinating Facts .... *Rashi* 47:29; *Yerushalmi Kilayim* 9:3
page 239 Torah in Our lives .... *Rashi* 47:31
"Come Quickly" .... *Rashi* 48:1

"Rachel Is Crying" .... *Rashi* 48:7
"Evil Descendants" .... *Rashi* 48:8-9
page 240 "The Sun Stops" .... *Rashi* 48:19
page 241 "Like Ephraim and Menashe" .... *Oznayim L'Torah*
page 242 Questions Anyone? (1) .... *MRB* 53:11
"A Gift" .... *Rashi* 48:22
Questions Anyone? (2) .... *Rashi* 48:22; *Sefer HaYashar* 34:13; *MRB* 80:10; *Bava Basra* 123a
"Exile would end" .... *MRB* 98:2, *Eitz Yosef*
"One and Only" .... *Pesachim* 56a
page 243 "Ripped their shirts in grief" .... *Sefer HaYashar*
Fascinating Facts (1) .... *Yalkut Me'am Loez* 49:33
"Was gone" .... *Rashi* 50:3
Fascinating Facts (2) .... *Rashi* 49:33, *Gur Aryeh*
"Can I Go?" .... *Sotah* 36b
page 245 "The Funeral" .... *Sefer HaYashar*
"To be at the funeral" .... *MRB* 100:5, *Eitz Yosef*
Questions Anyone? .... *Rashi* 50:13
Fascinating Facts .... *Rashi* 50:13
"Danger" .... *Sotah* 13a
"Feed them in the future" .... *Iyun Yaakov*, *Sotah* 13a
"Royal golden crowns" .... *Sotah* 13a
page 246 Fascinating Facts (1) ... *MRB* 100:6; *Pirkei D'R' Eliezer* 39
"Challenge" .... *Sotah* 13a; *Pirkei D'R' Eliezer* 39
Fascinating Facts (2) .... *Bava Basra* 17a
"Problem Solved" .... *Pirkei D'R' Eliezer* 39
"And he died" .... *Sotah* 13a
Fascinating Facts (3) .... *Targum Yonasan* 50:13
"Second only to Pharaoh" .... *Sotah* 13a
Questions Anyone? .... *Sotah* 9b
"Yosef Remembers" .... *Midrash Tanchuma* 17
page 247 "Dinner Invitations" .... *Rashi* 50:15
"Yosef Has a Problem" .... *MRB* 100:8
Peace Mission" .... *Rashi* 50:16
page 248 "Yosef Cries" .... *MRB* 100:8, *Eitz Yosef* & *Matnos Kehunah*
Torah in Our Lives .... *Yevamos* 65b; *MRB* 100:8
"Blow out ten candles" .... *Megillah* 16b
"Hashem wouldn't permit it" .... *Rashi* 50:19
"Can I destroy any of you" .... *MRB* 100:9
"Would he kill them" .... *Rashi* 50:21
page 249 "Leave Egypt had come" .... *MRS* 5:13
Fascinating Facts (1) .... *Sotah* 13b
Fascinating Facts (2) .... *Pirkei D'R' Eliezer* 11; *Rashi*, *Shemos* 6:16
"Stuck in Egypt forever" .... *MR Devarim* 11:7
"Out of the water" .... *Sotah* 13a
"Laid to rest" .... *Rashi* 13:19
Torah in Our Lives .... *Zohar II* 156a, *Elyah Rabbah* 292:17
page 252 "Reuven" .... *Rashi* 49:3-4
"Lost these privileges" .... *Shabbos* 55b
"Strong and powerful" .... *Kli Yakar* 49:3
"He would be forgiven" .... *MRB* 99:6
"Shimon and Levi" .... *Rashi* 49:5-7
"Control their anger" .... *Ohr HaChaim* 49:28
page 253 "Wouldn't make trouble" .... *Kli Yakar* 49:7
Fascinating Facts .... *Rashi* 49:6
"Yehudah" .... *Rashi* 49:8-12
page 254 "Business with other countries" .... *MRB* 99:9
"Time to learning Torah" .... *Rashi* 49:13
Torah in Our Lives .... *Shitah Chadashah* 2:13
Questions Anyone? .... *MRB* 99:9
"Yissaschar" .... *Rashi* 49:14-15
"Jewish law" .... *MRB* 99:10
"Dan" .... *Rashi* 49:16-18
"They travel alone" .... *MRB* 98:13
"Jawbone of a donkey" .... *Shoftim* 15:15
page 255 Fascinating Facts (1) .... *Rashi* 49:15
"Defeat his enemies" .... *MRB* 98:13, *Eitz Yosef*
Fascinating Facts (2) .... *MRB* 98:14
"Gad" .... *Rashi* 49:19
"Outstanding warriors" .... *Rashi* 49:19
page 256 "Great amounts of oil" .... *Rashi* 49:20
"Kohanim Gedolim" .... *MRB* 98:16, *Eitz Yosef*
"From Asher's shevet" .... *Midrash Aggadah Bamidbar* 1:13
"Will be made by Asher" .... *Shitah Chadashah* 2:19
"Naphtali" .... *Rashi* 49:21
"Shores of Lake Kinneret" .... *MRB* 98:17
"Yosef" .... *Rashi* 49:22-26
page 257 "That's called ayin hara" .... *Rav Dessler*, *Vol.* 4, *Geder Ayin Hara*
"Water their crops" .... *Devarim* 33:13, *Rashi*
Fascinating Facts .... *Rashi* 49:6; *Rashi*, *Devarim* 33:17
"Binyamin" .... *Rashi* 49:27
"First king of the Jews" .... *MRB* 99:3, *Eitz Yosef*
"Wolves are strong animals" .... *Shitah Chadashah* 2:22
"In charge of it all" .... *MRB* 99:3
"Dangerous as snakes etc." .... *Rashi* 49:28
Questions Anyone? .... *MRB* 99:4, *Eitz Yosef*